Negotiating Business Equipment Leases

Second Edition

Negotiating Business Equipment Leases

Second Edition

Richard M. Contino

AMACOM
American Management Association
New York . Atlanta . Boston . Chicago . Kansas City . San Francisco . Washington, D.C.
Brussels . Mexico City . Tokyo . Toronto

This book is available at a special
discount when ordered in bulk quantities.
For information, contact Special Sales Department,
AMACOM, a division of American Management Association,
1601 Broadway, New York, NY 10019.

This publication is designed to provide accurate and authoritative information in regard to the subject matter covered. It is sold with the
understanding that the publisher is not engaged in rendering legal,
accounting, or other professional service. If legal advice or other expert assistance is required, the services of a competent professional
person should be sought.

Library of Congress Cataloging-in-Publication Data

Contino, Richard M.
Negotiating business equipment leases, second edition / Richard M. Contino- 2nd ed.
        p. cm.
    includes index.
    ISBN 0-8144-0417-0
    1. Industrial equipment leases.   2. Negotiation in business.
I. Title.
HD39.4. C663   1998   97–49134
658. 15′242—DC21   CIP

Printing number
10 9 8 7 6 5 4 3 2 1

To Penelope, May-Lynne, Matthew, and my Mother

Contents

Preface . . . . *x*

Acknowledgments . . . . *xv*

1. Selecting the Best Lessor for Your Deal 1
 A Lessor's Capabilities and Objectives Set Your Deal   *1*
 Understanding How Various Lessors Operate Is Key   *2*
 What Types of Leases Are Available?   *15*
 Save Time and Money: Investigate Potential Lessors   *19*
 By Checking Financial Requirements Early,
 *   You Can Avoid a Turndown*   *30*
 The Best Deal May Be a Matter of Timing   *31*
 Some Lessors Use Bait-and-Switch Marketing;
 *   Don't Deal With Them*   *32*
 Conclusion   *33*

2. How Lessors Take Your Money 35
 Getting the Best Deal Means Finding Hidden Profits   *35*
 Lessors Profit in Many Ways   *36*
 Here's Why Leasing Companies Want Your Business   *64*
 These False Financial Programs Can Increase Profits   *66*
 You Now Have the Information to Negotiate Away
 *   Hidden Profits*   *68*

3. Bargaining Strategies and Tactics That Work 69
 To Win, Knowledge of Your Opponent Is Not Enough   *69*
 Don't Be Your Own Worst Enemy   *70*
 Avoid Friendships   *72*
 Avoid Social Situations   *73*
 Plan Your Equipment Financing Early   *74*
 Watch Out for Lessor Delays   *74*
 Use a Deal Timetable to Avoid Problems   *76*

Don't Offer a Last Look   78
When Requesting Bids, Provide Only Essentials   78
Never Make These Typical Lessee Statements   80
Avoid These Other Common Mistakes   86
Here's How to Handle an Initial Lessor Telephone Call   94
Make Sure Your Team Knows Your Strategy   97

4. Establishing Solid Negotiation Objectives 98
A Negotiation Plan Sets the Stage to Win   98
Get Internal Support   99
Identify the Key Business Areas to Address   100
Determine Your Specific Deal Priorities   102
What's Next?   116

5. Using the Bid Request to Outnegotiate a Lessor 118
The Proposal Negotiation—Where Your Deal Is Made   118
Gaining Control by Setting Bid Guidelines   119
Writing an Effective Request for Quotes   123
Handling an Overlooked RFQ Point   146
Getting the Deal You Want   146
A Lessee Proposal Stage Checklist   146

6. Evaluating the Lessor's Offer 151
A Key Step: Evaluating the Lessor's Offer   151
A Proposal Overview   153
Reviewing the Lessor's Offer in Detail   156
Proposal Issues to Address   162
The Lease Award   209
A Few Final Comments   210

7. Negotiating Your Lease Agreement 211
Your Ongoing Lease Negotiation Job   211
The Lease Agreement's Simple Objective   212
Advantages and Disadvantages of
    Common Lease Formats   212
Subjects to Address in Negotiating the Lease   214
Checklist for Drafting and Negotiating a
    Lease Agreement   256

8. Closing Your Lease Financing 264
Closing a Lease Financing   264
Legal Opinions   265
The Need for Current Financial Information   268

The Type of Financial Information That
  May Be Required   *270*
Transaction Authorization Documents That
  Are Part of a Lease Closing   *271*
Guarantees   *271*
Proof of Insurance Documents   *272*
Equipment Purchase Agreements   *273*
The Fundamental Importance of an
  Equipment Bill of Sale   *273*
Landowner or Mortgagee Waivers   *274*
Security Interest Filings   *274*
Participation Agreement Found in
  Underwritten Leases   *274*
Owner's Trust Agreement   *275*
Lender's Trust Agreement   *275*
Using a Partnership Instead of a Trust Arrangement   *276*
Underwriter's Fee Agreement   *276*
A Supplemental Document Closing Checklist   *276*

9. Some Wrap-Up Advice and Thoughts **280**

Putting What You've Learned to Work   *280*
Getting Leverage When You Have None   *281*
Some Comments About Issues Often Overlooked   *287*
The Results Are Now Up to You   *289*

Appendix A: Negotiation Objectives Checklist *291*

Appendix B: Request for Quotations to Lease Equipment *295*

Glossary *303*

Index *315*

Preface

This book has only one purpose: to enable you, as a prospective lessee, to negotiate the best possible equipment lease deals—whether you're a negotiating novice or an experienced professional, and whether you're involved with a $5,000 financing or a $100 million lease. It will coach you through every critical phase of a lease negotiation, step by step, in a way no other book on the market does. You'll learn, for example, when a lessor's bargaining leverage is weakest and the many tricks leasing company negotiators use to put you at a disadvantage.

This book is based on the author's extensive lease-negotiating experience as an attorney-negotiator representing both lessees and lessors, a lease marketing executive, and a leasing company owner. You'll learn what to do, when to do it, and why—to win in a lease negotiation. And you'll learn what not to do—to avoid crippling your bargaining power. You'll also learn lessor insider secrets that can make a negotiating difference. All of this is explained simply and in plain English. In a nutshell, it will enable you to negotiate as a leasing expert, even if you have no financing, or negotiation, background at all. And if you *are* an expert, the information offered will add even more power to your bargaining ability. Use it as your own personal lease adviser on your next deal.

For example, you'll learn:

- How leasing companies cleverly take your money
- About misleading marketing schemes that lessors use over and over
- When your bargaining leverage is highest
- How most lessees unknowingly hand lessors the negotiating edge
- What business and personal statements weaken your position
- About lease broker frauds
- To write requests for lease quotes that put you on top
- To identify leasing companies that can't be aggressive
- Insider secrets lessors don't want you to know

- What benefits are never offered but are always available if requested
- The most effective way to handle lessor telephone calls
- About the 0% interest rate scam
- Lessor-beating competitive bidding techniques
- Strategies that make a lessor want to do business with your company
- Effective bluffs that win points
- Proposal tricks lessors use
- The best way to create a winning deal strategy
- How hidden purchase discounts increase your lease rate
- The profit-grabbing, small-transaction lessor attitudes
- The risks of dealing with vendor leasing subsidiaries

As you proceed through the book, you'll be taken systematically through each aspect of the lease negotiation process so you can pick the right type of lessor for your particular deal, set solid deal objectives, get aggressive leasing company quotes, comprehensively analyze financing offers, spot hidden lessor profits, identify lease agreement traps, and efficiently handle the lease closing. At each critical stage, you'll be given lessor-beating tips, tricks, tactics, and strategies. For example, most prospective lessees don't realize that it's a lessee's market today: There are too many lessors competing for too few deals. You'll find out how best to take advantage of this fact to get the most aggressive deals possible. And examples have been included, where appropriate, to illustrate complicated concepts simply.

Some lessors are better than others for your deal. One of the biggest mistakes prospective lessees make is failing to realize that certain lessors are structurally unable to give them an aggressive deal on certain types of equipment financings. For example, you should never approach a money-over lessor, one that makes its profits by simply marking up its cost of funds, when your equipment historically has a high end-of-lease resale value. Instead, residual-sensitive lessors, ones that take potential end-of-lease proceeds into account in computing lease rents, should be invited to bid. Asking the wrong lessor into your deal will guarantee that you won't get a market-favorable offer. Chapter 1, "Selecting the Best Lessor for Your Deal," tells you how to pick the right type of leasing company for your particular needs.

Knowing how lessors profit will provide a negotiating edge. You can't beat a lessor unless you know how it makes money in a lease deal. Chapter 2, "How Lessors Take Your Money," explains the many ways lessors profit in a lease transaction so you will know what to look for and what concessions are possible. For example, some small-ticket lessors make as much money on documentation process fees and clever precommencement rent charges as they do on financing profit. And large-ticket lessors at times get unfair profits from unreasonable, up-front deal commitment fees, payable whether you lease or not. All these charges can unnecessarily increase your leasing costs. If you know enough to ask, however, the lessor will waive all, or a portion of, these added costs.

Lessee negotiators often unknowingly hand a lessor bargaining power. Leasing company representatives are highly experienced negotiators. They know what to look for to uncover a lessee negotiator's weak points. And they use every trick in the book to gain that edge. Worse yet, inexperienced lessee negotiators invariably hand these lessor representatives facts about themselves or their company that allow the lessor representatives to manipulate a deal in their favor. It's not unusual, for example, for a lessee negotiator to tell a lessor representative inadvertently that the lessee always leases, a statement that gives the lessor an unnecessary competitive advantage. Chapter 3, "Bargaining Strategies and Tactics That Work," shows you the best way to handle yourself to maintain a superior negotiating front.

Determining your overall negotiation objectives is critical. To negotiate from a position of strength, you must know what you want and what you're willing to compromise before the negotiations start. And because of the far-reaching impact a lease deal can have on your business, you must determine and balance your company's legal, tax, financial, business, accounting, and administrative needs. Chapter 4, "Establishing Solid Negotiation Objectives," helps you do that. It provides an effective methodology for determining and assessing lease needs so you will come to the bargaining table with solid and balanced negotiation objectives.

Take early bargaining control. Your negotiating position is inherently the greatest during the period of time before making the lease award, often referred to as the proposal stage. To win your lease business, a lessor knows that it must meet all your initial lease requests. This is the time to ask for everything you need and pin down a lessor's commitments. There is only one way to do this—by preparing and delivering a comprehensive, written request for lease quotes (RFQ). A sweeping RFQ will ensure that the lessor responds to your deal specifics and nothing is overlooked. If you forget to ask for something up front, you can bet you won't get it without a rate increase—if at all. Chapter 5, "Using the Bid Request to Outnegotiate a Lessor," shows you how to outbargain a lessor using an effective RFQ.

If you don't know how to analyze a lessor's offer, you'll be outsmarted. Lease proposal writing is an art. Sophisticated lessors know how to make an offer look better than it is. Tricky language, vague commitments, and misleading approaches are all designed to get you to think you've gotten a great deal—while leaving the door open to gain every advantage when the time comes to negotiating the lease agreement. If you know how to analyze a lessor's proposal properly, you won't get trapped. Chapter 6, "Evaluating the Lessor's Offer," shows you how to do this to protect yourself and avoid the many pitfalls.

You cannot let your guard down until all documents are signed. Chapter 7, "Negotiating Your Lease Agreement," and Chapter 8, "Closing Your Lease Financing," explain all you need to know to review and negotiate your lease documents and close your financing. All too often, prospective lessees mistakenly feel that documenting a deal outlined in a lessor's offer is a mere formality. Leasing companies know this, and some take full advantage of this misconception, hoping to quietly slip additional profit opportunities into the lease agreement. These chapters offer tip after tip to avoid the many snares that can increase your costs, reduce your flexibility, and threaten the deal you thought you had.

My Best Expert Negotiator's Advice

Chapter 9, "Some Wrap-Up Advice and Thoughts," offers key suggestions for pulling together the most effective negotiation approach, so that even if you're about to take on your first deal you'll have every advantage. For example, it lists my top twenty bargaining rules—ones that have successfully stood the test of hundreds of lease deal negotiations. Stick to them and you can't go wrong.

A key negotiation-stage checklist is included to help you effectively organize and negotiate your lease deals. A proven lessee request for lease quotes is included that will assist you in analyzing your needs and provide approaches to use in your next lease negotiation. And finally, you'll find a glossary of equipment leasing terminology that will be a useful and ready reference for unfamiliar terms.

In summary, this book provides you with everything you need in order to negotiate the best possible equipment lease financings in today's marketplace.

Richard M. Contino, Esq.

Acknowledgments

I wish to express my appreciation to everyone who has been of assistance in bringing this revised edition to fruition. In particular, I thank Tony Vlamis, formerly senior acquisitions and planning editor, and Hank V. Kennedy, publisher, at AMACOM for their help in formulating the revised edition, and Jim Kaylor, one of the smart leasing guys (who undoubtedly thought I'd forgotten all about him), for his initial support in the original project's infancy.

My special thanks to my wonderful wife, Penelope, for graciously, as always, putting up with my absences during the revision process; to my marvelous ten-year-old daughter, May-Lynne, for keeping my writing office cheerful with her many charming and colorful paintings; and to my delightful son, Matthew, for not walking on the manuscript pages that were always spread on my writing office floor.

Chapter 1
Selecting the Best Lessor for Your Deal

A Lessor's Capabilities and Objectives Set Your Deal

Leasing companies have different business capabilities and objectives. The lease deal you get depends on a lessor's management interests and profit objectives as well as its financial capabilities. Picking one whose business guidelines won't permit the type of lease you need will waste time and cost you money. For example, approaching a leasing company that specializes in leasing $1,500 to $50,000 telephone systems to finance a $200,000 conveyer system is a mistake. Choosing one that regularly leases industrial equipment in that price range will produce the best results.

Business capabilities and objectives differ from lessor to lessor for a variety of reasons. In order to profit in the highly competitive leasing business, companies have to develop financial niches. The niches are as different as the personalities of the people running these businesses. Some understand computers and know how to get the most out of re-marketing used systems, thereby enabling them to offer lower rents by relying more on end-of-lease profits. Some know how to cost-effectively check credit and document small lease transactions, allowing them to outprice many competitors not specializing in "small-ticket" leases. Others know the technical ins and outs of tax leasing, enabling them to maximize available tax benefits to both the lessor and the lessee. And the list goes on.

One of the key reasons for the wide range of differences among lessors is, as you will learn in Chapter 2, that there are many ways to profit in a lease transaction. Couple this with the fact that there is little industry or governmental regulation and you find a business sector whose participants have a diversity of capabilities, objectives, interests, ethical standards, and approaches.

Understanding How Various Lessors Operate Is Key

Leasing is a no-holds-barred, buyer-beware market. If you don't know whom you are dealing with and have a good idea of how the lessor operates, not only won't you get your best deal, but chances are you'll be taken for a financial ride.

A lessor's capabilities can be readily defined by the type of company it is. And there are many types, each with unique characteristics, benefits, and risks that must be taken into account in making your selection assessment. As you'll see below, some lessors are clearly the wrong choice in certain situations.

A quick word about unethical practitioners is in order here. Although most leasing companies are ethical, the stories of high lease profits and income tax loopholes have attracted shady business practitioners. For them, anything goes to make a profit. They have a financial field day with unsuspecting or inexperienced businesspeople. What makes matters worse is that these practitioners often provide opportunities for dishonest lessee employees to profit at their company's expense. It's not unheard of, for example, for unethical computer lessors to kick back money to corporate lease managers willing to approve deals with high-rate leases. And worse yet, many win business with deceitful promotions or set up situations that guarantee rate increases once the deal has been closed. If you're working for someone else, doing business with one of these lessors can cost you your job.

For discussion purposes, let's separate lessor types into five categories: individuals, independent leasing companies, lease brokers, captive leasing companies, and bank affiliates. In reality, the classes are not always this clear-cut. For instance, some independent leasing companies at times act as brokers, selling off their leases to lease investors.

Individuals

Prior to the 1986 Tax Reform Act (TRA), the role of the individual as lessor was limited because of tax rules restricting an individual from claiming investment tax credits (ITCs) on leased property. The TRA generally eliminated equipment ITCs, so wealthy individuals were able to be more competitive. In the past, a number of innovative equipment leasing companies and investment bankers put together interesting investment programs for individuals, making them an increasing part of the equipment financing business. For example, some computer lessors set up investment programs that offered individuals an opportunity to benefit from owning computer leases.

At the time of this writing, individual equipment lessors have one significant federal income tax issue to address: the passive loss rules. An explanation of these rules is outside the scope of this book. Suffice it to say, however, that the passive loss rules are of no concern to a prospective lessee, unless the lease agreement requires the lessee to reimburse the lessor for deductions lost under those rules.

Since the faltering economy of the late 1980s and early 1990s, there have been renewed discussions of federal tax incentives for business, such as equipment ITCs, and the possible elimination of the alternative minimum tax (AMT), a tax restricting the benefit of equipment ownership. If ITC incentives are reinstated containing pre-TRA–type individual restrictions, and if the AMT is eliminated, individual-type lessors could be less competitive than unrestricted corporate lessors.

Advantages and Disadvantages of Individual-Type Lessors

There are certain advantages, and certain disadvantages, for a prospective lessee in becoming involved with individual-type lessors.

Advantages. To be competitive, individuals often take greater business and tax risks than traditional leasing companies. The added risk taking makes them a good choice when:

- Credit problems exist. For example, start-up companies and ones with a history of credit difficulties may find individuals more receptive than traditional lessors.
- There is high end-of-lease equipment sale potential. Individuals are often willing to place greater emphasis on anticipated end-of-lease sale or re-lease profits, thereby lowering rent charges.
- Equipment has a high likelihood of obsolescence. Individuals, as opposed to corporate lessors, more readily assume risks that end-of-lease equipment values may not be as high as anticipated. This, in turn, means lower rent charges or a willingness to finance equipment that traditional lessors avoid, such as tanning beds.
- Less restrictive lease documentation is preferred. Typically, individual-type lessors are willing to take more business risks and therefore don't require the type of documentation detail on which, for example, institutional lessors insist.
- Attractive tax benefits may be available to an individual-type lessor.
- Transactions aspects put lessor tax benefits at risk, such as when a lessee wants the right to purchase the equipment for one dollar, because individual-type lessors are often more willing to take these risks. (Note: The IRS takes the position that a nominal end-of-lease

purchase or renewal price, such as one dollar, turns the lease arrangement into a conditional sale financing for income tax characterization purposes. If the IRS successfully so characterizes a financing arrangement, the tax rules state that the lessee, not the lessor, is the only one entitled to claim equipment ownership tax benefits. If the lessor, for rent-pricing purposes, anticipated having the equipment ownership tax benefits available to shelter certain transaction profits and is prevented from claiming them by the IRS, the lease will not be as economically attractive to the lessor.)
- A quick lease financing commitment is necessary. An individual-type lessor's investment decision doesn't require a credit committee or board of director approval.

Disadvantages. There are risks in dealing with individuals as lessors. For example, they:

- May fail to pay proper taxes, ultimately resulting in property seizures by taxing authorities. Even when a lease agreement protects a lessee's right to an asset's use, there may be some difficult or embarrassing moments.
- Can be arbitrary when negotiating initial lease documentation or exceptions needed after a lease is signed.
- Are typically street-smart businesspeople who know how and when to take advantage of a profit opportunity to its fullest.
- Are hard to find and are typically accessible only indirectly through lease brokers or investment bankers.

Independent Leasing Companies

Independent leasing companies, sometimes referred to as nonbank leasing companies, provide a major source of equipment lease financing. The smaller ones are generally privately held companies owned by one or two businesspeople, while the larger ones are typically *Fortune* 1,000 company affiliates. Their success depends on their ability to generate a large volume of highly profitable equipment lease financings, as opposed, for example, to that of a bank-affiliated lease operation, whose success may be measured more in terms of readily providing regular banking customers with an equipment lease financing accommodation at reasonably acceptable levels of profit. Except in the individual consumer area, their leasing activities are not subject to state or federal regulation like that governing bank-affiliated leasing companies.

Two Ways in Which Independent Lessors Operate

There are two types of independent leasing companies: those that merely buy and lease equipment to the user, referred to as finance lessors; and those that also offer other services, such as equipment maintenance and repair, referred to as service lessors. Let's take a look at each.

Finance Leasing Companies. Finance leasing companies—lessors of millions of dollars of equipment each year—operate in much the same manner as banks or other lending institutions. They do not maintain an equipment inventory but rather, after agreeing to provide financing for a particular lessee, purchase and lease specific equipment ordered from the lessee's equipment vendor.

Finance lessors typically write leases—referred to as finance leases— that run from 70% to 80% of the equipment's useful life. The total financial benefits received under these long-term leases—including the rents payable, the tax benefits, and the proceeds from the sale or re-lease of the equipment at lease end—are usually sufficient to provide the lessor with a full return of its equipment investment and a solid profit. If the lessor borrows a portion of the equipment cost from a third-party lender, under what is referred to as a leveraged lease arrangement, the rents will be sufficient to cover full debt repayment.

The long-term leases entered into by finance lessors are net leases, ones in which the lessee must assume substantially all the equipment ownership responsibilities, such as maintenance, taxes, and insurance. This is in keeping with the lenderlike approach of a finance lessor, providing long-term financing without assuming equipment ownership obligations.

Service Leasing Companies. Service, or specialized, leasing companies provide nonfinancial services in addition to the equipment financing. There is a separate charge for these services, which might include, for example, equipment maintenance or repair or ongoing operational advice. The service charge is often bundled into the rent payments.

Service lessors typically limit their activity to a single type of equipment, such as computers, or to a single industry, such as the rail transportation industry. The in-depth experience gained through specialization enables them to reduce many leasing risks. For example, those that concentrate on certain equipment gain extensive experience in its specialized equipment sale and re-lease market, thereby enabling them to maximize the dollars received from this equipment when it comes off lease. By being able to reduce their re-leasing and sale risks, they are often willing to provide attractive lease termination or equipment exchange privileges as well as take greater credit risks.

Because of their equipment remarketing capabilities, service lessors are willing to write leases with terms much shorter than finance leases. Since these short-term leases, often referred to as nonpayout leases, generally don't permit the service lessor to recoup its entire equipment investment during the first lease term, it must effectively re-lease or sell the equipment to make a profit. If the equipment becomes obsolete sooner than expected, the service lessor may incur a loss. To offset this risk, the service lessor builds a premium into the rent charge, generally resulting in rent charges considerably higher than those payable under a finance lease.

Advantages and Disadvantages of Independent Leasing Companies

There are certain advantages, and certain disadvantages, for a prospective lessee in becoming involved with independent leasing companies.

Advantages. Because success is dependent on lease profits, independent lessors have to be extremely aggressive in the highly competitive leasing market. They're a good choice because:

- Significant deal concessions may be offered to win business. Many, for example, are willing to bend the tax rules to get a lease award, such as providing low end-of-lease fixed-price equipment purchase and renewal rights—a practice that can result in the loss of ownership tax benefits for a lessor.
- They're easy to find. Industry trade associations, such as the Equipment Leasing Association in Arlington, Virginia, make available lists of regional and national leasing company members.
- Financing for virtually any type of equipment is available.
- When they need business, they'll dramatically drop lease rates and take greater credit risks.
- Many look heavily to what equipment may be worth at lease end for profits, which, in turn, means lower rent payments.
- Some offer services that lessen the burden of equipment use, such as maintenance and repair services.
- Short lease terms, attractive early termination privileges, and equipment exchange programs may be available through service lessors.
- High equipment obsolescence risks can be avoided through short-term service leases.
- Their standard lease documentation can speed the deal-closing process.
- Their lease experience enables them to identify and resolve problems early.
- They are generally current on financial and tax structures that benefit lessees.
- Success often depends greatly on their market business reputation, so they're less likely to take arbitrary positions when problems arise or concessions are needed.

Disadvantages. Independent lessors are the backbone of the leasing business, but there's risk for a lessee. For example:

- Independent lessors are out to make as much money as possible as quickly as possible, so they'll aggressively go after every profit opportunity. Inexperienced lessees are the most at risk.
- Their commission-motivated sales representatives are often opportunistic, frequently shifting from job to job. The representative you trust may not be on hand when you have a problem.
- Lessees without fixed-price purchase options written into their leases are often charged top dollar for equipment they want to buy at lease end.
- They're experienced financial negotiators, often able to outmaneuver prospective lessees easily.
- Their standard lease documents often contain many hidden traps.
- Those offering collateral equipment-related services, such as maintenance, often use service charges to hide excessive lease interest rates.
- In their pursuit of profits, some take unreasonable financial risks, which can result in bankruptcy, leaving their lessees to negotiate lease problems or requests with arbitrary and indecisive bankruptcy trustees.

Lease Brokers

Also referred to as lease underwriters or syndicators, lease brokers package lease transactions for the account of third-party lessors. Put simply, brokers match up prospective lessees with prospective lessor-investors. They charge a fee for their service—usually ranging from 0.75% to 12% of the leased equipment's cost—typically paid by the lessor-investors.

To cover the broker's fee, the rent charge is marked up. Here's one way this is done. The equipment cost is increased by the amount of the fee, and then the new rent is computed by multiplying that sum by the rent factor. For example, assume that a lessor wants $100 per month to finance a $10,000 computer. The rent factor, 0.01, is determined by dividing the $100 monthly rent by the $10,000 equipment cost. Assume that the lease broker wants a $1,000, or 10%, fee. To compute a lease rent that will cover this fee, the fee desired, $1,000, is added to the equipment cost, $10,000, and that sum is multiplied by the rent factor. In this case, the rent necessary to pay the desired fee is $110 ($1,000 + $10,000 = $11,000 x .01 = $110).

A broker's involvement adds an increased level of funding risk not found with direct lessors. To understand the added risk, let's look at how a broker normally operates. Generally, a lease broker begins by contacting all types of equipment users and vendors to determine whether they have any leasing needs. In the case of a prospective lessee, it will define the rough parameters of a financing offer through discussions with the prospective lessee. At this juncture, the broker may perform a credit check on the prospective lessee to make sure the transaction is marketable. If there aren't any problems, it will formulate a concise lease structure, including rental rate, and offer it to the equipment user, generally through a formal proposal letter.

If the user finds the proposed arrangement acceptable, the broker asks for a formal award letter and then proceeds to find one or more parties interested in acting as lessor. The party or parties may be individual investors, private or public companies looking for tax shelter–type investments, independent leasing companies, or bank-affiliated lessors. If a leveraged lease is contemplated—that is, a portion of the equipment purchase cost is to be supplied by a third-party loan— it may also put out feelers for prospective lenders, commonly referred to as debt participants. In most leveraged lease situations, however, investment bankers are called in to find the debt participants. Once the lessor-investor (also referred to as equity) and debt participants are identified, the broker proceeds to shepherd the transaction through documentation to completion.

Although generally acting exclusively as a broker, a lease underwriter may, on occasion, invest some of its own funds in the equipment along with other third-party lessor-investors and thereby become a part owner. By doing so, the lease underwriter adds credibility to the investment and thus is able to sell the lease transaction to potential investors more readily.

One of the lease broker's major assets is its knowledge of the leasing business. Because it is continually in the market, it will know where to find competitive, cooperative, and realistic equity participants. And it will know how to get lessee-required concessions from lessor participants effectively, including, for example, optimal lease rates, favorable transaction structures, and acceptable document provisions.

As you can see, the added risk is one of funding. If a broker can't find interested funding participants, financing won't be available when equipment arrives. And a prospective lessee may not know this until it's too late.

Brokers' Reluctance to Disclose Their Role

Lease brokers often hide the fact that they're acting in a broker capacity for fear a prospective lessee won't deal with them. Their concern is well-founded. Many companies simply won't work through intermediaries, insisting on offers from actual money sources. As a result, some unethical brokers lie about their role, claiming they are principal lease investors. So a prospective lessee relying on a lessor's word that it's not acting as a broker can be in for quite a surprise when advised that the deal won't be funded as promised because no lease investors were interested in it.

The solution, of course, is to uncover brokers in hiding. To do so, you have to know what questions to ask and how to evaluate the answers given. Finding out that you're dealing with a broker after it's too late to get other proposals can be embarrassing if not costly. If you know a broker is involved, and you choose to deal with it, at least you can protect against risks by, for example, having a contingency plan in the event the broker can't perform. Ways to uncover a broker in hiding are discussed in the following subsection.

How to Determine Whether You're Dealing With a Broker in Hiding

As mentioned above, some leasing companies won't disclose that they're acting in a broker role. The key is to be able to act quickly to uncover those hiding this fact from you.

The inexperienced lessee has the greatest challenge. Brokers often refer to themselves as leasing companies, leading people to believe that they have money to buy and lease equipment. This is reinforced by their use of terms such as *Leasing, Credit, Capital,* or *Financial* in their company name. Those more open about their role call themselves lease underwriters or syndicators, which, although less misleading, at times creates an appearance of greater capability than deserved.

There is nothing wrong with dealing with a broker, provided you know it and take steps to avoid the intermediary risk and provided you keep in mind that brokers are interested in one thing: earning as big a fee as possible as quickly as possible. And they do this by increasing rents to cover fees; the higher the lease rate, the more in it for the broker.

Asking a leasing representative whether his or her company is a broker may not uncover the truth, particularly if the representative believes he or she will be excluded from participating. So you have to look for clues. One of the best clues is a vague, unclear, or confusing response to a direct question about the company's role in a financing, such as:

"No, we are a syndicator."

"No, we are a lease underwriter."

"We are a lease financing source."

Silence and a change of subject.

At times, the responses are half-truths, designed to mislead a lessee into a false sense of security. Classic examples are:

"We may make a partial investment in your deal, but we have someone that we work with regularly that is quite interested in putting up all the funds."

"Our lender-investors put up the money for us."

Another effective way to determine whether you're dealing with a broker is to ask for the company's financial statements. A broker in hiding won't want to let you see them because it would be self-evident that the company doesn't have the financial strength to make lease investments.

If you ask a broker in hiding for financial statements, don't be surprised if the representative offers one of the following responses:

"We are privately held, and as I am sure you can understand, our financial statements are something we simply don't let out."

"It's against company policy to give financial statements out."

"Our accountants are in the middle of updating our financial statements. Our earlier statements don't give an accurate picture of our business, so we're unable to give them to you because they would be misleading."

"The financials are consolidated with our parent company's statements and don't give a true picture of our financial position."

"We can't give out our financials, but we can put you in touch with our company owner's bank. It'll give you a feel for his financial substance."

Qualified Offer—A Broker Clue. If you get a qualified financing offer, one that doesn't firmly commit to provide lease financing, chances are you're dealing with a broker. For example, many brokers submit "best-effort" proposals, obligating themselves merely to make an effort to arrange the financing as stated. A best-effort proposal might start out stating something like: "We will use our best efforts to arrange financing for your equipment under the following terms and conditions. . . ." It then goes on to set out the deal offered, including the rent to be paid. If the company is unable to find interested lessor-investors, it can walk away without liability.

Qualified offers can be disastrous for an unsuspecting lessee, particularly if equipment is about to be delivered and the broker was unable to find a lessor-investor to pay for it. Tactics and suggestions for handling qualified proposals are discussed in Chapter 6.

Be alert for the possibility of a broker in hiding if a leasing company hedges when asked about any offer qualification by saying something like:

"It's simply a form proposal. Don't worry about it."

"It's boilerplate language written by our lawyers. I'm not sure what it means. You know those lawyers. They always make everything confusing."

The key is to make sure you fully understand what you're being told. If you're not happy with any answer, pin it down. And get it in writing, something unethical brokers will resist to avoid exposing themselves to legal liability.

Advantages and Disadvantages of Lease Brokers

There are certain advantages, and certain disadvantages, for a prospective lessee in becoming involved with lease brokers.

Advantages. The involvement of a lease broker in your deal may have certain advantages because lease brokers:

- Are often the most informed on tax, financial, and lease structures that benefit a lessee. Their survival depends on adding value for their fee.
- Are continually in the lessor market and often know what lease investors and lenders offer the best rates.
- Will push hard for concessions you need. If the deal doesn't go through, they don't get paid.
- Can be excellent project managers, ensuring that all your financing gets done in a timely manner.
- Can provide helpful negotiating tips and tactics.

Disadvantages. There are risks in dealing with brokers. For example:

- Brokers generally don't have the money to buy equipment, so if they can't find interested investors, your financing won't get done.
- Their fees add to the cost of your lease financing.
- They may mislead you to get your business. Nonbroker lessors can rely on ongoing lease profits to keep their doors open, so they're less likely to make risky promises they may not be able to fulfill in order to win business. Brokers need continual fee income to survive.
- It takes little investment to set up a broker operation, so it's easy for anyone to enter the business, even those with little experience or low ethical standards.
- Brokers appear to act as your representative, which can throw you off guard. In fact, their first allegiance is to themselves.
- Once the deal closes, chances are you won't get any meaningful assistance from them if problems arise.

Captive Leasing Companies

In increasing numbers, equipment vendors are setting up leasing companies, generally referred to as captive leasing companies or simply "captives," to facilitate their equipment sales. In today's market, a vendor offering financing on equipment it sells has a marketing edge.

Captives have a pricing advantage. Not only do they have the traditional lease profit ingredients to work with, but they also have their vendor-affiliate company's equipment sale markup to rely on. For example, on a consolidated basis, the combined companies can make a profit even if financing is offered at break-even rates. This, coupled with their knowledge of the equipment's resale market, can make captives very competitive.

But all captives are not what they seem. It's not unusual, for example, for them to act as a lease broker, getting the lease signed and then selling it off to a third-party lessor, in which event the defaulting lessee may be faced with an equipment repossession by the purchasing lessor. Those willing to pay a higher rate to lease from a captive, thinking that doing so can provide negotiating leverage if equipment problems occur, can also be in for a surprise. For example, some captive leasing company lessees have withheld rent when equipment malfunctioned, only to discover that being in default under a lease has unexpected implications. For instance, it's not unusual for a company's general corporate working capital loan agreements to be deemed in default if the borrower is in default under any other loan or lease agreement. So withholding rent and throwing the lease in default may trigger a loan payment acceleration under another agreement. As a result, the rent premium paid to the captive gains the lessee nothing.

Although typically set up to provide lease financing on equipment sold by an affiliated company, some captives will also finance equipment sold by a nonaffiliated company. In these situations, they are no different than independent leasing companies, with the same advantages and disadvantages.

Advantages and Disadvantages of Captive Leasing Companies

There are certain advantages, and certain disadvantages, for a prospective lessee in becoming involved with captive leasing companies.

Advantages. Leasing equipment sold by a captive lessor's affiliated company has its advantages. For instance:

- The rents offered may be the lowest, particularly if the affiliated company vendor is competing for the equipment sale.
- The company may offer a more flexible lease, permitting, for example, easy equipment upgrades or exchanges.
- There may be enhanced negotiating leverage to restructure a lease if future problems occur, particularly if the vendor wants to maintain a good reputation in the sales market. Many are willing to provide

after-the-fact lease concessions to ensure the possibility of future equipment purchases.

Disadvantages. Captives historically have a number of disadvantages. For example:

- Although their vendor-affiliate connection provides a theoretical rent pricing advantage over other lessors, they frequently fail to take advantage of it. Often this is due to vendor management's failure to support its leasing operations fully.
- Their apparent rate advantage is generally offset by a high cost of investment funds, often due to weak financial management typically found in captives.
- Their lease offers are often above-market, particularly if they believe that the customer has decided to acquire their affiliate's equipment and is willing to pay a rent premium to lease from the vendor's affiliate.
- Captives often broker their leases to third-party lessors, eliminating the perceived comfort of leasing from a vendor's captive.
- Doing business with a captive may create unexpected problems. For example, if the lease is in default, the affiliated equipment vendor may refuse to perform necessary maintenance or warranty repairs.

Bank Leasing Companies

Today, banks, particularly national banks, are actively involved in equipment leasing, generally through bank-affiliated leasing companies. Their leasing approach, however, is limited. Bank regulations require leases written by banks to be full-payout, net finance leases. These net leases place the entire equipment ownership responsibility on the lessee, and their full-payout nature, whereby the lease rents return substantially all the equipment purchase cost, assures them of the lowest possible lease risk. Net finance leases are discussed in more detail later in this chapter.

Bank lessors have had an interesting history in equipment leasing. In the 1970s, bank lessors operated with limited lease-marketing staffs, and as a result, the transactions they saw were fundamentally those coming in through existing customers or lease brokers. As lease profit opportunities grew, circumstances changed. Through the early to mid-1980s, bank lessors established strong marketing organizations and, as a group, became a solid factor in the marketplace.

The faltering economy of the late 1980s and early 1990s caused widespread and general bank losses. In an effort to survive, banks adopted a "let's get back to basics" turnaround approach. Since traditional bank management views leasing as a secondary business line, it summarily terminated or sold off leasing operations. Chase Manhattan Bank's sale of its profitable, and well-run, leasing subsidiaries in 1991 is a good example of what can happen when a bank experiences general financial problems.

All that said, however, bank-affiliated leasing companies do have one distinct advantage in the leasing business: Their cost of investment funds is extremely low. The lower a lessor's cost of funds, the more competitive it can be in the leasing market. For example, if a lessor's cost of money is 10% per annum, it would make an annual 2% profit on a lease with a 12% per annum interest charge. If the cost of funds is 9%, it could drop its rate to 11% and still make a 2% profit or keep the rate at 12% and increase its profit to 3% per annum.

The cost-of-funds advantage, however, is often offset by several factors. Bank leasing activities fall under certain regulations that restrict the risks that banks can assume. For example, banks have top limits on how much end-of-lease sale revenues they can anticipate in pricing their rent charge. The less profit that can be assumed from potential residual revenues, the higher the rent charge must be to maintain rent pricing profit levels. See Chapter 2 for an explanation of how the residual revenue assumption affects the lease term rent and see a pricing example given later in *this* chapter.

Another strong influence adversely affecting a bank's rent aggressiveness is the attitude of traditional bank management. Typically, its business approach to leasing is far more conservative than that of non-bank lessor management.

Finally, it is worth mentioning that banks directly participate in the leasing market in another major way: They frequently act as lenders in leveraged lease transactions. This can create hidden risks for an unsophisticated lessee, because the lease loans are typically nonrecourse to the lessor, granted solely on the credit of the lessee. Couple this with the fact that the easiest lender for a lessor to approach is the lessee's own bank, which is familiar with the lessee's credit, and that, typically, a lessor can take out such a loan under a lease without a lessee's knowledge, the lessee's future borrowing capacity can be adversely impacted without the lessee's knowledge. Bank regulations restrict how much banks can lend to any one customer, and a nonrecourse leveraged lease loan is viewed as a loan to the lessee, not the lessor. The solution is to negotiate a lease requirement forcing the lessor to get your permission to borrow leveraged lease funds from your bank.

Advantages and Disadvantages of Bank Leasing Companies

There are certain advantages, and certain disadvantages, for a prospective lessee in becoming involved with bank leasing companies.

Advantages. Bank-affiliated lessors should always be invited to bid on your lease financing because:

- There is little risk that the bank-affiliated lessor won't have funds available when the time comes to pay for your equipment.
- Bank-affiliated lessors' lower cost of investment funds advantage can make them very rate-aggressive.
- Banks can often make better use of equipment ownership tax benefits than most nonbank lessors, which can translate into lower lease rents because, typically, conservative management assures greater likelihood of profits necessary to maximize equipment tax benefits.
- Bank regulators are constantly looking over a bank's shoulder, so a bank is less likely to take unfair advantage of lessees.
- Leasing from your existing bank can be easy: Little additional credit and business investigation will be required.
- Bank lease documentation is generally the fairest in the lessor industry.

Disadvantages. As with other types of lessors, bank-affiliated leasing companies have some disadvantages. For instance:

- Lease rates offered, particularly in transactions in excess of $1 million, vary widely from time to time. More so than nonbank lessors, when bank-affiliated leasing companies want business, they're very aggressive, and when they have all they need, their rates go up dramatically.
- Their interest in lease business is inconsistent—from year to year and sometimes from month to month. Management whims, unrelated business problems, and a general lack of commitment to leasing often make them an unreliable source of competitive financing.
- You can't count on getting their full attention if problems occur, because leasing is not their main line of business.
- Although bank lease documentation is generally the fairest in the industry, concessions or modifications can be hard to get, in part because bank management tends to be less flexible than nonbank lessor management.

What Types of Leases Are Available?

A look at the various types of leasing companies would not be complete without a discussion of the types of leases that are available. Although an in-depth discussion of the various types of leases that lessors offer is beyond the scope of this book, it is worthwhile briefly going over the various ones available so you have a firm foundation for evaluating prospective lessors. In most situations, you will be considering only one type—a financial lease. If you want to know more about the various lease types, I suggest that you obtain one of the many technical equipment leasing books available today, such as my *Handbook of Equipment Leasing—A Deal Maker's Guide*, second edition (published by AMACOM).

As you read, keep the following in mind: The industry jargon used to label the different types of leases is sometimes less than precise. Add to this problem the fact that there are many hybrid lease arrangements that cross over the lines of the typical structure and you have the potential for unintentional misunderstandings. Armed with a basic knowledge of the fundamental characteristics of different "standard" lease arrangements, however, you can protect yourself against any last-minute, and embarrassing, problems.

To begin with, it will be helpful to separate all equipment leases into two main categories: financial leases and operating leases. The financial, or finance, lease typically represents a long-term lease commitment in which the sum of the rents due will approximate the equipment's purchase cost. Decisions to enter into a financial lease should be part of a company's financial, as opposed to operating, policy considerations. All equipment leases not fitting within the financial lease category can be put into the operating lease category. Because operating leases involve shorter-term financial commitments, decisions as to their use typically come within the scope of a company's operating policy.

Within these two general categories, you will find a number of basic variations: leveraged leases, nonleveraged leases, and service leases. These variations are sometimes improperly considered to be separate lease types rather than what they are: descriptive forms of the basic types. For example, a finance lease can be a leveraged lease or a nonleveraged lease, and a service lease can be financial or operating in nature. They will, however, be explained individually to give you a working perspective.

The Financial Lease

Finance leases are considered to be long-term leases because the primary lease terms usually run for most of the equipment's useful life. Generally, the total cash made available to the lessor over the lease term—from rents, tax savings, and equipment residual proceeds—will be sufficient to pay back the lessor's investment, pay off any equipment-related debt obligations and commissions, take care of its administrative expenses, and provide a profit. Because they are entered into by lessors as long-term financial commitments, lessors typically impose a substantial repayment penalty for a lessee's early lease termination in an amount that will assure the lessor of a return of its investment and a profit, at least up to the date of termination.

Consistent with its financial character, a finance lease is generally a net lease, one that imposes the fundamental ownership responsibilities—such as maintaining and repairing the equipment; paying for the necessary insurance; and taking care of property, use, and sales taxes—on the lessee. A net finance lease is comparable to an equipment loan because the lessor, like a lender, is involved only in asset funding. The lessor's only basic responsibilities are to pay for the equipment, lease it to the lessee for the agreed-upon term, and not interfere with its use.

Since the term of a finance lease runs for most of the equipment's useful life, the lessee bears virtually all of the equipment's obsolescence risk. If, for example, the lessor assumed in its rent computation that at lease end the equipment would be worthless, not relying on resale or re-lease proceeds for a portion of its transaction profit, the lessee would have assumed all of the equipment obsolescence risk. As a practical matter, however, a lessor must generally assume that it will receive some residual proceeds in order to be price-competitive. In this case, the risk of obsolescence would then be on the lessor to the extent of the value estimated. And to the extent that its profit is dependent on the anticipated residual value, the greater the risk of obsolescence, the greater the chance that the transaction will not turn out to be as profitable as anticipated.

A principal concern is the protection of the lessor's investment in the event of a lease default or an equipment casualty. Toward this end, finance leases usually include provisions to make the lessor whole if any of these events occur. From a casualty loss standpoint, the lease may include stipulated loss (sometimes referred to as casualty) value provisions, which set out the amount the lessee must pay the lessor if an equipment casualty occurs. The stipulated loss value amount is generally designed to guarantee the lessor a return of its investment, reimburse it for any tax benefit losses, and ensure that it profits at least to the date of loss. Stipulated loss values are also, at times, used as a measure of lease default damages.

Finance leases contain a "hell-or-high-water" rent commitment. In effect, this commitment forces a lessee to pay the full rent when due without offset for any reason, even including, for example, if the lessee has a legitimate claim against the lessor for money owed. A lessee, however, is not prevented from bringing a lawsuit against the lessor for any such claim.

The hell-or-high-water rent provision is a key to putting together the typical leveraged lease transaction in which the lessor wants to borrow equipment purchase funds on a nonrecourse basis. The reason is simple: In a nonrecourse loan, the lender agrees to look only to the lessee, the lease rent payments, and the equipment for a return of its investment. With a hell-or-high-water provision, the lender is assured that any dispute between the lessor and the lessee won't result in the lessee's withholding rent.

The Operating Lease

Leases whose primary term is significantly shorter than the equipment's useful life are referred to as operating leases. Their terms typically run anywhere from a few months to a few years, although some are as short as a few hours.

Because the lease terms are short, typically the lessor is unable to earn much of its equipment investment back through the rents from one lease transaction. So when the initial term ends, the lessor must either sell or re-lease the equipment on attractive terms to come out ahead. The lessor's risk, of course, is that the equipment's market value won't be enough to permit a sale or re-lease on economically favorable terms. In other words, the lessor has the risk of equipment obsolescence. To offset this risk, the lessor will attempt to earn its money back faster, thereby lessening its investment exposure, by charging higher rents than, say, in the case of a finance lease.

From a lessee's perspective, the short lease terms and easy cancellation provisions make operating leases attractive in several situations. One is when the user anticipates using the equipment only for a short time. Another is when the user wants to be able to change equipment if something better comes out. For this reason, computer equipment is often leased under operating leases because of constant technological improvements available virtually every year.

The Leveraged Lease

A leveraged lease is one in which a percentage of the funds to buy the equipment, usually 70% to 80%, is loaned by a bank or some other lender. Because the lessor has put up only a small percentage of the equipment's cost, its investment is said to be leveraged because its return is based on 100% of the cost. Leveraging generally enables a lessor to provide a lessee with relatively lower rents while at the same time maintaining its return. Frequently, net finance leases are structured as leveraged leases.

The debt used to leverage a lease transaction is usually nonrecourse debt. As mentioned above, a nonrecourse lender has no recourse against the lessor for nonpayment of the loan and must look only to the rental stream, the lessee, and the value of the equipment for its loan repayment. The lender, as a result, requires the lessor to assign to it all of its rights under the lease, including the right to the rental payments. This creates some investment risk for a lessor because, although it has no loan repayment obligations, its rights against the lessee and the equipment are subordinated to the lender's repayment rights. And if funds available are only enough to satisfy the debt obligations, the lessor loses its equity investment.

The Nonleveraged Lease

A nonleveraged lease, also referred to as an unleveraged or straight lease, is one in which the lessor pays for the equipment from its own funds From a prospective lessee's point of view, it is often the preferable lease structure, because only two principals are involved, the lessor and the lessee. And the fewer the participants, the lower the risk that problems will arise that will get in the way of the lessee's having its equipment financed in a timely manner—or worse yet, not at all. In addition, because of the limited number of parties, the mechanics of putting together a transaction are simpler, saving time and documentation costs, such as legal fees. There is one disadvantage: Typically, the rent is higher than it would be if the lease were leveraged.

The Service Lease

Leases in which the lessor assumes equipment ownership responsibilities—such as maintenance, repair, insurance, record keeping, or payment of property taxes—in addition to providing the asset financing are usually called service leases. Service leases have short lease terms and can be viewed as operating leases with services attached.

Save Time and Money: Investigate Potential Lessors

Making an early assessment of leasing companies with which you are about to deal will save time and money. Don't waste your efforts talking to those unlikely to give you your best deal. Stay away, for example, from those with poor performance reputations, ones with weak ethical standards, ones that notoriously overcharge, and ones that are financially or structurally unable to provide the best rate possible.

This is true even in a competitive bid situation, where five to ten lessors may be invited to submit offers. Inviting lessors unable or unwilling to bid aggressively or honestly will reduce or eliminate the competitive bid process benefits. If, for instance, three of five lessors invited to bid are clearly noncompetitive, in effect, you're only working with two leasing companies. And if the remaining two don't happen to be offering market rates, little is gained from having a competitive bid. Worse yet, the noncompetitive rate lessors may make it appear that the lower bidders are extremely aggressive.

Very simply, to get the best lease deal, the first step is to ensure that each lessor invited to submit an offer is likely to propose the type of financing you want. This means carefully checking out each lessor's market reputation as well as its general strengths, weaknesses, interests, and business capabilities.

A Poor Market Reputation
Guarantees Problems

Business never runs as smoothly as we hope. Problems occur. Equipment requirements change. So you need as much flexibility as possible. When you sign a lease, you're entering into a long-term, contractual relationship with the leasing company, one negotiated on the basis of existing business and needs—and one that often puts the lessor in control.

Even if a lessor would agree to all document requests, it's virtually impossible to anticipate every conceivable turn of events. For example, you may discover one year into a four-year computer lease that the leased computer won't perform applications now required in your expanded business. Or you may find that your competition has just acquired an upgraded computer system that will enable it to cut prices dramatically and that, to compete, you should also. Or you may realize that in order to stay competitive in a market slump, getting rid of nonessential leased equipment early could help profits.

Dealing with a lessor interested in maintaining an excellent market reputation will give you flexibility. To keep customers happy, some allow lessees to break contracts without penalty or agree to favorable changes that they have no legal obligation to make. On the other hand, notoriously difficult lessors try to take advantage of every situation they can, including interpreting lease language that you thought gave you leeway in a manner that benefits them.

Remember, even the clearest-appearing lease provisions can create problems when unexpected events occur. For example, leases provide that equipment must be returned in good operating condition, subject to normal wear and tear. This seems clear enough until, for example, your operations manager asks whether the equipment's condition resulting from use for 12, rather than 8, hours a day would violate the return condition obligation. There are often no easy answers.

Therefore, regardless of what you think your rights may be under your lease agreement, the caliber of leasing company with which you deal can make a difference. Accommodating lessors have a reputation of working problems out with lessees, even when they have no contractual obligation to do so, simply because it's good business practice. Unethical, or notoriously difficult, lessors take shortsighted positions, just to keep near-term money rolling in. So expect the unexpected in your lease situation and keep your flexibility at its maximum. Make the effort to find lessors with good market reputations that are likely to work with you to solve problems.

A Word of Caution: Never Let Your Guard Down

Even through you've found lessors with good reputations, don't let your negotiating guard down. Get as much flexibility as possible written into your lease contract. And never let a leasing sales representative dissuade you from getting what you need in writing for any reason. The cooperative lessor with which you signed on may no longer be so because, for example, of management changes or financial difficulties. And a verbal promise from a lessor that regularly provides, say, equipment upgrade financing is worthless if the lessor changes its business practice after you've signed a lease.

The risk of verbal promises was brought home to a bank client of mine several years ago. Its data-processing manager was about to enter into a computer lease line of credit that guaranteed a specific lease rent for equipment delivered up to three months after the contract was signed. After reviewing the lease situation, I suggested that a five-month commitment be negotiated to leave a cushion for a late equipment delivery, even though the vendor assured us that the equipment under consideration would be delivered in two months. Our initial request to the lessor for a lease extension was met with a rate increase. The data-processing manager felt that pushing the lessor too hard would result in the loss of what was a favorable rate deal. I suggested that we take the chance and insist on an extension, but he refused to do so, stating he had been assured by the lease sales representative that if a problem arose, she could talk management into an extension without a rate increase.

As luck would have it, the computer was delivered two days after the commitment period ran out, and between the lease signing and equipment delivery, there was a lessor management change. The lessor refused to finance the equipment under the old rate, claiming that an increase was necessary because its funding costs had increased, something we later learned was not the case. In any event, since the commitment period had run out, there was nothing we could do to force the lessor to finance the equipment at the initial lease rate. My client had no time to look elsewhere for lease financing. It agreed to the increased rate.

Follow These Suggestions for Checking a Lessor's Industry Reputation

There are many ways to check out a lessor's reputation. Here are some suggestions:

- Get a Dun & Bradstreet financial report on the lessor. Check it for a reporting of customer disputes or lawsuits. Call those involved in the disputes and see what they have to say.
- Contact your industry trade association or look in industry trade manuals, such as the *Million Dollar Directory*, for companies in your line of business and call them to see whether they've had dealings with the lessor you're considering.
- Call someone you know in the leasing industry and see what he or

she knows. If you don't know anyone, network with business contacts to find a leasing industry contact.

- Talk to your equipment suppliers. They often have valuable information on leasing companies. Also, see whether they'll give you names of customers that lease. Check with them.
- Check with lessor trade associations, such as the Equipment Lessors Association in Arlington, Virginia. They may be able to provide leads for getting information on the lessor.
- Call your bank and see what it knows about the lessor or whom it suggests contacting to get information.

Make Sure Your Deal Fits a Lessor's Capabilities and Interests

If you can match a lessor's capabilities, interests, and objectives with the type of lease you need before you ask for lease bids, you'll come out ahead. For example, if you want a tax-oriented lease, one that gives you credit for the equipment ownership tax benefits, avoid lessors that determine rent without taking tax benefits into account. See Chapter 2 for an overview of why tax benefits can be an important aspect of a lease. And if you want to lease a computer, it's unlikely you'll get your most economic deal from a lessor interested in financing printing presses. The way a lessor approaches a transaction, therefore, may automatically rule it out of your particular lease situation.

The key to assessing early whether a particular leasing company should be in the running is to find out how it operates. For example, is the leasing company a money-over lessor or a residual-sensitive lessor? And in what type of equipment or transaction size, if any, does it specialize? Discovering this may take some work, but it will pay benefits.

The problem facing lessees is that many lessors aren't willing to disclose how they approach a lease financing. Some fear, for example, that a competitor will learn their secrets. Others are concerned that they'll be excluded because, for example, they don't take tax benefits into account in rent pricing. Some are concerned that disclosing their approach will tip you off to something you've overlooked in your lease analysis.

Residual-sensitive lessors, for example, may not want you to know that your equipment has high value at lease end for fear you'll determine that it's better to purchase rather than lose resale revenues. As a rule of thumb, not factoring high potential residual value into a lease-versus-buy analysis can result in the wrong decision, one improperly favoring leasing over purchasing.

Worse yet, even if a lessor tells you that it is, for example, a tax-oriented, residual-sensitive, or money-over lessor, you still may be unable to make a valid assessment. It's not unheard of, for instance, for sales representatives to say whatever they think you want to hear, particularly if it can't be verified. A few money-over lessors, for example, are notorious for telling lessees that they're tax-oriented lessors to make it appear that they're more competitive.

So what do you do? Do some homework on each leasing company you're considering, such as:

- Find someone in the leasing industry not involved in your deal and ask what he or she knows about how the lessor approaches a lease transaction.
- Ask to see the company's financial statements. The use of tax benefits and other pricing approaches can often be determined from an informed review. Lease brokers are the easiest to spot. Typically, they have a small net worth and no lease investments. Pay particular attention to any financial statement footnotes. They often contain facts not readily apparent in the statements themselves.
- Get an annual report if one is available. If you're lucky, the company's manner of structuring transactions will be described sufficiently to enable you make an assessment of its capabilities.
- Listen carefully to what you are being told and how your questions are answered. For example, if a reasonable request is resisted, be on your guard.
- Spend time talking to lease salespeople. They often inadvertently disclose enough information about their company and transaction structure to enable you to determine what transaction aspects are looked to for lease profits.
- Run a Dun & Bradstreet or other business credit report on the lessor. Although the information contained in these reports, particularly for privately owned lessors, is basically supplied by lessor management and may not be accurate, they can provide helpful insights. The most aggressive and innovative lessors will often disclose what you need to know.
- Talk to people most likely to give you accurate information, those less likely to "market" you, such as the lessor's lawyers, accountants, or financial analysts.
- Keep up with leasing industry news by subscribing to trade newsletters or magazines, such as the *Monitor* (published by Molloy Associates, Ardmore, Pennsylvania). Lessor trade associations also publish newsletters or magazines that may keep you up to date on information that can assist in your assessment. Trade association listings can be found in trade association directories.
- Ask your prospective lessors for customer and vendor references. Get a name and department. Then call the department and see whether you can talk to someone else, someone who doesn't expect

a call from you. Or call a different department, such as the finance or legal department, and see whether someone there will provide some insights.

- Check industry listing publications, such as the *Leasing Sourcebook* (published by Bibliotechnology Systems and Publishing Company, Lincoln, Massachusetts). The book contains a comprehensive listing of U.S. leasing companies and details about their leasing activities and interests. Another good source of leasing company listings is available through the Equipment Leasing Association in Arlington, Virginia, the leasing community's national trade association.

If you're still not clear on how a particular lessor operates, hire a leasing expert to help you out.

Follow These Tips for Picking the Right Lessor

There are many variables to consider in determining whether a particular lessor may be right for your deal, so care must be taken in following any general selection guidelines. Experience has shown, however, that the following suggestions are good rules of thumb.

For Weak Credit and High Residual Value Equipment Situations, Use Residual-Sensitive Lessors

Lessors that place great emphasis on the value of equipment at the end of a lease, referred to as residual-sensitive lessors, are the right choice in situations involving equipment with high potential sale or re-lease value. These lessors look to end-of-lease sale or re-lease proceeds for part of their lease profits and, as a result, are able to offer lower rents.

Residual-sensitive lessors that specialize in particular types of equipment, such as printing presses, can offer even better deals on equipment they handle. Because of their familiarity with the equipment on which they concentrate, they often anticipate greater end-of-lease sale or re-lease values than nonspecialized lessors, which, in turn, could mean even lower rents. For this reason, it's well worth the effort to find residual-sensitive lessors that specialize in the type of equipment you're considering.

Residual-sensitive lessors are a good choice in weak credit situations. Their equipment familiarity enables them to sell or re-lease equipment at maximum value, reducing their risk of loss in the event of a lease default. So they'll often finance prospective lessees that other lessors turn down.

Here's how potential residual proceeds impact rent pricing. Assume that Simon Tool Corporation wants to lease a $36,000 lathe for three years. To make this analysis simple, let's assume that the time value of money is unimportant to Simon Tool and that the lessor is willing to offer financing at a 0% lease interest rate. A lessor not assuming any end-of-lease equipment proceeds would need to set monthly rents at $1,000 to get its $36,000 investment back (36 months x $1,000 per month = $36,000). A leasing company taking a residual position could charge a lower monthly rent. Assume, for instance, that the lessor anticipates receiving $18,000 from an end-of-lease sale of the lathe. To be economically whole, the lessor needs to charge only $500 a month for three years (36 months x $500 = $18,000 added to an end-of-lease $18,000 equipment sale = $36,000).

Residual-sensitive lessors are easy to spot. They typically have strong equipment-remarketing departments. And they're usually so proud of how well they do that they'll readily volunteer information about their remarketing activity. Those that aren't residual-sensitive generally have no remarketing staff.

When Credit or Residual Value Is Weak, Use Money-Over Lessors

Traditional money-over lessors, ones that simply borrow money at one rate (say, 9% per annum) and mark it up (to, say, 15%), are not the best economic choice for good-credit lessees. Good-credit lessees can typically borrow money to buy equipment at equivalent or better interest rates than money-over lessors, so after the lessor adds its profit markup, a lessee would pay far more than necessary to lease the equipment.

Financially weaker companies, such as small businesses, or ones with little credit history, such as start-up companies, are another story. Typically, their interest cost on equipment loans is much higher than a money-over lessor's cost of funds. Even after the lessor adds its profit markup, the lease may still be economically attractive. So a money-over lessor may be a good choice for them, particularly since there is less red tape in getting lease financing than in getting an equipment loan.

If the equipment does not have high potential end-of-lease value, a money-over lessor might also be considered. With no potential for residual proceeds, the money-over lessor is more able to offer competitive rents.

Finding a money-over lessor is easy. Generally, they're the ones that specialize in small ($1,500 to $100,000) and, in a few cases, middle-market ($100,000 to $750,000) lease transactions. If they know they have no basic rent pricing disadvantage, they'll readily disclose their money-over approach.

If You Can Use Tax Benefits, Avoid Money-Over Lessors

If your company is profitable and currently able to use equipment ownership tax benefits, traditional money-over lessors are the wrong choice.

Because it doesn't take tax benefits into account in computing lease rents, a lessee loses its benefit completely by leasing from a money-over lessor. Not considering tax benefits results in higher rent charges.

As already mentioned, some leasing companies hide the fact that they're money-over lessors when they're aware that a lessee is looking for tax-oriented lease pricing. If you're unsure whether a lessor is in fact a tax-oriented lessor, ask for a rate quote on a lease containing a fair market value purchase option, one giving you a right to buy the leased equipment at lease end for a price equal to its then market value. Once you get it, ask for a quote on a lease with a nominal fixed price purchase option, such as one dollar. If the rental rates are the same, or very close, tax benefits are unimportant in rent pricing, and the lessor is taking a money-over approach.

Good-Credit Lessees Should Always Use Tax-Oriented Lessors

If you're a good-credit lessee and can currently use the equipment ownership tax benefits, leasing long-term is not the best choice unless the lessor is willing to pass the benefits on indirectly through lower rent charges. An explanation of why this is so is beyond the scope of this book. Suffice it to say, however, that incorporating available equipment ownership tax benefits as a part of its lease profit enables a lessor to lower rent while maintaining its economic return.

Identifying tax-oriented lessors is easy: Simply ask. They're more than willing to tell you. But remember, it's always a good idea to verify what you're being told.

If You Need Equipment for a Long Time, Avoid Rental Companies

If you need a long-term lease, avoid companies, referred to as rental companies, that specialize in short-term leasing, offering, for example, month-to-month or daily arrangements. A rental car company is a good example of this type of lessor.

Long-term lessors, such as finance leasing companies, buy equipment only after a lessee commits to lease it for an agreed-upon period. Their initial transaction approach anticipates a full return of investment and a profit. Rental companies, on the other hand, buy equipment for inventory, hoping to find lessees willing to use the equipment long enough so the companies will get their investment back and make a profit. Because they have little assurance when they purchase equipment that they'll find necessary lessee business, they charge high rates in an effort to recover their investment as quickly as possible. For example, it's not unusual for a rental company to fully recover its entire asset purchase cost in 12 months, providing it with solid profits for the remainder of the equipment's useful life—which, in the case of a computer, could be five or more years. Their short-term profit orientation coupled with their borrowing structure typically inhibits rental companies from competing effectively in the long-term leasing market.

Long-term lessors, on the other hand, set up their bank loans to match their long-term leasing approach, borrowing at fixed interest rates for periods matching the lease terms on equipment they finance. For example, a long-term lessor entering into a three-year lease with a 9% lease interest rate might buy the equipment using a three-year 7% per annum equipment loan. In this way, the lessor locks in a 2% per annum profit spread.

If You're a Good-Credit, Small-Ticket Lessee, Avoid Brokers

Brokers make money by building fees into lease transactions. As discussed earlier, the rent offered by a lessor-investor is marked up by the amount of its fee. So if a broker is involved, you will pay higher lease rents. That, however, may not always be detrimental. In certain situations, you may not be able to find a lessor-investor willing to accept as low a lease rate as that found by the lease broker. In this case, the benefit added by the broker in finding a little-known and extremely aggressive lease investor may offset the fee charged.

As a general rule, brokers may add value only in transactions involving more than $1 million. Below that, it's not difficult to find competitive lessors, so involving brokers is not usually advisable. For example, brokers rarely add any benefit in small transactions, typically in the $1,500 to $100,000 range. Only when a lessee does not have the time to talk to direct lessors may the rate premium be justified. If your company has substantial small-ticket leasing needs, dealing through a small-ticket lease broker is a mistake.

Small Leasing Companies Have a Pricing Disadvantage

As you'll see in Chapter 2, one way a lessor profits is by marking up its cost of funds. So the higher the lessor's funding cost, the higher the rent charge. Small leasing companies, because they lack the financial strength to borrow lease investment funds at the best available rates, are often forced to charge above-market rates simply to cover their cost of borrowing. Think carefully about using one if you need aggressive lease rates.

Reviewing financial statements or touring a lessor's office is an easy way to determine whether you're dealing with a small leasing company.

Watch Out for Small-Ticket Lessors That Don't Publish Rate Sheets

Generally, financially strong regional and national lessors, or ones affiliated with major corporations or banks, that offer small-ticket lease financing assure you of the best deal. But be careful. Although most have standard rates, a few don't. *Those that don't have standard rates* attempt to make the most out of each situation.

Companies that offer fair standard lease rates in small-ticket lease situations periodically publish "rate sheets." These rate sheets specify charges for the various financing terms and equipment costs. Opportunistic lessors that gouge don't publish rate sheets. So if a rate sheet is unavailable, be on your guard.

Vendor Leasing Subsidiaries Often Overcharge

Equipment suppliers often finance equipment they sell through company-owned leasing subsidiaries. But be careful. More so than independent lessors, they're always on the lookout for profit-grabbing opportunities. If, for example, you have decided to purchase their affiliate's product and they think you won't take the time to seek competitive lease quotes, they'll charge as much as they think they can get away with.

Local Bank Leasing Companies Are Often Not Aggressive

Rates charged by local bank leasing companies are generally higher than market, often because their customers, typically local businesses, expect leasing to be more expensive than borrowing.

There are two additional reasons that rates can be high. Many small banks take a money-over approach to rent pricing, often overlooking tax benefits and residual revenues simply because they don't know how to maximize lessor profits and thereby lower rents. And some are run by bank traditionalists who believe that leasing is a low-class form of lending, offering it only as a customer accommodation at high take-it-or-leave-it prices.

Local Leasing Companies Go After Every Profit Opportunity

Privately held small, local leasing companies, often owned by one or two businesspeople, typically take advantage of every opportunity to charge as much as they can. They rarely publish rate sheets to avoid limiting a potential opportunity for windfall profits.

In fairness to the small companies, it must be pointed out that the economic realities of a small business often force them to take a deal-by-deal opportunistic approach. Larger, national leasing companies with high, consistent business volume are assured of better aggregate profits at lower rates. The small, local lessor, with considerably less business, must cover overhead by making as much as possible on each lease.

Niche Lessors Often Overcharge for Non-Niche Leases

Niche leasing companies, ones specializing in certain dollar size transactions or in certain equipment types, typically refuse to finance leases outside their specialization, unless, possibly, they can make windfall profits. Small-transaction money-over lessors, for example, never actively seek out multimillion-dollar leases. If one comes along, some will entertain financing it, but only at rates that provide the type of profits they're used to in the small-ticket market, a market that supports returns far in excess of those found in the big-ticket lease market.

By the same token, large-ticket lessors avoid small-ticket leases, unless, possibly, very attractive economic returns are likely. There are a number of reasons for this. Large-ticket lessors can rarely process small lease transactions cost-effectively. In addition, large-ticket lessors generally don't have the credit expertise to evaluate a small-ticket lease situation effectively. And possibly most important, the big-ticket leasing produces greater dollar inflows. Big-ticket economics are plain to see: A 2% profit margin on a $10 million lease is $200,000, but on a $10,000 lease, it's only $200.

Lessors that specialize in certain equipment avoid unfamiliar equipment transactions. For example, not knowing how to maximize end-of-lease sale or re-lease profits increases investment risk. To minimize investment problems, those willing to finance unfamiliar equipment don't rely heavily on end-of-lease revenues for profits, thereby increasing rents. And to ensure that they don't make a bad deal, they'll build in a greater-than-normal profit cushion. So if you want the best deal on a printing press lease, for instance, don't approach a lessor specializing in telephone systems.

Watch Out for 0% Lessors

Beware of leasing companies or equipment vendors offering 0% financing. These offers are often deceitful marketing gimmicks. Every business must make a profit to survive, and you can be sure that 0% offers have profits hidden somewhere.

Automobile dealers and manufacturers often use this trick. Once you're in the door, you find out that the 0% offer applies only to a car purchased at full list price. And you also learn that the company will heavily discount the car's purchase price if you buy it outright. In effect, under the 0% financing offer, a dealer is leasing discounted cars at market interest rates. Most consumers are completely taken in by this soft deception, never realizing that the 0% offer is a scam.

Here's how the scam works. Assume you want to buy a $36,000 car. The dealer offers to sell it to you for $30,500, a $4,500 discount. You ask about lease financing. The dealer offers a three-year, 0% lease, calling for monthly, in advance, rent payments of $1,000 ($36,000 ÷ 36 months = $1,000 per month). Since the dealer would have sold the car for $30,500, your real lease interest is 11.78% per annum, determined by finding the interest rate that will discount the $1,000 monthly payment to a $30,500 purchase price.

By Checking Financial Requirements Early, You Can Avoid a Turndown

In order to get your deal approved, your company must meet a lessor's financial, or credit acceptance, requirements. Knowing them early in the lease process will save you time if there are ones you cannot meet and will increase your chances of approval if there are problems you can overcome. There's nothing worse than investing time talking to a lessor, requesting a bid, reviewing form documents, and submitting an application, only to learn that your company doesn't meet its standard financial hurdles. Some lessors, for example, require audited financial statements or a minimum time in business. If you don't have audited financial statements or don't meet the minimum-time-in-business requirement, your efforts would best be directed elsewhere.

Knowing the financial requirements before submitting a lease request has another advantage. Although the requirements may not be met, you may be able to structure your transaction in a way that will overcome the problem. For example, if audited financial statements are not available, solid financial support from a related company, shareholder, partner, or other third party may be the solution. Once a deal is turned down, human nature makes it difficult to get it reconsidered, even if what you offer after the turndown would have been enough to get it approved had it been done at the time of initial submission.

Knowing the financial requirements before submitting a deal to a lessor is important for still another reason: A formal financing turndown taints a deal in the eyes of the next lessor that reviews it. Credit managers at times refuse business they would otherwise accept merely because someone else turned it down before them, often being afraid there's a problem they couldn't find.

Although specific credit criteria can vary from lessor to lessor, certain basic areas will always be of review interest in the lessor's approval process. Let's take a look at the types of criteria found on a typical lessor's credit information sheet for small lease transactions:

- *Minimum time in business:* The applicant must have a minimum verifiable time in business of two years. Three years is required in the case of applications over $25,000 and four years in the case of applications over $100,000.
- *Existing banking relationship:* The applicant must have a business banking relationship of at least two years, and the bank account must show a minimum low-four-figure average balance. In the case of transactions exceeding $25,000, the minimum average account balance must be in the low-five-figure range. There can be no overdrafts or check returns for insufficient funds.
- *Trade references:* The applicant must provide three significant trade

references, each involving a relationship that goes back at least six months. COD trade references will not be acceptable.

- *Good personal credit:* The applicant must be able to provide personal credit reports that contain no derogatory information.
- *Financial statements:* Financial statements must be supplied for transactions exceeding $25,000. Current assets must exceed current liabilities, and for transactions in excess of $50,000, a minimum equity of $75,000 must be present.

It's not unusual for other requirements or restrictions to exist that could affect your transaction. For example, many lessors have lists of prohibited equipment that exclude items such as security systems and tanning beds. It pays to ask for information on all requirements early.

The Best Deal May Be a Matter of Timing

At times, leasing companies go on drives for business. Some do it infrequently, others every year. If you're talking to a lessor at one of these times, you can get a rock-bottom deal with little or no effort. But remember, the leasing company that gave you the lowest bid six months ago may not do so today.

How can you tell when a business drive is in progress? Typically, a lease sales representative will tip you off. But be cautious: Many are inclined to tell you anything you want to hear. Another clue is receiving a lease-marketing letter. They're often sent at the start of a drive. If you can cultivate an acquaintance in the leasing industry, checking with him or her may provide that information. Word gets around the industry quickly when a lessor is aggressively seeking business.

The reasons for these competitive drives are many. At times, lessors want to manage their income tax bill. Equipment ownership provides tax benefits, benefits that can reduce taxes on income from nonleasing and leasing sources. An in-depth explanation of how these benefits work can be found in many of the equipment leasing books that discuss the technical aspects, such as my *Handbook of Equipment Leasing—A Deal Maker's Guide,* second edition (published by AMACOM).

Sometimes leasing companies go on drives for a particular type of equipment with high potential residual value, hoping for windfall profits at lease end. For example, in the 1970s, a few lessors specialized in financing aircraft. When these leases ended, lessors were able to sell the used aircraft for 60% to 110% of original cost—even after ten or more years of use. Market demand and inflation had kept prices at their peak. As a result, the early aircraft lessors made windfall profits. The word spread quickly, and every major leasing company went on drives to lease aircraft. As competition increased, lease rates dropped and lessees benefited.

Lessors go on business drives for particular types of lessees when the word gets around that they're generally good credit risks. Doctors are a good example. The first medical equipment lessors had favorable payment experiences with doctors. As other lessors became aware of that fact, there was a rush for doctors' business. Once again, rates plummeted. Today, doctors, medical clinics, and related health care businesses can get some excellent lease deals, provided they do a little rate shopping.

Some Lessors Use Bait-and-Switch Marketing; Don't Deal With Them

In the highly competitive, no-holds-barred leasing marketplace, some unethical lessors use a bait-and-switch tactic to win business: the lowball offer. These lessors have no intention of honoring the below-market offer. They use the offer to get the other bidders out of the picture, giving them a one-on-one opportunity to manipulate the rate upward. Seem impossible? It's done all the time—without lessees' suspecting what is happening.

Here's how the lowball tactic works. A rate is offered that's so far below the market that an award is guaranteed. Once the lessee takes the bait and signs on with the lessor, the lessor begins to develop opportunities to increase the lease rate. These lessors know that lessees will tolerate changes, including rate increases, when accompanied by a plausible rationale. The reason is simple: Lessees simply have their guard down once an award is made. They think that nothing remains but to formalize what was agreed upon. In addition—it's a fact of negotiating life—people become psychologically committed once an award is made. Experienced negotiators have a field day. They know people don't like throwing away invested time. And the more time a lessor gets a lessee to invest, the less likely the lessee will walk away, even in the face of rate increases. And the nearer the equipment delivery, the less time for a lessee to find alternative financing.

Here's how unethical lessors work these situations. To ensure that rate increase opportunities will arise, they omit details or use vague or misleading language in their lease offer. They might, for example, not offer an end-of-lease purchase option. If it's overlooked and requested after the award, the lessor has an opening for a rate increase. The lessor will claim that a rate increase is necessary, for instance, because the rent was priced without an option and granting it reduces the lessor's profit opportunity. Inexperienced lessees, and even some experienced ones, all too often go along with this plausible, but invariably untrue, rationale.

So if an offer looks to good to be true, be on your guard. If you accept the offer, take some precautions. For example:

- Don't accept an offer unless it's in writing.
- Read the offer conditions carefully. Look for lessor loopholes in, for example, vaguely written paragraphs.
- Make sure you understand the meaning of every sentence. Put clarifying language in the proposal if you don't.
- Have a contingency plan. Consider your alternatives if the lessor doesn't deliver as promised. For example, keep your second-place bidder around until the lease is signed.
- Don't rely on legal remedies. A right to sue for a performance breach is nice to have, but it won't solve your immediate financing problem if the lessor doesn't deliver as promised.
- Make sure you're dealing with a direct funding source, not a lease broker, or your funding risk will go up.
- Set a timetable for documenting your lease transaction. If the lessor delays the process, get another bidder involved. Lowball lessors often delay documentation until there's no time for a lessee to find other financing.

Conclusion

If you keep the following points in mind in approaching prospective lessors, your chances of finding the right lessor for your deal will be improved:

- Don't use lease brokers.
- Don't use your main bank if keeping maximum lines of credit is important.
- Immediately cut off relations with lessors that mislead you in any way.
- Don't do business with leasing companies that won't put everything they offer in writing.
- Avoid lessors that justify higher costs with claims of value-added service, unless the service offered is clearly unique.
- Don't deal with leasing companies that won't let you review their financial statements.
- Be extremely wary of leasing companies offering substantially below-market rates.
- Lease from lessors that emphasize what your equipment's residual value will be when pricing lease rents.
- Avoid leasing companies that don't specialize in the equipment you want to lease.

- Give award preference to tax-oriented lessors, ones that take advantage of equipment ownership tax benefits and pass them on through rent savings.
- Avoid equipment rental companies if you need equipment for an extended period of time.
- Don't lease from a small local bank. Such banks rarely understand how to structure a lease for your benefit.
- Don't deal with small local leasing companies if you want the lowest possible lease rate.

Chapter 2

How Lessors Take
Your Money

Getting the Best Deal
Means Finding Hidden Profits

If you don't know how a leasing company makes money, you won't get your best deal. Worse yet, you may not even get a fair one. Leasing looks straightforward, but there are many hidden profit areas. Missing any can be costly.

To beat a lessor, you have to find where the profit is buried in the deal you are making. Sometimes it is obvious, such as in high lease interest rates, but more often it's hidden in less obvious areas, such as in insurance markups or end-of-lease equipment sale revenues. Once you know what the lessor has to trade with, you'll gain negotiating control.

The money-grabbing provisions in lease agreements present the greatest challenge for lessees. Leases can be difficult to read, often tangled with legal jargon that even lawyers at times don't understand. Attorneys who draft leases are masters at making profit-gouging provisions look harmless. Misleading approaches are not unusual. Innocent-looking paragraph headings steer people away from key obligations that increase leasing costs. Confusing sentence structure discourages thoughtful reading. All this is intentional. Lessors know that businesspeople don't give their full attention to boring, complex paragraphs, particularly when they appear standard. And that's where many financial traps are hidden. The answer is to know what to look for. And that's the purpose of this chapter: to help you identify the many ways a lessor can take your money.

Lessors Profit in Many Ways

Most lessees don't realize how extensive the profit opportunities in a lease transaction are. They think that a lessor, at most, makes money from:

- Interest charges
- Tax benefits
- Equipment sales or re-leases

But there are more opportunities, including:

- Interim rent
- Prepayment penalties
- Casualty occurrences
- Insurance cost markups
- Upgrade financing
- Documentation fees
- Filing fees
- Maintenance charges
- Repair costs
- Excess use charges
- Equity placement fees
- Debt costs and placement fees
- Commitment fees
- Nonutilization fees
- Remarketing fees
- Late payment charges
- Collection telephone charges
- Deal rewrite fees
- Equipment redelivery charges

Now let's examine each profit area, so you'll be prepared to get your best deal.

The Obvious Profit Areas

The obvious lessor profit areas are: interest charges, equipment tax benefits, and residual earnings. Overlooking any one can significantly add to the cost of a lease.

Interest Charges

The most apparent way lessors make money is through financing profits. Financing profit, sometimes referred to as financing spread, is the difference between a leasing company's cost of money and the lease interest rate charged. The higher the interest rate charged, the greater the financing profit. Assume, for example, that a lessor borrows money at a 12% per annum interest rate and charges a lease interest rate of 14%. Its financing spread is 2% per annum. By increasing the lease interest rate to 15%, the lessor increases its financing profit to 3%.

Watch Out For: High Lease Interest Rates

Since there is virtually no limit on what lessors can charge commercial lessees, lessors ask for as much as they can get away with, limited only by competition and the lessee's sophistication. The greater the competition and sophistication, the more creative a lessor must be. For example, if a lessor knows that a prospect is concerned about monthly cash flow, it will offer a longer lease term to keep monthly rent payments as low as possible. A longer lease gives the lessor an opportunity to build in higher financing profits.

Here's how the cash flow scam works. A $15,000, three-year computer lease with monthly, in advance, rent payments of $513 would provide the lessor with an annual interest rate of 15%. If the rent payments are lowered to $407 per month but the lease term is stretched to five years, the annual interest charge would increase to 22%. A lessee concerned about monthly cash flow may jump at the lower monthly payment five-year lease, not realizing that the interest charge is substantially higher.

Here's What to Do: Use Your Market Leverage

To beat a lessor at the financing rate game, you must be aware of your market leverage and not hesitate to take full advantage of it. Many lessees don't know that they are in a superior bargaining position and readily accept what they're offered. The fact is that high potential profits have attracted many companies into leasing. Too many companies are competing for too few deals, turning it into a buyer's market for good-credit lessees.

A lessee's leverage further increases in times when corporate equipment acquisitions are slow, as in recessionary periods. And when corporate downsizing occurs, as in the early 1990s, available financing business is drastically reduced, and a lessee's position is unbeatable. So if you understand your leverage and use it, you can get rock-bottom pricing.

Even in a lessee's market, however, you can't rely on competitive fears to ensure the best offer. Lessors are a tough group. To begin with, never give a prospective leasing company an exclusive right to provide your equipment financing.

> If you do, there's one thing you can count on: not getting the lowest possible offer. Keep in mind that a lessor's objective is to *make a lot of money, quickly and without credit risk. The solution is to introduce open competition, inviting at least three companies to bid and letting each know that others are involved.*

Here's a Technique for Getting Low Rates. Open competition, in which lessors know that others are bidding, ensures aggressive quotes. And using a tiered bid approach makes lessors stretch for business. The time you invest will depend on the size of the transaction. Saving 1% on a $5,000 lease is rarely economical, but it is on a $1 million lease.

In approaching the lessor market, keep the following three points in mind. A leasing company:

1. *Never* gives its best rate in its first offer.
2. *Rarely* gives its best rate in its second offer.
3. *May* get close to its lowest rate by its third offer.

It's always a good idea to let each lessor know that you may purchase the equipment if rates aren't acceptable. That possibility creates greater pressure than competition; lessors feel that they have a chance against others but that they have little chance if a lessee is inclined to purchase because of factors they can't argue against, such as that the manufacturing executive simply feels more comfortable owning his or her equipment.

Another key to getting the deal you want is to get the prospective lessors to invest time. The more time invested, the more likely they'll stretch to reach the goal—if only to avoid wasting their work investment. In the heat of battle, winning often becomes more important than making a profit.

Here's the tiered bid technique:

1. Use open competitive bidding.
2. Invite five to eight leasing companies to bid.
3. Don't initially tell them that rebids will be requested.
4. Get rebids as often as practical.
5. In the final rebid:
   a. Name the other bidders.
   b. Disclose their individual ranking.
   c. Disclose the other lease quotes.
   d. Don't tell who submitted what bid.

For example, assume you received the following three finalist bids:

Lessor	Lease Rate (per annum)
Apex Leasing Company	7.500%
Bison Credit Company	7.445%
NYC Leasing Company	7.555%

Call Apex and tell its representative that Apex came in second and that the other two quotes were 7.555% and 7.445%. Let the Apex representative know that Bison and NYC finished in the top cut but not who submitted what quote.

6. Don't follow a pattern if you're in the market regularly. For example, get two rebids one time and three rebids another time. You must vary your bidding procedure to keep lessors off guard.
7. Don't tell the leasing companies more than necessary to keep them motivated.

Here's an example of how this technique works. Several years ago, I was hired to negotiate a lease for a $750,000 computer. We invited eight leasing companies to bid, letting each know up front that it would be a competitive bid situation and that we were considering purchasing. We said nothing about our intention to ask for rebids.

After evaluating the bids, we asked the five lowest bidders to rebid, stating that the closeness of the offers made it necessary. They were also told that we would narrow the field down to the lowest three and ask for rebids. They were not told how they ranked or who the other bidders were.

After the rebids were received, we advised the top three how they ranked and who the other contenders were, and we disclosed the offers. We didn't disclose who submitted what offer.

We requested a second rebid, stating that an award would be made the day after the bids were due. All could see the goal and had a feel for what they had to do to win. The process ended in an attractive proposal.

To summarize:

- *It's a lessee's market today.* Lessors are starving for business.
- *Never limit bidding to only one lessor*—or you won't get its best offer.
- *Open competitive bidding assures the best offers.* Lessors won't offer their best deal unless they know there is competition.
- *If you don't ask for something, you won't get it.*

There Are No Interest Rate Limits. Lease interest rates (referred to as simple interest rates) vary considerably. There are no general profit limitations or fairness guidelines for the business lessee, so a lessor charges whatever the market will bear.

Typically, the smaller the lease dollar size, the higher the rate. For example, interest rates on $5,000 to $50,000 equipment transactions at the time of this writing generally range from 12.5% to 22% per annum. As transactions approach $100,000 and over, simple interest rates are in the 10.5% to 13.5% range. Once the deal size hits $1 million, rates run 2% to 4% below the lessee's equivalent long-term borrowing rate. In the latter case, for example, a $4 million, three-year computer lease for a company that borrows long-term money at 10% per annum could run anywhere from 6% to 8% per annum. Shopping the market is the key to finding the best rate.

As a rule of thumb, small-ticket lessors determine rent by marking up their cost of money by a minimum of 6% per annum. Of that, 2% is allocated to overhead, 2% to a loss reserve, and the rest to net profit. Typically, many larger companies can operate effectively at a 6% markup. Ones with less business volume, however, often need higher returns, targeting financing spreads of 10%, which often push lease interest rates over 22% in today's market.

In small deals, lessors take *full* advantage of a lessee's inclination not to invest much, if any, time in reviewing or negotiating rates. Those that object to high rates are told that they're necessary to offset administrative and documentation costs. Although documenting a $1 million lease costs more than documenting a $10,000 one, the relative economics don't require excessive rates.

In large-dollar leases, rates are lower for two reasons: Transactions are closely examined, and competition is intense. Accepting low rates, however, is not as bad as it seems for lessors because, even at smaller financing spreads, greater absolute dollar profits are available. For example, a profit of 1% on a $1 million lease is $10,000, whereas on a $10,000 lease, it is $100. In some cases, to win business, a lessor has to offer lease rates that are less than its cost of money, forcing the lessor to look to other transaction aspects to offset negative cash flow, such as tax benefits and equipment residual proceeds.

Those Who Can Least Afford It Are Charged the Most. Unfortunately, companies that can least afford it, small businesses, are charged the highest rates. In a few cases, some lease interest rates are in the 30% to 40% range. The rationale: Less creditworthy lessees must be charged more to offset risk. Higher rates return investments faster. However, excessive rents increase credit risk because available lessee cash is reduced, putting additional pressure on what may be already strained finances.

Some analysts suggest charging a uniformly fair rate and declining weak-credit business, but greed and business realities push the market to increased rates and risks. The fact is that lessors that turn away marginal business often lose good business. A high turndown rate, regardless of the reasons, stigmatizes a lessor. So marginal business is justified with high rates, in the hope that all will balance out. It rarely does.

Lowball Rate Deals Can Be Expensive. A leasing company's first objective is to take the deal off the market quickly by getting a lease award while offering only the minimum necessary to win. When a lessor has an award, its negotiating control increases: The other bidders are out of the picture, and the lessee is psychologically, if not legally, committed to the financing offered.

Providing a below-market rate, referred to as a lowball rate, alone is often enough. Once in the door, the lessor jumps on any opportunity to increase profits. For example, if a lessee makes additional deal requests, such as asking for a right to purchase the equipment at the end of the lease for a bargain price, a rate increase is virtually guaranteed. In the case of bargain purchase right requests, lessors justify rent increases by claiming that they're needed to offset the loss of end-of-lease sale or re-lease earnings, something that can't be verified.

If the rate offered seems too good to be true, don't forget:

- The lowest rate gets a lessor in the door and buys an opportunity to work a deal to the lessor's economic advantage.
- A seasoned marketing representative will attempt to manipulate a lease commitment to make up lost profits or to increase profits.

If You've Been Overcharged, Check the State Rules. Although commercial, as opposed to consumer, leases are not generally regulated by federal or state laws, times are changing. If you find that you've signed a lease containing a high rate, have your lawyer check the governing state laws. A few states have enacted, or are considering implementing, rules that protect commercial, in addition to consumer, lessees. For example, unconscionable profit laws, referred to as usury laws, originally designed to protect individuals have, in Texas, been extended to corporations in installment sales-type financing. Included are low-fixed-price purchase option leases.

If your lease runs afoul of state law, generally your options are to:

- Walk away without penalty.
- Walk away unless you're given a rate reduction.

Pointing the problem out to a lessor usually gets a fast response.

A word of caution: Even when state governments get around to regulating commercial lease financing—and they will—it will take time before the rules will cover all areas of potential abuse. Leasing companies are a smart group, and they are years ahead of regulators and politicians. The evolving federal tax rules covering equipment leases are a good example. Initially they were weak and provided little to forestall abuse. Although they are much improved, there are still areas for manipulation.

Equipment Tax Benefits

Although any type of equipment can be leased, the critical question for the prospective lessee is, at what cost? While the answer is complex, as a threshold matter, leasing often is not the least expensive way to acquire equipment unless the lessor can take advantage of certain tax benefits and indirectly pass them on, at least in part, in the form of relatively lower lease rents.

An in-depth analysis of the tax aspects of an equipment lease is beyond the scope of this book, but you can consult the many excellent technical leasing books available today. However, in order to ensure that you have a full understanding of how lessors use the tax issue to manipulate a lease to their financial advantage, it will be helpful to take a quick look at the relevant tax aspects.

As explained in more detail later in this subsection, by leasing equipment, a lessee loses its right to claim equipment ownership tax benefits, such as depreciation and any available investment tax credits. Rents, however, are deductible. A lessee must balance what it gives up against the benefits it receives. For a company unable to use ownership tax benefits, the decision to lease or buy is not as complex; a lease in which the lessor uses the tax benefits, and passes them on through lower rents, is often the best choice.

Although the following example is admittedly oversimplified and not completely realistic, it shows why leasing may not make any economic sense for a lessee unless the lessor is able to use and pass on the available ownership tax benefits.

Example: Losing Tax Benefits Will Increase Costs

Tri-It Corporation wants to acquire the use of a $20,000 telephone system. It can borrow funds from its bank for five years at the prime rate, assumed for this example to be 10% a year. If Tri-It were able to borrow 100% of the funds required, its cost to finance the telephone system would be the cost of the $20,000 loan.

As an alternative, Tri-It could lease the telephone system from Steller Leasing Corporation. Assume that Steller Leasing also borrowed at prime from the same bank and that it would fund the telephone system purchase entirely from its bank borrowing. If there were no telephone system ownership tax advantages, the only way Steller could make a profit would be to charge a lease rate greater than its cost of funds. Thus, Tri-It would have to pay something over prime rate to Steller Leasing—not a very attractive arrangement.

The Lessor's Tax Benefits. What tax benefits are available to the lessor as an equipment owner? For equipment placed in service before 1986, the lessor could obtain both investment tax credit (ITC) and depreciation deductions as an equipment owner. With limited exceptions, the 1986 Tax Reform Act (TRA) did away with the ITC for equipment placed in service after 1985. Thus, the tax benefits for the lessor as of this writing are the depreciation deductions available under the modified accelerated cost recovery system (MACRS), introduced by the 1986 TRA.

Under MACRS, a lessor generally can write off its equipment's cost over a period significantly shorter than the equipment's actual useful life and at an accelerated rate. For example, a lessor can deduct the cost of leased computer equipment over a six-year period, with the percentages for each year being 20%, 32%, 19.2%, 11.52%, 11.52%, and 5.76%. In a typical lease, the lessor's deductions in the early years will exceed the rental income, permitting the lessor to offset other income with those excess deductions.

If investment tax credits generally become available in the future, it is likely that the equipment owner will have direct offsets to federal income tax owed in the amount of the available tax credits. Assume, for example, that an 8% investment tax credit was allowed on all new equipment acquired and put into use in a given year. An investment tax credit equal to 8% of equipment cost would permit an $8,000 tax offset for each $100,000 of equipment acquired. So if a lessor had an $80,000 federal income tax bill before considering investment credits and had purchased a $100,000 truck, its tax payment due would be reduced to $72,000 ($80,000 – $8,000).

The Lessee's Tax Benefits. A company deciding to lease rather than purchase equipment typically decreases the value of its available tax benefits. As lessee, the equipment user can deduct its rental payments, but those will be less than the depreciation it could have deducted in earlier years. Then why should leasing be considered? There are numerous financial and business reasons for a prospective lessee to lease rather than buy, such as cash management considerations, inability to use tax benefits, financial statement reporting issues, capital budget restrictions, borrowing problems, and equipment obsolescence concerns. Once again, you can refer to one of the many technical books available today for a discussion of the pros and cons of leasing, such as my *Handbook of Equipment Leasing—A Deal Maker's Guide,* second edition (published by AMACOM).

Tax Benefits as a Source of Extra Lessor Profits. The availability of equipment tax benefits, such as depreciation, can be an important lessor profit ingredient. If the lessor borrows a portion of the equipment purchase cost from a third-party lender, taking advantage of interest charge deductions can also provide profit advantages. All have a predetermined dollar value to a lessor.

By taking into account equipment-related tax benefits, a lessor is able to offer lower rents while achieving its profit objectives. For example, typically a lessor offering an annual lease rate of 14% could easily reduce its lease interest rate to 12% without reducing its economic return by incorporating depreciation benefits in its rent pricing.

One final point: Never tell a lessor that you can't use ownership tax benefits. It may not make the appropriate pricing adjustment.

Residual Earnings

Watch Out For: False Claim of a Tax Benefit Pass-Through

Some lessors falsely claim that they're taking tax benefits into account and state that they have made an appropriate downward rent adjustment. Lessees that don't independently verify whether a particular lessor is telling the truth often pay more than they should.

Here's What to Do: Verify Tax Pass-Through by Requesting Two Quotes

An easy way to determine whether a lessor will pass tax benefits on to you in the form of relatively lower rent charges is to ask for a quote on a lease in which you have the right to purchase the equipment when the lease is over for its fair market value; then, after you get that quote, ask for one containing a right to purchase the equipment at the end of the lease for one dollar. The one-dollar purchase option forces the lessor to treat the lease as a conditional sale for tax purposes. Under a conditional sale arrangement, the lessee, not the lessor, may claim the equipment ownership tax benefits. If the conditional sale rate quoted is the same as the fair market quote, the lessor did not take tax benefits into account.

Watch Out For: Tax Benefit Pass-Through Illusions

The illusion of a tax benefit pass-through in the form of relatively lower rent charges can be created with hidden equipment purchase price discounts. If the lessor provides a quote based on an equipment price higher than actually paid, the lease interest rate, and thus the rent charge, appears relatively lower. If the lessor offers to supply the equipment rather than purchase it from your selected vendor, or offers to buy it under its master purchase contract, be careful.

Doing this makes it easy for a lessor to hide purchase price discounts.

Here's how the scam works: You request a three-year lease quote on a $36,000 truck needed in your business. Your leasing company quotes a monthly, in advance, rent of $1,000, provided you let it purchase the truck from one of its affiliated dealers. So far, it seems like a great deal: The lease interest rate works out to be 0% ($36,000 ÷ 36 months). When you question the leasing company about the low rate, it responds by saying that it took the truck ownership tax benefits into account in pricing the rent.

Now assume that the leasing company secretly negotiated to purchase the truck for $28,800, a 20% price discount. Based on the $28,800 purchase price and a $1,000 monthly payment, the real lease interest rate would be 16% per annum. If the leasing company took out a three-year loan, at a 10% interest rate, the financing profit would be 6% (the 16% lease interest rate minus the 10% loan interest rate). The tax benefits are simply added profits.

Here's What to Do: Always Control the Equipment Purchase

To avoid being taken in by a hidden purchase price discount scam, make equipment purchase arrangements directly with the equipment seller. Once you've negotiated your best purchase deal, then ask the leasing company to provide a financing quote on the basis of your buy price. And go one step further: Make the lessor represent in the lease agreement what price it actually paid for the equipment and provide that, if it turns out to be less than stated, your rent payments will automatically and appropriately be adjusted downward.

A leasing company's first choice is to get its entire investment back, pay off any equipment loans, and make a profit, without considering end-of-lease sale or re-lease earnings, simply referred to as "residuals." In other words, it would determine the lease rent using a zero-residual assumption. In this case, sale or re-lease earnings, less remarketing costs, are windfall profits.

In small-ticket leases, the residual assumption is often zero. In larger-ticket transactions, competition dictates assuming higher residual values. And it's not unusual in large-ticket situations for a lessor to base its entire profit strategy on what it expects to receive from an end-of-lease equipment sale or re-lease.

Watch Out For: Loss of
Residual Upside

When a lessee leases equipment, it often forgoes the possibility of realizing a gain if the equipment appreciates in value during the lease term. Any such gain instead goes to the lessor. For example, through inflation or buyer demand, a ten-year-old river barge may be worth more than it originally cost. If it was leased, the lessor would benefit from its end-of-lease market value.

Lessees not having any right to purchase or renew can be in for an unfortunate surprise if equipment is needed when leases end. Lessors maximize residual income by holding out for high prices. Even when lessees have the option to buy or re-lease equipment for its fair market value, residual upside is lost. If the fair market value turns out to be high, the purchase price or renewal rent, coupled with the rent paid, can result in a very expensive transaction, and the lessee would undoubtedly have been better off if it had originally bought the equipment. The problem is that there is no way of telling what future values are going to be.

Here's What to Do: Negotiate
Fixed-Price Options

Negotiating fixed-price purchase and renewal options can prevent you from paying too much for old equipment you continue to need when the lease ends and, in addition, provides an opportunity to share in any residual upside.

Under a fixed-price purchase option, a lessee has the right to buy the equipment at the end of a lease at a fixed price—say, 25% of original cost—that was agreed on at the time the parties entered into the lease. If the equipment's market value at the lease term's end is high—say, 75% of cost—the lessee can take advantage of the favorable market by buying it for 25% of cost and selling it for 75% of cost.

Fixed-price renewal options work the same way. Under a fixed-price renewal option, a lessee could elect to renew the lease at the end of its primary term for a fixed percentage of original lease rent—say, 25%—agreed upon when the lease was signed.

There are two problems with fixed-price options. First, not all lessors are willing to grant them and give up their residual upside. Second, fixed-price options may jeopardize a lease's true lease status for tax purposes, and your tax attorney should review any significant dollar equipment lease containing any option of this nature.

Example: Residual Profit

Here's how a lessor can make up lost dollars—and more—with equipment residual earnings.

As you now know, residual earnings come from:

- Re-lease income and/or
- Equipment sale proceeds

When equipment is re-leased or sold at lease end, windfall profits may be available. Assume the following deal:

1. You sign a three-year lease for a $1 million computer with First Credit Company.
2. First Credit borrows $1 million at a 9.5% interest rate to buy your system.
3. It charges you a lease interest rate of 11.5% per annum.

The financing profit (spread) is the difference between 9.5% and 11.5%, or 2% per year. In this example, the rent is sufficient to pay off the lessor's equipment loan and provide an annual financing profit of 2%.

The financing spread produces $20,000 per year (2% x $1 million = $20,000), or a total of $60,000 over three years.

So far, your rents will:

- Pay off the lessor's entire $1 million loan.
- Provide a financing profit of $60,000.
- Leave the lessor with a computer free and clear.

If you had no purchase or renewal rights, the lessor would have the most bargaining leverage if you needed the equipment. And even if you had fair market value purchase and renewal rights, the residual profits would still be very acceptable since any proceeds would be windfall profits in this case.

The fact is, residual earnings have had such a dramatic effect on lessors' earnings that many lessors have adopted a low-rent pricing strategy to win business. They set rents to just cover overhead, hoping to ring the financial bell when equipment comes off lease.

Let's take a closer look at the residual economics. Assume that First Credit Company sells the computer at the end of the lease for 15% of original cost. This puts an additional $150,000 in the lessor's pocket. Couple that with what has already been earned—$60,000 in rent financing profit—and the lease has produced a total of $210,000. Not bad for taking a credit risk on your company. And the profit story is not over, as you shall see later in this chapter.

Here's a real example of what can happen: The first lease deal one of my client lessor companies did was with a large foreign bank, as lessee, located in New York City. The bank signed a three-year lease for a $50,000 computer system without purchase or renewal options. The rent was priced to pay off the lessor's entire $50,000 investment, plus its profit, by the end of the lease. In other words, in pricing the lease, the lessor assumed a zero residual value. A few months before the lease was over, the bank's data-processing department decided it needed the equipment, and since my client refused to sell, the bank renewed for one year at 80% of the initial term rent. At the end of each of the next three years, the bank again renewed. When the final term ended, not only had my client's $50,000 investment been paid back, with a profit, but it ultimately received an additional $80,000 in residual earnings.

Don't Lose Your Residual Perspective. A prospective lessee must keep its concern over the loss of residual value upside in the proper economic perspective. All too often, the residual concern is more emotional than practical. One way to do this is to attempt to put a realistic value on the residual worth of the asset by, for example, bringing in a qualified appraiser to give an opinion as to what the equipment is likely to be worth in the future and discounting the value to its present worth.

Example: A Residual Perspective

Rayburn Manufacturing Company is considering whether to lease or buy a heavy-duty crane. Rayburn's financial vice president recommends that it be leased; however, the operational vice president believes that it should be bought because of its potentially favorable market value at the end of the period of use.

The facts are as follows:

Crane cost:	$3 million
Lease term:	20 years
Depreciated book value at end of 20 years:	$300,000

If the market value of the crane turned out to be $500,000 at the end of the lease term, Rayburn would lose the chance at a $200,000 upside gain ($500,000 − $300,000) if it leased the equipment.

What if, however, the potential loss is considered in terms of current dollars? The present value of such a loss 20 years out, computed using an annual discount rate of 10%, is approximately $30,000. Compared to the original cost of $3 million, and considering the fact that the upside gain may not materialize, the residual concern may be overstated, particularly if any down payment that would have been required if the crane had been purchased was put to productive use.

The Less Obvious Profit Areas

As already mentioned, additional earnings can come from less obvious transaction aspects, such as interim rent, prepayment penalties, casualty occurrences, insurance cost markups, upgrade financing costs, documentation fees, filing fees, maintenance charges, repair costs, excess use charges, equity placement fees, debt costs and placement fees, commitment fees, nonutilization fees, remarketing fees, late payment charges, collection telephone call charges, deal rewrite charges, and equipment redelivery charges. Now let's examine each of these areas.

Interim Rent

Interim rent, sometimes referred to as precommencement rent or stub period rent, is rent payable for a period running from the start of the lease to the beginning of its primary, or main, term. For example, a five-year lease might provide for the primary term to begin on the first day of the month. If the equipment is not accepted on the first of a month, there will be an interim rent period. If equipment was delivered, for instance, on December 15, the five-year period would begin on January 1, with an additional interim term of half a month, running from December 15 through December 31.

Watch Out For: Costly Interim Rent

Leases with interim rent provisions defer the start of the primary term until a predetermined date following equipment acceptance. Since the rent is priced on the agreed-upon primary term—say, five years, as in the preceding example—the additional rent is a windfall for the lessor and adds to the cost of a lease.

Lessees that object to interim rent often acquiesce when told that the extra use entitles the lessor to be compensated. Rarely, however, is the extra use of value to a lessee. And if the extra use argument doesn't work, lessees are told that internal billing procedures require leases to begin uniformly on the first day of a month. And that usually quiets the objection.

Here's What to Do: Delete Interim Rent Provisions or Account for Costs

The best approach is to eliminate any potential interim rent periods by insisting that the primary term start when the equipment is accepted. If a lessor claims that administrative reasons require a first-of-the-month payment cycle, and that an interim rent term is therefore necessary, request a waiver of interim rent charges.

If the lessor refuses to waive interim rent charges, factor the potential additional rent into your analysis of the cost of the lease. There is nothing wrong with agreeing to pay interim rent, but you must make sure that doing so does not unduly add to your cost. When long interim terms are possible, it may be cheaper to purchase rather than lease. Lessors offering, for example, quarterly rental payments at times attempt to build in long interim periods by stating that the primary term will start on the first day of a calendar quarter, with an interim period for equipment not on lease as of the first day of a calendar quarter running from the date of equipment acceptance to the first day of the following calendar quarter. In these situations, an interim term close to three months could result, providing the lessor with a three-month rent windfall.

Watch Out For: Unfair Rent-Invoicing Practices

Unethical lessors pick up extra interim-type profits by invoicing rent on a specific date each month, regardless of when it's due. For example, a typical monthly lease provides for rent to be paid 30 days after the lease begins. Assume that a lease begins on March 25. The next rent payment would be due on April 25. These lessors invoice all lessees for payment on, say, the fifteenth of the month. Lessees that have leases beginning before the fifteenth come out ahead; those that have leases beginning after the fifteenth and that pay on the fifteenth incur a time-value-of-money loss.

A word of caution: Lessors are beginning to request rights to withdraw rent from lessees' checking accounts electronically rather than wait for payment by check because it eliminates costly billing procedures and assists collection. Unless the withdrawals are strictly controlled, there is room for lessor abuse by, for example, premature rent grabbing in an attempt to pick up time-value-of-money profits.

Here's What to Do: Check Your Lease and Set Up a Rent Calendar

In order to prevent an unethical lessor from picking up interim rent-type earnings, you must ensure that invoice payment due dates correspond with your due date obligations under the lease. The best way to track proper billing is to set up a tickler file as soon as each lease is signed. Don't trust lease invoice due dates.

Prepayment Penalties

If you have the right to end your lease early, you can count on paying an exercise penalty. The penalties, referred to as prepayment, or early termination, penalties, are designed to make the lessor economically whole and sometimes more—returning its entire investment, with a profit; providing funds to pay off any equipment purchase loans; and adding a fee for exercise. An early termination guarantees the lessor lease profits by eliminating future credit risk.

Watch Out For: Excessive Prepayment Penalties

Prepayment penalties can be excessive and unfairly enrich a lessor. When a lease is terminated early, the lessor sells or re-leases the equipment and, if the equipment has a high residual value and the lessee receives no credit for sale or re-lease proceeds against the termination payment due, realizes windfall profits.

Termination amounts are sometimes arbitrarily set. They look mathematically precise and thus are often assumed to be industry standard. That assumption can cost a lessee a lot of money.

Here's What to Do: Get Comparison Quotes

A simple way to keep lessors honest is to get competitive lease quotes and require termination payment schedules to be included with all financing bids so they can be compared. Unless forced, many lessors will not supply termination amounts until a lease is ready to be signed, knowing they probably won't be checked at the last minute.

If you are unable to get competitive bids, call the lessor and flatly state that, based on your calculations, the termination amounts are too high. That alone may be enough to get a reduction, particularly if the lessor had unfairly built in profits. And if you can, purchase a lessor lease analysis software program and run the termination amounts. You won't be able to verify them precisely unless the lessor provides you with its deal assumptions, but you can see whether they are in an acceptable range.

Lease termination payments are usually incorporated into a termination payment schedule, with the amounts often being expressed as a percentage of equipment cost for each rent payment period. Payment of the applicable termination amount on any rent date allows the lessee to terminate a lease as of that time. For example, a monthly lease might provide for a termination payment of 99% of equipment cost when the second rent payment is paid, 97% of equipment cost when the third rent payment is paid, and so on.

One final point: Always get an early termination right, even if its exercise is unlikely.

Casualty Occurrences

Leases require a predetermined casualty value payment if equipment is destroyed. These payments are usually prescribed by formula in a lease provision or in a casualty payment schedule. They, like termination payments, are designed to make a lessor economically whole, including payment for loss of anticipated residual profits.

Casualty payment obligations are approached in the same manner as termination payment amounts: Typically, a schedule of payment amounts, expressed as a percentage of equipment cost, is incorporated into the lease.

Watch Out For: Excessive Casualty Payments

Although a lessee may insure leased equipment against loss, it is not unusual for lease casualty loss payments to exceed insurance proceeds, such as when replacement value is low. Unless otherwise specified, insurance only covers the current market value at the time of loss. In that case, a lessee will have to pay the difference.

Without proper insurance, even if replacement value is high, a lessee may still have to pay a casualty shortfall. Some lessors aggressively mark up casualty values to provide opportunities for windfall profits. An add-on markup totaling 5% of equipment cost can go unnoticed, particularly in the rush of closing a lease deal. Some lessors purposely avoid submitting casualty value schedules until the lease is ready to be signed, hoping there won't be time for careful review.

Here's What to Do: Insure Casualty Value Amounts and Get Comparison Quotes

To avoid unexpected casualty payment exposure, insure equipment for the higher of the equipment casualty amounts or the replacement value. This puts the risk of low replacement values, or aggressive casualty value markups, on the insurance company.

If your insurance company will not insure the higher of replacement or casualty value, approach the casualty value issue in the same manner as suggested with termination values above: Compare values among bidders or, if you have only one bid, try the "values are too high" bluff and see whether that gets a reduction. And consider verifying the casualty values by running a casualty schedule on a lessor profit analysis software program. One more suggestion: Compare casualty values against any submitted lease termination values. The amounts should be reasonably close.

Insurance Cost Markups

Leases require lessees to insure equipment at their expense. Tracking compliance is an administrative burden, particularly in small-dollar leases, so some lessors offer to supply coverage at an additional cost.

Watch Out For: Excessive Insurance Markups

It may not now surprise you to learn that lessors offering to provide insurance required under your lease make a nice profit on it—at times as much as 200% over cost. And most lessees rarely suspect it.

In fairness, a lessor's volume purchasing power often enables it to buy insurance at rates lower than those available to a lessee. In some cases, the charge may be in line with what a lessee would have to pay, but don't rely on it. All too many lessors have discovered that insurance rates are not checked, and gouging is possible, particularly in small transactions. For example, a lessor might charge $14 a year for a $2,000 casualty insurance policy costing $8 a year, making a $6 profit. On a $20 million equipment portfolio, this means $60,000 annually.

Here's What to Do: Get Independent Insurance Quotes

The solution to potentially excessive insurance charges is simple: Get your own insurance quote and compare it against what the lessor offers. If the quotes are close, ask the lessor for a reduced rate. You'll probably get it.

If you find after you sign a lease that you've paid too much for insurance coverage, suggest that you are going to look into whether the lessor has complied with the state insurance laws. Insurance is a regulated industry, so unless the lessor is a licensed insurance broker, it may run afoul of the insurance laws. A careful lessor, however, will have avoided that problem, but it's worth a try.

Upgrade Financing

Equipment upgrades—when a lessee adds to or modifies existing leased equipment—can provide leasing companies with significant profit opportunities. If the upgrade is not readily removable or has no stand-alone value, only the existing lessor is generally willing or able to finance it.

Some Think Early Termination Is the Solution. Some lessees feel that asking to terminate a lease and purchase the equipment is a viable approach when the existing lessor refuses to provide reasonable upgrade financing. They assume that they can then bring in another leasing company to finance the entire package economically. Those that have tried this approach know it rarely works.

Here's an example of what can happen: Suppose you're in the third year of a five-year telephone system lease and additions are needed to meet office growth. An internal parts upgrade is required. You ask for a five-year refinancing on all equipment, including the upgrade, to keep monthly payments low. You don't have an early termination right.

The lessor comes back with a five-year refinancing offer. It includes, however, payment of a termination penalty, which it offers to roll, along with the upgrade cost, into the new lease. The overall refinancing seems too expensive, so you ask the cost of simply terminating the lease and buying the equipment, hoping to get a more aggressive quote from another lessor. The response is an even higher termination penalty, with the lessor claiming that part of its loss was to be offset by the upgrade-financing profit. This reasoning is plausible but invariably untrue. The result: Even if you find an aggressive financing offer, the higher stand-alone termination makes the refinancing cost more than accepting the lessor's package refinancing. Typically, the lessor anticipates the dilemma and prices the refinancing to effectively eliminate the economic choice.

Documentation and Filing Fees

Many leasing companies, typically those in the small-ticket business, charge transaction processing, documentation preparation, and security interest filing fees.

Processing fees ensure the seriousness of the lessee and can range from a nominal amount to hundreds of dollars. Small lease transaction documentation fees generally run from $50 to $200 per transaction. In larger leases, however, a lessee may have to pay all of the lessor's outside counsel fees, which can easily run into thousands of dollars. Security interest filing fees, such as state uniform commercial code filing fees, are generally nominal, ranging from $15 to $25 per filing.

Watch Out For: Excessive Documentation and Filing Fees

Documentation, filing, and other lease transaction fees can be a profit area for a lessor, in small leases actually doubling up-front proceeds.

The problem with fees of this nature is that lease sales representatives often avoid mentioning them, as with any issue that may create deal objections, until the lessee is committed. A sales representative working for one of my lessor clients did this continually. He never asked the prospective lessee for required documentation fees before a lease was signed, always telling my client that they would be collected at equipment delivery and always hoping my client would forget about them. Lessees that spotted the fee payment requirement and objected would be assured that he could get the fees waived. In fact, he never tried to get a waiver and, after the lease was signed, would simply tell the lessees that he was unable to do so.

**Here's What to Do: Get Fees Itemized
Early and, Where Necessary, Ask for Waivers**

The payment of documentation, filing, and other lease transaction fees is often negotiable, particularly if your financing is attractive to a lessor. The best approach is to have all required fees itemized before you sign your lease. If you've missed a fee obligation before signing a lease, there is no way out.

Equipment Maintenance and Repair Charges

Most lessors only finance equipment; that is, they buy equipment for lease under what are referred to as finance leases, imposing on the lessee all ownership responsibilities. These finance leases require lessees to pay, for example, for all normal equipment upkeep, such as maintenance and repair.

Although there is no maintenance or repair expense exposure during the equipment warranty period, the story changes once it ends. If there are equipment problems, the lessee must pay to have them corrected. A few lessors, referred to as service lessors, offer, for a fee, equipment maintenance and repair services following the warranty period. Many lessees sign up for these services.

Watch Out For: Costly Lessor-Provided Service

Lessors providing repair and maintenance services can make substantial profits. For example, computer lessors offering maintenance service typically wrap service and lease rents into one payment, thereby disguising high lease rates. And some make their statement of services offered so general that meaningful comparisons with third-party service providers are impossible.

Automobile fleet lessors were notorious for bundling maintenance with rent and refusing to identify the various components. Competition and lessee pressure, however, have forced them to separate the different charges, but only if you ask.

Here's What to Do: Get Service Charge Breakdowns and Use Third Parties

To avoid overpaying for maintenance or repair servicing, ask the lessor to itemize all financing and service charges separately. And get detailed specifics on all services offered. In many cases, you'll find that the financing rate is high and that it will be cheaper to use a separate third-party service provider, other than the lessor.

Watch Out For: Tricky Maintenance and Return Provisions

Some lessors substantially increase lease profits by inserting ambiguous maintenance and return provisions in leases that in effect require equipment to be returned in like-new condition. To the uninitiated, these provisions look innocent. For example, a provision might require the equipment to be maintained in good operating condition, with nothing said about normal wear and tear. Like-new return conditions guarantee maximum sale or re-lease profits and increase your lease costs.

Here's What to Do: Limit Maintenance Obligations

If equipment maintenance obligations appear ambiguous or too broad, you may end up in a financial battle if the lessor claims that you have not returned the equipment in proper condition. To avoid this, limit maintenance obligations to keeping equipment in good operating condition, subject to wear and tear normal for your business. In addition, get the lessor to inspect, and sign off on, the equipment's return condition while the equipment is under your control so you can correct any legitimate problem before sending the equipment back. If a lessor makes the repairs, you can bet it will profit on them.

Excess Use Charges

As mentioned earlier, the better the equipment's return condition, the more likely a lessor will make residual windfall profits. One way to ensure the best possible return condition is to put use restrictions on the equipment, which, if exceeded, call for penalty charges payable at the end of the lease.

Watch Out For: Unrealistic Use Limitations

Lessors increase profits though clever equipment use limitation provisions. They offer unbeatable financing rates and then couple them with use limitations likely to be exceeded. For example, aircraft leases often limit use to a predetermined number of flying hours or landing and takeoff cycles. Mileage restrictions in auto leases, such as limiting use to 10,000 miles a year, can be equally onerous. When these limits are exceeded, the excess usage penalties produce extraordinary profits and can turn a good financial deal into a bad one for a lessee.

Here's What to Do: Consider Higher Rents and Expanded Use Limits

In order to avoid excess charges from exceeding unrealistic equipment use limitations, carefully review what your needs may be. Very often it's less expensive to negotiate a somewhat higher lease rent and get extended use rights rather than having a lower rate with unrealistic equipment use limitations.

Equity Placement Fees

Leasing companies sometimes act as brokers, matching lessees with lease-funding sources, charging what is typically referred to as an equity placement fee or a brokerage commission. Although lease-funding sources, often referred to as equity participants or lease investors, pay these fees, rents are marked up to cover them. The net result is that the fees are paid indirectly by the lessee.

Lessees frequently refuse to deal through brokers, feeling that they can do just as well finding lease investors. So brokers generally hide the fact that they're not investing principals.

Watch Out For: Unknown Broker Fees and Risks

All too often, leasing companies don't disclose that they're acting in a brokerage capacity. There is nothing wrong in dealing with a broker, as long as you know it. In some cases, brokers create additional deal risks and their fees unduly add to leasing costs.

**Here's What to Do: Get Proper
Disclosures and Look for Clues**

Always require lessors to disclose in writing whether they are acting as broker or principal. If a lessor says that it's not acting as a broker, be alert for clues that indicate otherwise. For example, lessors that act as brokers often give evasive answers, such as "We may broker part of the lease, depending on what happens."

Knowing that a leasing company is acting as a broker allows you to take action to get additional proposals or pursue other remedies if it can't perform as agreed or in a timely manner. It is not unheard of for brokers to misrepresent your lease transaction initially to a funding source to get an approval and then confront you at the last minute with a deal issue that you must concede to finalize the financing. If you know you are dealing with a broker, you can independently verify all deal aspects directly with the funding source. If you don't, you may learn too late that necessary financial commitments or key requests were never considered or approved. There is nothing worse than learning, on the day your equipment must be paid for, that there are financing problems.

Debt Costs and Placement Fees

At times, leasing companies borrow a portion of the funds necessary to purchase the equipment from a third-party lender in transactions referred to as leveraged leases. Typically, the leasing company charges a fee, referred to as a debt placement fee, for arranging the transaction debt. At times, the lessor hires a third party, such as an investment banker, to identify a potential lender. In this situation, some or all of the fee goes to the third party.

Watch Out For: High Debt Placement Fees

Many prospective lessees agree to pay debt placement fees higher than necessary because they have no idea of market rates. As a rule of thumb, fees ranging from .25% to .5% of the loan amount are considered reasonable. Some lessors, however, will attempt to charge as much as 1%.

**Here's What to Do: Check Fees
With Your Investment Banker**

There is only one way to keep proposed debt placement fees under control: Get quotes from several investment bankers, preferably including one regional and one national organization.

Watch Out For: Unfair Debt Change Rent Adjustments

Leveraged lease rents are quoted based on a specified assumed debt interest rate. For example, a lessee may be offered a particular lease rent—say, $1,000 per month—based on a stated assumption that the leasing company can borrow 80% of the equipment purchase cost at 9% per annum.

Some lessors reserve the right to raise rent, but avoid the obligation to lower it, if the loan interest rate differs from that assumed in their proposal. If the rate is lower, these lessors pocket the interest savings.

**Here's What to Do: Provide for
Appropriate Rent Adjustments**

Leveraged lease proposals must provide that rents will be appropriately adjusted upward or downward in the event that loan interest charges or principal amount varies from that assumed.

Watch Out For: Excessive Debt Charges

Rent adjustment provisions aren't the entire answer to over-payment risks if the lessor is responsible for finding the debt. A leasing company is primarily interested in closing the deal, taking its profit, and moving on to the next deal. Under adjustment provisions, the profit is the same regardless of debt interest cost, so there is little incentive for the lessor to find the lowest possible rate. The higher the interest rate, however, the greater the lessee's cost.

Here's What to Do: Require Veto Rights Over Debt Rates

In a leveraged lease situation, a lessee must not only have a rent adjustment provision, but it must also control the debt placement or it may pay more than necessary. To avoid giving a lessor a windfall profit, include in your lease award the right to veto any third-party debt.

Commitment and Nonutilization Fees

Leasing companies sometimes ask for commitment or nonutilization fees, particularly when equipment won't be delivered in the near future. Commitment fees, nonrefundable in nature, are designed to compensate a lessor for holding funds available and reduce the risk of lessor yield deterioration through adverse changes in its borrowing cost.

Commitment fees are typically imposed when equipment deliveries are more than six months away. They must be paid up front and can range anywhere from .5% to 2% of equipment cost. Some lessors, however, attempt to charge commitment fees even when deliveries are imminent. Once a lessee puts up money, a lessor knows its control has increased because a lessee will tolerate many problems before walking away.

A nonutilization fee—payable only if the equipment is not leased and due when the commitment period is over—is less onerous. For example, a lessor may require that the lessee pay a fee equal to 1% of the available funds unused at the end of, say, six months. If all committed funds are used, the lessee owes nothing.

A word of caution: If the equipment is leased but the actual cost is less than the full financing commitment, a nonutilization fee must be paid on the unused portion. A fee of 1% would require payment of $500 (1% x $50,000 = $500) if the funding commitment was $1 million but the delivered price was $950,000. The solution is to provide for cost leeway—for example, by stating that the fee is payable only if a minimum of 90% of the funds committed are not used.

**Watch Out For: Unnecessary
Commitment and Nonutilization Fees**

A leasing company will charge a commitment or nonutilization fee anytime it feels it can get away with it. When deals are plentiful and competition is low, lessors use such fees to get extra profits. There are no industry guidelines for amounts charged or for when they're appropriate.

Here's What to Do: Resist All Fees

Commitment fees and nonutilization fees are generally highly negotiable. A good general approach is always to refuse to pay them. If a fee seems likely, as in situations in which equipment will not be delivered for at least six months, use competitive bidding to minimize or eliminate any requirement.

Remarketing Fees

Many lessors charge fees to remarket equipment if, for example, the lessee terminates its lease early. These fees are in addition to any other charges that may be payable, such as termination penalties.

Watch Out For: Excessive or Unnecessary Remarketing Fees

Remarketing fees are often arbitrarily set and rarely questioned by lessees. It's not unusual for leasing companies to have equipment-remarketing departments. Their cost is built into a lessor's original lease pricing, and as a result, the fees are added profit.

**Here's What to Do: Limit Payment to
Third-Party Remarketing**

If a lessor insists on a remarketing fee, limit payment to fees that must be paid to third parties. Better yet, control the equipment remarketing, including having the right to hire a remarketing agent. This ensures maximum value if the remarketing price impacts lease costs, such as when, for example, higher sales proceeds will reduce early termination penalties.

Late Payment Charges

Leases always incorporate late payment charges. If, for example, rent is not paid when due, penalties as high as 5% to 10% of the rent charge may be imposed.

Watch Out For: Unfair Late Payment Charges

Late payment fees can substantially increase the lessor's lease profits, often being more than necessary to maintain its economic return. If payment is late, a lessor is entitled to a charge that will maintain, not substantially increase, its economic return. Unfortunately, excessive charges are rarely questioned by prospective lessees.

Here's What to Do: Request Reduction of Unfair Penalties

Before signing a lease, make sure any late payment charges are reasonable. If you discover after you've signed a lease that these charges appear excessive, check your state laws to see whether there are any statutory limits that have been exceeded. If so, you may be able to void your lease without penalty. And if you don't want to do so, the right will enable you to negotiate a reduction easily.

Collection Telephone Charges

To maintain profits, lessors are increasingly finding ways to pass on overhead costs. For example, many lessors now require lessees to pay telephone charges on collection calls.

Watch Out For: Collection Call Charge Pass-Throughs

In many cases, lease charges for collection calls substantially exceed actual costs. Although intentionally delinquent lessees have little right to complain, lessors still should not profit unfairly from these charges. However, if they can, they will.

Here's What to Do: Negotiate a Direct Charge Pass-Through

Make sure lease charges imposed for lessor collection calls are limited to a direct pass-through of actual call charges. Then, if the charges appear excessive, at least you have grounds to argue.

Deal Rewrites

Lessors increase profits by charging a fee for lessee-requested deal changes after a lease is signed. For example, if you need a lease extension but have no right to it, a lessor will attempt to throw in a deal rewrite fee. Most lessees agree without objection.

Watch Out For: Rewrite Gouging

Some lessors charge a substantial rewrite fee and offer to finance the fee in the refinancing. In these cases, not only does the lessor get added profits, but the lessee ends up paying interest at a hefty rate on these profits. When questioned, lessees are told that these rewrite fees are standard, but the fact is they are totally arbitrary.

Here's What to Do: Challenge Rewrite Fees

Rewrite fees are highly negotiable. A good negotiating tactic when calling a lessor to discuss a deal rewrite fee is to mention casually early in the conversation that you are considering leasing additional equipment later in the year. At the end of the conversation, ask the representative to waive the fee. Chances are good that it will be waived.

Redelivery Charges

Leases typically contain equipment return obligations requiring payment for shipment to a specified, or later lessor-chosen, location. Some obligate the lessee to pay for shipment anywhere in the world.

Watch Out For: Unfair Equipment Redelivery Charges

Lessors make extra profits by charging twice for equipment redelivery: They have the new party buying or leasing the equipment pay for shipping as well as the original lessee. In addition, lessees at times unfairly pay high shipping charges when there are no destination charge limits. For example, if the lessee must pay for shipping anywhere in the world, the lessor has little incentive to limit costs by selling or re-leasing to a party near the lessee.

Here's What to Do: Limit Redelivery Obligations

Read lease redelivery obligations carefully and limit your exposure. Insert a lease clause that prevents the lessor from collecting delivery charges twice for the same shipment, once from you and once from the party to which the equipment is

> being sent. In addition, agree to pay only for equipment return to the nearest point of general transportation, not to exceed, say, 50 miles from your place of use.

Here's Why Leasing Companies Want Your Business

Aside from the profits discussed, your long-term lease deal offers a leasing company a number of additional benefits. This section discusses the key ones.

The Chance to Purchase Assets With Your Money

How would you react if a wealthy neighbor asked you to lease him or her a $60,000 Porsche? Assume that you could borrow the entire purchase price from your local bank at a rate giving you a $50 monthly profit. In addition, assume the loan to be based on your neighbor's credit, having no impact on your future borrowing capabilities. And if your neighbor defaulted on his or her lease payments for any reason, you would no longer be responsible for paying off any remaining loan balance. Assume also that the lease would be for five years, the rents due would pay off the entire loan, and when the lease ended, your neighbor would return the car to you. You would then own free and clear a well-maintained Porsche to do with as you wish. Sound good? Most people would agree that it does.

You might think it would be impossible to get a bank to lend you money to invest without holding you responsible for repayment. But so-called nonrecourse equipment loans are available because banks and other lenders will lend money on the strength of a strong lease contract, without checking the creditworthiness of the owner-lessor. The leases must contain hell-or-high-water clauses that state that the entire term rent must be paid without offset for any reason, including a claim against the lessor. So if you have a hell-or-high-water lease with a good-credit lessee, nonrecourse equipment loans are available. The most interesting aspect of nonrecourse loans is that they, in effect, provide an unlimited borrowing capacity.

Now what if nine more wealthy neighbors approached you to lease Porsches under the same terms? Your profit would be $500 a month, and you would own ten Porsches free and clear at the end of five years. Not a bad return for a no-money-down investment.

That's the strategy of the leasing business: getting creditworthy companies to pay for and maintain assets that can be sold or re-released at a profit, all the time making a profit while waiting for their return. All the lessor has to do is to remember to send rent bills and deposit the checks when they come in. And if the lessor doesn't want to wait, the leases can be sold to another lessor for a profit.

The Possibility of Windfall Profits

Assume in the preceding subsection's example that, at the end of the five-year lease, each Porsche was worth 50% of original cost. In addition to a $50 monthly profit, selling each car at the end of lease would bring in $30,000 in residual profits.

It is not unusual for residual values to range anywhere from 10% to 100% of the asset's original cost. The values, of course, depend on the type of asset, its return condition, inflation, and market demand. For example, in the early to mid-1980s, some ten-year-old aircraft would sell for prices in excess of their original cost.

Lessors quickly caught on to the residual "end game." Some even adopted a strategy of acquiring millions of dollars of equipment solely for the residual potential. They cut their lease term profits to a minimum to win business, with rents often covering little more than basic transaction and overhead costs, in anticipation of profits when the equipment came off lease. Once through the initial start-up phase, the cash flow squeeze is over, and yearly residual profits provide bottom-line returns.

Lessors using this business strategy run the risk that equipment won't be worth much more than scrap if there is no market demand or if the equipment is obsolete. If rents just pay overhead, there is little return for the effort. Aircraft lessors encountering a market demand problem, for instance, stored equipment waiting for the used equipment market to turn around. Equipment and industry diversification can reduce this type of risk.

So what does this mean to a lessee? Very simply, if the potential future value of an asset under lease consideration is high, and if a prospective lessor does not take at least a significant portion of the asset's future residual value into account in computing its lease offer, the rents will not be as aggressive as they should be. In addition, if the anticipated residual value is high, the lessee should give serious consideration to purchasing rather than leasing the asset.

Attractive Repeat Business Opportunities

Developing an extensive customer base is a strategic business objective of virtually every leasing company. Qualified prospects are valuable. Customers that lease once often lease again, at times forgetting about competitive bids. Noncompetitive bid situations assure lessors of solid returns.

Good customer lists add to profits; new business can be originated with little expense: Often a simple letter offering preapproved lease financing is enough. In addition, credit risks are reduced when dealing with known customers. There is no substitute for firsthand payment experience. Financial statements and discussions with trade references and lenders don't always tell the whole credit story.

So never forget, your business is valuable for two reasons: present deal profits and future deal profits. Aggressive lessors sometimes offer break-even, or even loss-producing, financing just to get in the door.

Buying Customers With Low Rates

Below-market rates are the most effective way for a leasing company to buy a potentially long-term customer relationship. And rates often stay low on future financings until the customer is lulled into a sense of deal fairness. Satisfied lessees let their guard down, often giving incumbent lessors exclusive deals from time to time. Those are the deals on which lessors go to work to make up for lost profits.

Once the first deal is accepted, a lessor makes another strategic effort: It strives to put a master lease in place. A master lease is, in effect, a boilerplate document that permits future business to be added simply by attaching short, often one-page, schedules that incorporate the new equipment under the term of the master document. This allows future financings to be handled with minimal effort on both sides. It's a fact that the easier the documentation process, the more attractive a prospective lessor becomes. Lessors with master leases in place are given an edge over competitors not having such leases in place, often getting the last opportunity to win by matching the lowest bidder. In some cases, they can win even at higher rates simply because documentation is easy.

Example: Winning Customer Relationships With Low Rates

The lowball rate strategy to buy a customer relationship can be very effective. A foreign bank client of mine decided to get into equipment leasing in the United States. It offered below-cost rates for two years. The loss was considered part of its start-up expenses. To help offset the loss, the bank kept office expenses and salaries to a minimum. The strategy worked, and it built a profitable business. American leasing companies rarely consider adopting this type of approach—low rates and low overhead—possibly because of the traditional pressure to show a profit as soon as possible. And typically, they invest endless dollars in office facilities and advertising, hoping to attract business by looking successful.

These False Financial Programs Can Increase Profits

There are two common value-added approaches that leasing companies reinvent every year to justify, or hide, excessive profit taking: offering flexible lease programs and better service. They are designed to convince lessees that they are getting more than what is actually offered. And every year, many lessees get taken in by them.

Flexible Leases

Equipment leases are typically long-term financial commitments, locking a lessee in for most of the equipment's useful life. Rent payments, however, are significantly less than in shorter-term rental arrangements.

Lessors prefer long-term arrangements because investment returns, and therefore anticipated profits, are guaranteed subject,—of course, to credit risks. Lessees, on the other hand, would prefer the attractive rates offered by long-term leases and the flexibility of short-term commitments. A long-term lease that can be canceled anytime without penalty would be very attractive to a lessee.

In an effort to induce lessees to sign long-term leases, some lessors periodically offer what appear to be low-payment, easy-out lease programs, often called "flexlease programs." These programs create the false impression that a lessee can walk away anytime during the lease term without penalty. Flexleases, better characterized as crawl-away leases, generally impose heavy penalties for early termination and don't provide any real advantages.

Watch Out For: Unfair Lease Cancellation Rights

Be careful of long-term leases that appear to permit no-penalty cancellation. Chances are you'll find provisions that impose significant restrictions. For example, termination may be permitted, without penalty, provided the terminated equipment is replaced with new leased equipment at a lessor-determined rate. In addition, the lease may require that the remaining balance due under the old lease be rolled into the new lease financing.

Here's What to Do: Ask How It Works

Have the lessor provide you with specific examples of how cancellation would work.

Better Service

Leasing companies unable or unwilling to offer competitive rates develop value-added programs to justify higher rates. Typically, the value-added services offered are little more than services provided in the regular course of the leasing business.

The services offered usually address areas of uncertainty. For example, lessors know that certain equipment is likely to require upgrading before lease end. In this case, the value-added service offered would be assurances that upgrades will be financed. Although the financing rate offered is typically high, lessees are often willing to accept it to eliminate financing uncertainty. Rarely, however, is it a fair deal.

You Now Have the Information to Negotiate Away Hidden Profits

Now that you know how a lessor profits in a lease deal, you know what to look for to get the best possible financing offer. The obvious profit areas are interest charges, tax benefits, and equipment residual earnings. The less obvious profit areas are interim rent, prepayment penalties, casualty occurrences, insurance cost markups, upgrade financing, early termination rights, documentation and filing fees, equipment maintenance and repair charges, excess use charges, equity placement fees, debt costs and placement fees, commitment and nonutilization fees, remarketing fees, late payment charges, collection telephone charges, deal rewrites, and redelivery charges.

Keep in mind, however, that leasing companies are clever and innovative. They're always looking for new ways to increase their lease profits. Your only protection against paying more than you have to for lease financing is to question every cost and charge provided for in the lessor's lease offer and lease agreement—and ask the lessor to provide you with an example, in writing, of how each questioned cost or charge works.

Chapter 3
Bargaining Strategies and Tactics That Work

To Win, Knowledge of Your Opponent Is Not Enough

So far, you've learned how a lessor profits in a lease transaction and what leasing company characteristics to look for to get a better deal. All this will put you on the right track, but it's far from enough to ensure superiority in a lease negotiation.

All too often, lessees, even experienced ones, inadvertently hand lessors information that allows them to gain the advantage. In a lease negotiation, you must never forget that lessor representatives are financing experts, often with many years of negotiating experience. Because they're continually in the negotiating trenches, they know how to make the most out of every lessee slip to gain an advantage. And they know how to work a deal aggressively to reduce, or eliminate, any lessee deal advantage.

To ensure the upper hand in a lease negotiation, you must be aware of everything you, and members of your negotiating team, do and say. Innocent-appearing statements and actions often can provide an experienced negotiator with information that can seriously damage your negotiating position. For example, casual comments about news events or your family or social life can provide invaluable insights into your negotiating blind spots. An unhappily married person is often very receptive to discussing business after work over drinks or dinner, a setting in which he or she is likely to relax and say too much.

And be careful of casual questions. Experienced negotiators will try to draw you into personal conversations to learn the best way to handle you. For example, asking your impressions about President Bush and President Clinton may appear innocent, but it can provide solid clues on how to manipulate you. If negotiators sense that you're politically liberal, they will appeal to your sense of fairness to win points. Typically, liberal people want to do what's right for everyone. At a deal impasse, the negotiators may reason, for instance, that you should concede to their request because of all the concessions they've made. The fairness approach is powerful, and many liberal people easily fall victim to it.

For many, doing what's necessary psychologically and strategically to avoid losing any advantage, by maintaining an arm's-length business relationship and saying only what's absolutely required to get the deal done, is difficult. The fact is, however, that the less your opponent knows about you, the harder it is to outnegotiate you.

Don't Be Your Own Worst Enemy

Without realizing it, most people make negotiation concessions before talking to their opponent. They fail to understand that the give-and-take process begins the moment they start thinking about an impending transaction. As a result, they weaken their negotiating posture by, for example, becoming predisposed to accepting compromises before their opponent asks for them.

Hard to believe? Well, consider this. Most people begin compromising while formulating their deal requests. They put themselves in their opponent's shoes and guess how he or she will react. If they believe they'll get a favorable response, they're comfortable in making the request. If not, they may not make the request at all or, if they do, are apt to withdraw it readily if met with resistance. To make matters worse, any fearful feeling about a prospective response is often projected by a slight hesitation before the request is made. An experienced negotiator will look for clues to any concession predispositions.

The mistake most of us make in guessing whether an opponent will go along with a request is thinking he or she knows what we know, particularly if it's something favorable to our position. For example, if we think that equipment will have a high resale value at the end of the lease term, we assume that the lessor knows this as well and would refuse to grant a low end-of-lease fixed-price purchase option because of it.

Some people's emotions take them one step further. They feel they can never get what they want in business. If you feel this way from time to time, be careful. Negative thinkers are easy to spot and even easier to manipulate.

If you're not sure whether you have a general negative inclination, here's a good way to test yourself: Think about the last time you were negotiating a purchase, such as a house or a car. Did you try to guess whether the offer you wanted to make was too low? If so, did you then raise the offer before making it simply because you thought it would be rejected? If you did, was there any factual basis for assuming it would be rejected? If there wasn't, you may have been the victim of your own negative thinking.

Let's take a closer look at how negative thinking can get in your way in a situation most people encounter in a home purchase. Assume you're shown a $150,000 house that's exactly what you want. You're excited but are afraid of being disappointed. Inevitably, thoughts creep in about why you might not get the house: "The seller won't agree to taking a second mortgage," or, "The price I'm willing to pay will clearly be unacceptable." You ask your broker to submit an offer of $135,000, with the seller taking back a $15,000, 12% per annum second mortgage. Unknown to you or your broker, the seller knows nothing about second mortgages.

If you assumed that the seller wouldn't take back a second mortgage simply because *you* wouldn't, chances are you will not persist if your second-mortgage request is initially denied. It's an unfortunate fact that when our own preoffer assumptions are confirmed, we're more inclined to acquiesce quickly. This, of course, is a mistake in any negotiation, because the refusal may not be based on what we think it is. In the case just mentioned, the seller was uncomfortable with the second-mortgage offer because he didn't understand it fully.

If, on the other hand, you weren't psychologically predisposed to a turndown, you would be less likely to concede. For example, you might ask again and, if refused again, request a face-to-face meeting to go over your offer. Then you would find that the seller did not understand the concept of a second mortgage.

A lease situation is no different. Going into a negotiation thinking that a particular request will be denied makes it unlikely that you'll get what you request. And never forget, experienced lessor negotiators often initially refuse requests to make you feel you've won something when they finally grant them. The point to keep in mind is not to fall victim to constructing your deal request in a way that you think will be acceptable to a leasing company.

Here's What to Do: Take a Break

If you're beginning to experience negative thoughts about your success in a particular negotiation, immediately take a break and put these feelings into their proper perspective. Realize that your anxieties have nothing to do with reality unless you so choose.

The solution is to be honest with yourself. Write down every random thought you have about why you may not get what you ask for. Look at your reasons and see whether they're based in fact or in fear. Then accept that there is nothing wrong

> with how you feel, even if you must admit that you are gener-
> ally pessimistic. That will allow you to be fully conscious of
> your inclinations and compensate during a negotiation. The
> key to winning in a negotiation is to test your requests out on
> your opponent, even if you think they'll be denied.

Avoid Friendships

The most successful salespeople make friends easily. Building a solid personal rapport, or friendship, is salespeople's first priority. The better the
relationship, the more likely you'll provide information that will enable
them to beat their competition—and you.

Making friends with a lessor representative compromises your negotiating ability. The stronger the personal rapport, the harder it is to negotiate
effectively because needs are often tempered in an effort to maintain the
rapport. Lease salespeople know this, and they use it to their advantage.

The reason that keeping an arm's-length relationship is difficult is that
we're taught from childhood that it's good to make friends. In addition,
establishing a personal rapport with someone with whom we're dealing
makes us feel more comfortable. The more we know about someone, the
less anxiety we experience when dealing with him or her. We know what
to expect. And we often feel we're going to be dealt with fairly.

Salespeople capitalize on this inclination and use it to their advantage. For example, the stronger the personal relationship, the harder they
know they can push on a deal point before you'll walk away from the
transaction.

Here's what you can expect from a salesperson. Watch for it. Invariably, in your first meeting, the salesperson will steer the conversation
away from business, hoping to get into a personal conversation. He or she
will ask you about yourself and your family, or about your personal interests. The salesperson may, for example, ask whether you like country-and-
western music. If so, a subsequent meeting to discuss business at a
country-and-western bar may be suggested. The process of building a
rapport begins.

More likely, it will be done indirectly. For example, the salesperson
may tell you something personal, about a hobby or special interest, hoping to drag you into a casual conversation. If you bite, chances are you'll
begin opening up, relaxing your guard, and again, the rapport-building
process will begin.

Keeping an all-business, arm's-length relationship with a lessor will
pay solid negotiating dividends. The less a lessor representative knows
about you personally, the less chance aggressive or overreaching requests

will be made and the less likely you'll inadvertently compromise your negotiating ability in order to maintain a personal relationship. An arm's-length relationship keeps your opponent off guard, a key to effective negotiation.

Here's What to Do: Keep to Yourself

Ensure an appropriate negotiating relationship by:

- Never appearing too friendly.
- Never discussing anything of a personal nature with, or in front of, a lessor's representative. If you must take a personal call, for example, while meeting with a lessor, do it in another office.
- Always making it clear that your time is limited. State, for example, that you're due in another meeting in, say, an hour.
- Always appearing busy. The busier you seem, the more important you look. And the more important you look, the less inclined someone will be to take advantage of you.

Avoid Social Situations

You're always better off keeping away from lessor cocktail or holiday parties, along with any social situation in which you may have idle time with lessor representatives. Their purposes are to provide an opportunity to build a relationship to put them on an inside track with you and your company and to get information that can provide a negotiating or competitive edge. Since it's impossible to avoid casual talk in these situations, it's likely you'll say something that can help your opponent.

Business lunches or dinners should also be avoided. They're particularly revealing because your table manners can expose personal aspects that can be used against you. If you're overly polite, for example, insisting that your food order be taken last, you're probably the type of person who always wants to do or say the right thing, and you're someone who might be concerned with appearances. This information can assist your negotiating opponent.

Here's What to Do: Limit Personal Involvement

Use the following strategies to keep an arm's-length business relationship:

- Avoid social meetings or situations, such as lunches or dinners, where idle time might lead to personal conversations. This includes sports events.
- If a lunch or dinner is necessary because you're in the process of negotiating a lease, have sandwiches sent in, and keep working while you eat.
- Never travel with a lessor's representative. If you have to meet at an equipment vendor's or lawyer's office, go on your own. If you must fly to a meeting, don't sit next to the lessor representative. Remember, lessors need your business to stay in business. How socially appropriate you are won't affect how good a deal you can get.

Plan Your Equipment Financing Early

All too often, companies acquiring equipment rush out at the last minute for financing. Not having enough time to shop the lessor market comfortably for competitive lease rates or negotiate the lease agreement after a lease award puts these companies at a negotiating disadvantage. People with little time take negotiating shortcuts, often accepting what's offered without objection and overlooking details. Don't put yourself in that spot if you want the best possible deal.

Here's What to Do: Plan Your Financing Needs

To maximize negotiating leverage, ensure maximum lead time before equipment delivery by planning your equipment financing needs at the beginning of each business year, well in advance of equipment deliveries, and put together an action schedule that avoids a last-minute financing rush.

Exhibit 3-1 will help you plan the lead time you'll need.

Watch Out for Lessor Delays

Even with good lease-financing lead-time planning, many lessees still get caught in a time squeeze, losing critical negotiating leverage through clever lessor delays. The closer the equipment delivery date, the more pressure on a lessee to take what's offered. If your lease hasn't been signed when the equipment arrives, the lessor won't make the vendor payment—forcing you to pay the supplier directly, sign the lease promptly, or risk having the vendor take the equipment back. Companies that need equipment and can't, or prefer not to, make payment have no option but to sign the lease without further negotiation.

A common lessor delay tactic is to slow the document negotiation process down intentionally. Leases, for example, don't arrive when promised. When you call to check, the lessor invariably blames the delay on its lawyers, hoping to cover up what's being done.

There are other ways a lessor can create delays. If you ask for a deal modification after you've made a lease award, for example, many will use this opportunity to erode your lead time. Let's say you ask for a longer lease term. Expect the sales representative to tell you that it seems possible but that it will take a few days to get approval, hoping to lull you into a false sense of security. If you're like most lessees, you'll put the transaction on hold waiting for the representative's response. The lessor, however, often has no intention of calling you as promised, waiting instead until you call to check. Again, if you're like most lessees, you'll wait at least a week before calling. When you finally call, your salesperson will attempt to buy a little more time, telling you, for example, that his or her boss has been out of town. If you're not too upset, the representative will again promise to get back to you in a few days. And once again, he or she will do nothing and wait for another call from you. This process will go on as long as the representative thinks he or she can get away with it, using one plausible excuse after another to erode your negotiating time. When you finally get upset, the representative will offer the concession and wait for another opportunity to build in more delays.

Exhibit 3-1. Recommended lease transaction lead time.

Anticipated Type of Transaction	Number of Lessor Investors	Anticipated Number of Lenders	Recommended Lead Time* (months)
Direct lease†	1	0	2
Direct lease	1	1 or more	3
Underwritten single-investor‡	1	0	3
Underwritten leveraged lease	1	1	4
Underwritten leveraged lease	1	2 or more	5

(continues)

Exhibit 3-1. *(continued)*

Underwritten leveraged lease	2 or more	1	6
Underwritten leveraged lease	2 or more	2 or more	6

*Lead time is the period between the lessor's proposal due date and the lessee's antici-
pated first equipment delivery under the lease. These estimates assume a one-month
proposal analysis time.

†A direct lease transaction is one in which the prospective lessee deals directly with the
prospective lessor and not through a lease broker.

‡An underwritten single-investor lease transaction is one in which the lease broker
arranges the financing with one lessor-investor who puts up 100% of the equipment cost.

Here's What to Do: Keep Pressure On

Use these techniques to avoid clever lessor delays:

- Make sure a lessor responds in a timely manner to every request you make. Keep track of all requests, together with
the agreed-upon time for response, and make follow-up
calls. And sound annoyed each time a delay excuse is offered. The point is to keep the lessor under pressure.

- If the lessor blames a third party for a delay, such as the
company's lawyer or an equity participant's credit committee, ask to talk directly to the third party to verify the delay.
Keep in mind, however, that when you're talking to someone on the lessor's payroll, such as the company's attorney,
you may have to read between the lines to get at the truth.
Very often, asking to confirm a third-party delay directly is
enough to correct the problem, particularly if you sound
upset or threaten to take your business elsewhere.

Use a Deal Timetable to Avoid Problems

Use a written deal timetable to keep your lease transaction on track and
avoid losing valuable negotiating lead time. Deliver it to the lessor and
stick to it. With a timetable in the lessor's hands, tactical delays are less
likely. A timetable also ensures that you won't forget about something
critical to completing your deal in a timely fashion.

Although most lessees using timetables hand them to the lessor, a few
experienced ones deliver them along with their request for lease quote
letters (which are discussed in Chapter 5). In my experience, providing a
timetable as soon as possible is preferable. It can always be revised.

> ### Here's What to Do: Use a Deal Timetable
>
> Deliver a deal timetable covering the key transaction milestones to lessors on every deal in which you're involved. Exhibit 3-2 sets out a typical timetable I send along with written request for lease quotes in competitive bid situations.
>
> When you use a preaward timetable, such as the one in Exhibit 3-2, it's essential that any necessary revisions be made at the time you make a lease award. For example, I like to deliver a revised timetable detailing every important aspect of the documentation process. In a leveraged lease situation, this would mean setting deadlines for obtaining formal equity and debt participant commitments, as well as cutoff dates for the appointment of equity and debt counsel. The strategies and tactics of what items should be covered and why are discussed in detail in Chapter 4.

Exhibit 3-2. Transaction timetable.

ABC Corporation will adhere to the following time schedule in connection with evaluating submitted proposals, making the award decision, and negotiating the equipment lease document(s):

Action	Date
Lessor proposal intent notifications due	_____
Lessor proposals due	_____
Lessor proposal commitment cutoff	_____
Lessor notification of initial qualification	_____
Form lease document(s) sent to qualified lessor(s)	_____
Lessor comments to form lease document(s)	_____
Selection of lessor(s)	_____
Award announcement	_____
Lease negotiations—start	_____

(continues)

Exhibit 3-2. *(continued)*

Lease signing   _____

Anticipated equipment delivery   _____

Anticipated equipment acceptance for lease   _____

Don't Offer a Last Look

Lease sales representatives often try to get the last look, an opportunity to come in and match, or beat, the lowest financing offer received from another lessor. Giving such a last look makes it easy for a lessor and can create problems for a lessee. A last-look lessor doesn't have to get aggressive until another lessor comes in with a lower offer. If a competitor's offer is too low, the lessor looks good by confirming that it's a great deal and suggesting that the lessee take it. If it's not too low, the last-look lessor knows what it will take to win, without having to stretch. In effect, a last-look lessor isn't part of the competition.

There's another reason why giving a last-look opportunity is a mistake. If the word gets around the leasing community that you provide a particular lessor with a last look—and word inevitably does get around—competing lessors won't submit their best rate, feeling that it's a waste of time.

Here's What to Do: Keep Everyone Competitive

Here's how to proceed if asked for a last look:

- Flatly refuse to give it.
- If you're concerned that flatly refusing to grant a last-look request will damage your relationship, blame the refusal on your management. Tell the lessor, for example, that you'd like to accommodate the request, but it's against company policy—something with which no one argues. This will take the sting out of the refusal. But if you think that looking as if you're in control will strengthen your negotiating posture, say that it was your decision.

When Requesting Bids, Provide Only Essentials

Telling a lessor more information than necessary to make an offer is a strategic mistake. The more information a lessor has about your deal and your company, the greater the possibility of finding a weakness that can be used against you, and the greater the possibility of alerting the lessor to something it overlooked.

Inexperienced lessees frequently do this simply because they don't realize the advantage it can provide a lessor. For example, novice computer equipment lessees often blurt out in the first meeting with the lessor that they're leasing because the equipment will be worthless in a few years. When the lessor comes back with what the lessee thinks is too high a lease rent, the lessor points to the lack of residual potential to justify it. The lessee then has no room to negotiate for lower rates by arguing that the lessor's residual estimate is wrong. Worse yet, if the lessor wasn't aware of the resale value problem, the lessee would have lost an opportunity for a good deal.

At times, even experienced lessee representatives make the same mistake by failing to appreciate a lease analysis nuance or, in a relaxed moment, simply slipping. Here's a good example: Most lessors assume that the equipment will be used during normal business hours, 8 hours a day, 5 days a week. They rarely verify whether this *is in fact true* in a particular situation. In one of the first deals on which I ran the bids, an experienced lessee negotiator casually volunteered during a negotiation break that he was amazed at how great an offer my client was able to make considering what the equipment condition would be at the end of the lease term. The equipment was considered a high residual value asset, and since my client had anticipated that in its rent offer, I naturally asked what he meant. He had assumed that we knew the equipment would be used 24 hours a day, 7 days a week. We didn't, and needless to say, we took that opportunity to renegotiate a very profitable, last-minute rate increase.

Here's What to Do: Give the Minimum

Whether you're experienced or not, the best way to avoid weakening your negotiating position is to provide a lessor only what's absolutely necessary to make an offer. If you're not sure, wait until you're asked for something before providing it. What to provide is discussed extensively in Chapter 5. Here's a quick overview that you can use as a checklist:

- The equipment description, cost, and any trade-in arrangement.
- The estimated equipment delivery and lease acceptance date.
- The date the equipment vendor must be paid.
- Where the equipment will be located while on lease.
- The lease term desired.
- The rent payments desired (for example, monthly, quarterly).

- Whether the rent payments should be in advance or in arrears.
- Whether an interim lease term will be acceptable.
- Whether interim lease rents will be acceptable.
- What lease options are desired (for example, purchase option, renewal option).
- What insurance requirements will be acceptable, such as self-insurance.
- What schedules must be submitted with the lease quote, such as casualty or termination value schedules.
- What fees will be unacceptable (for example, commitment or nonutilization fees).
- The preferred lease accounting treatment. (Will, for example, an operating lease be given preference?)
- The type of lease structure preferred, such as a single-investor lease or leveraged lease.
- Whether lease brokers may submit bids.
- Who will pay what transaction expenses, such as documentation expenses.

Never Make These Typical Lessee Statements

I've negotiated hundreds of lease transactions, ranging from $2,000 to $200 million. To my amazement, most lessees, their lawyers, or advisers made statements that seriously damaged their negotiating leverage. Saying something that hands a lessor negotiator more power is like insisting on paying more than a lessor asks.

Although most damaging lessee statements appear to result from inexperience, many seem motivated by overriding personal issues or anxieties. For example, some lease negotiators self-conscious about their lack of tax expertise compensate in a way that telegraphs this fact to a lessor negotiator, apparently in an effort to avoid looking foolish. Their requests are often preceded with statements such as, "I know that you may not be able to grant us the following request, but . . ." Some go even further, flatly stating that they are unfamiliar with the relevant tax issues, apparently hoping to engender some sympathy or understanding. People who make statements like this often unconsciously view the lessor representative as a lease authority, thus effectively eliminating their *own* negotiating power.

Everyone, including successful negotiators, has uncomfortable personal issues. And everyone feels inclined to do or say something to avoid being judged too harshly. That's a mistake in a negotiation. If you can't control your personal anxieties, you'll be at a disadvantage. The key is to understand the effect of statements you make in the process of a negotiation.

What type of statements can get you into trouble in a lease negotiation? Read on. And as you read, think about the impression hearing these statements would create if you were a lessor representative. Once you get the idea, you'll be able to think about anything you might say to a lessor—and edit those remarks before it's too late.

Never Say, "Purchase Funds Aren't Available"

If the lessor knows that you cannot, or are unwilling to, pay for the equipment at delivery, it will have a negotiating advantage. When leasing is your only alternative, a lessor has a better chance of holding out for higher rates and better terms without risking losing the deal. Don't put the lessor in the driver's seat.

Here's What to Do: Suggest the Possibility of Purchase

Even if funds are not available to purchase necessary equipment, use these strategies to keep your negotiating leverage at its maximum:

- Never state that you cannot, or prefer not to, purchase the equipment. All too often, lessees tell lessors that they must lease because they're trying to conserve existing funds for other equipment purchase needs.

- Always tell the lessor affirmatively at the start that you're seriously considering purchasing the equipment under consideration. Nothing keeps a lessor strategically off guard more than stating that you may purchase, rather than lease, your equipment. Lessors know that they have a reasonable chance against competitors but feel less optimistic when competing against a purchase decision.

- If your company always leases a particular type of equipment, such as computers, and the lessor knows it, telling the lessor at the beginning that your management has decided to make an exception in this case is a must. And give a plausible reason why, such as that it's felt that the equipment will have a high end-of-lease value or your chief financial officer feels that it's more economical to purchase than to lease. And don't let facts indicating anything to the contrary cause you to admit otherwise. Keep the lessor off guard and stand firm in your bluff.

- Always tell the lessor firmly that if your lease is not negotiated to your satisfaction and signed by a specific date (comfortably in advance of the equipment delivery so you can find backup financing if necessary), the deal is off. A signing deadline that provides sufficient time to find another lessor adds credibility to your statement; one that doesn't indicate that you either have no intention of looking elsewhere or don't know what you're doing.
- Instruct every member of your negotiating team not to disclose the unavailability of purchase funds.
- Purchase the equipment if you run out of negotiating time, rather than accede to unfavorable demands, and then immediately look for a lessor willing to enter into a sale/leaseback. A word of caution: Some lessors won't do sale/leasebacks because they complicate the financing, so finding a willing lessor may take some effort. A sale/leaseback lessor, for example, must check whether existing creditors have liens that give them a prior right over the rights of a sale/leaseback lessor and that automatically attached when your company purchased the equipment. Liens of this nature are commonly imposed under bank loan agreements.
- Bluff if your financial statements show that you have limited working capital available to purchase equipment and the lessor points that out. State, for example, that you've made arrangements with an institutional lender to provide the necessary funds. If you're not willing to play negotiation poker, you will hurt your negotiating leverage.

Never Say, "There Are Capital Budget Restrictions"

Companies often restrict how much equipment may be purchased by a particular department in a given year. Once the budget limit has been reached, leasing is typically the only alternative available to acquire use of the equipment.

Telling a lessor that you have capital budget restrictions is a mistake. Doing so guarantees that the lessor will attempt to increase its leverage by, for example, creating document delays, in hopes of extracting concessions on the eve of an equipment delivery.

Here's an example of what can happen if you're not careful: In my role as a lessor, I received a call a few years ago from the chief financial officer of a large U.S. airline requesting a lease quote on a computer system. The CFO, whom I'll call Mr. Jones, started the conversation by saying, "Like other companies in today's economy, we have a zero capital budget." When I asked how large the transaction was, he hesitated a moment and then said, somewhat awkwardly, "It's small." I asked how small. He replied, "$12,000."

It so happened that my company was a small-ticket lessor, specializing in computer equipment, so the deal was perfect. In addition, inasmuch as my company generally financed companies of a much lesser credit standing, the opportunity of doing business with a major airline, even with some financial problems, was very attractive.

Mr. Jones's discomfort made it clear that he would be happy to get the financing and probably would accept whatever rate my company offered—as long as it wasn't ridiculously high. My company offered a premium lease rate, citing the problems in his industry. Not only was the offer accepted, but Mr. Jones thanked the company for providing financing so quickly. It was also clear that if he had known how my company viewed the lease opportunity, he would have attempted to negotiate the rate downward.

Here's What to Do: Don't Disclose Restrictions

If you have capital equipment acquisition budget restrictions, follow these guidelines:

- Don't state that any restrictions exist.
- If you don't have funds available under your capital budget to purchase the equipment, and you or someone else accidentally discloses that fact to a lessor, immediately let it be known that your management has made a budget exception that will allow you to purchase if you're not satisfied with the lease deal offered.
- Once you've made a lease award to a particular lessor, set a transaction closing deadline—one that gives you adequate time to find another lessor. And if your deal hasn't closed when it should, immediately start negotiations with another lessor. If you want to give the original lessor more time, tell it that you have started simultaneous negotiations with another lessor. A simultaneous negotiation, if used judiciously, is an effective way of getting what you need.

Never Say, "I'm Not Getting Competitive Quotes"

There's no substitute for competitive bids, asking a cross section of leasing companies to make proposals on your equipment financing, if you want to get the best possible deal. See Chapter 2 for a discussion of how to set up and manage an effective competitive bidding. Suffice it to say, it should be a part of your negotiating strategy.

Statements like "We are not going to other leasing companies for quotes because we have little time, so give us your best deal" are an open invitation to have a lessor take your money. Apparently, lessees that make statements like this hope to appeal to a lessor's sense of fairness. That's a mistake. If a lessor knows there's no competition, you won't get offered its lowest rate.

Here's What to Do: Never Say You're Giving an Exclusive Deal

If there's no time for competitive bids, protect your negotiating leverage by:

- Never stating that you're giving a leasing company an exclusive deal or that there is no competition.
- Never confirming to a lessor that there is no competition.
- Making it clear up front that your management may purchase the equipment unless the lease offer is very favorable. This will eliminate any perceived advantage a lessor thinks it has if it's discovered that you're not shopping the lessor market.

Never Say, "Equipment Tax Benefits Can't Be Used"

If a lessor finds out that you can't take full advantage of equipment ownership tax benefits, such as depreciation, you're not likely to be offered its most aggressive lease rate. As a general rule, leasing is clearly the right economic choice if tax benefits can't be used, particularly if some of the ownership tax benefit advantages are passed through to a lessee in the form of relatively lower rent charges. A lessor knowing that tax benefits can't be used also knows that it can charge relatively higher rents without upsetting the leasing advantage. See Chapter 2 for an explanation of how this works.

Here's What to Do: Claim That Benefits Are Valuable

Here's how to proceed if your company cannot currently use available equipment ownership tax benefits:

- Never tell a lessor that your company can't take full advantage of equipment ownership tax benefits in your current fiscal year.
- If it's apparent from your company's financial statements that equipment ownership tax benefits can't be used, claim that you've figured out a way to take advantage of them— even if the lessor's tax experts can't see how you'll do so. The tax rules are so complicated that even experts can be bluffed at times. For example, state that your company in-

tends to purchase the asset jointly with a partner that is willing to lend you funds at a rate that, in effect, will put you in the same position economically as if you could use the tax benefits. Or say that your company has devised a unique way to use tax benefits. If you're asked for proof, simply state that you've been advised not to disclose your position because of the risk of highlighting an issue that might initiate an IRS audit, one in which you would prevail but that might result in legal or accounting costs. Negotiating bluffs are most effective in technical areas.

Never Say, "Equipment Is Needed Immediately"

Telling a lessor that you need equipment immediately will leave you open to tactics that can weaken your negotiating position. All too often, lessee representatives tell lessors in the initial leasing telephone call that they need the equipment "yesterday." In virtually every situation, lessors ask for, and get, concessions that they wouldn't ordinarily have gone after if they didn't know a lessee was in a hurry.

Here's What to Do: Don't Act Rushed

To maintain negotiating leverage:

- Never tell the lessor that you need the equipment immediately.
- Make sure your anxiety doesn't show. Act as if you have plenty of time, but set a tight timetable to close the financing. Tell the lessor, for example, that you want to be sure that there is plenty of time to look elsewhere if you can't negotiate a satisfactory deal. Or state that your work schedule is tight, you have little time to devote to the financing in question, and if the deal is not closed by the specified deadline, management wants you to purchase the equipment.

Never Say, "Lease Rate Is Not Important"

There are times when companies are willing to pay a higher-than-market lease rate, such as when they are having financial problems. In these situations, management often feels that the lease rate is secondary to getting the equipment financed.

Stating that an aggressive lease rate is not a primary consideration is a negotiating mistake, no matter what the reason. If you do, you'll be overcharged because it will be clear that you don't know what you're doing. Saying, for example, that you'll pay a higher rate to get a favorable purchase right gives the lessor permission to take your money. It also may work against you for another reason: Most leasing companies have little equipment residual value expertise, and asking for a low purchase option in return for your willingness to pay an above-market rate will alert them to high residual possibilities, something they may not have considered. As you now know from Chapter 2, earnings expected from end-of-lease equipment sales can be an attractive lessor profit opportunity. It's like telling a used-car dealer how wonderful the car is before you make a below-asking-price offer.

Here's What to Do: Claim That Rate Is Key

To ensure that you get the best lease deal possible, never:

- State that lease rate is not a primary consideration.
- Alert the lessor to anything that could cause it to reexamine the value of the equipment at the end of the lease term, unless it could work in your favor. For example, if you want the lowest rent payment possible and the lessor states that, in computing your lease rate, it anticipated little profit from the end-of-lease resale, convincing it that the equipment has high potential resale value may get you a lower rate, but it may also increase any possible fixed-price purchase option.

Avoid These Other Common Mistakes

In addition to avoiding the statements discussed in the preceding section, you must be careful not to make any of the mistakes discussed in this section.

Avoid Disclosing Future Equipment Upgrade Needs

Statements like "We're probably going to have to upgrade the leased equipment in a little while" can get you into trouble. Equipment upgrades are additions or modifications that typically enhance performance or increase efficiency.

When upgrades are needed, the equipment lessor, as discussed in Chapter 2, is generally in the superior negotiating position. In most cases, it's because the lessee failed to negotiate an effective and meaningful upgrade financing right in its original lease. Lessors don't like meaningful upgrade rights. They fix future financing rates and therefore cut down on a lessor's opportunity to profit.

Saying that you may need to upgrade your equipment alerts a lessor to an opportunity to back you into a corner by, for example, slipping an innocent-looking provision into your lease giving the lessor the exclusive right to provide all upgrade financing at virtually any rate it chooses.

Here's What to Do: Pin Down Upgrade Financing

To avoid losing negotiating leverage in situations in which you may have to upgrade leased equipment:

- Never give a lease award unless you've negotiated the specific business terms of an upgrade financing right and those terms have been included as part of the lessor's written financing offer.
- Never sign a lease for equipment you may need to upgrade unless an upgrade right has been incorporated into your lease agreement.
- Never agree to a lease provision that obligates you to lease all equipment upgrades from the lessor, unless the financing rate is very attractive.
- Make sure that any upgrade financing right you negotiate is meaningful. In most cases, the right offered by a lessor offers nothing substantive, allowing the lessor to elect not to provide the upgrade financing or, if it does provide the financing, to dictate the financing rate.

Avoid Confirming the Severity of Existing Financial Problems

People representing companies with financial problems are often self-conscious about how they'll be received by the leasing community. As a result, they frequently make statements like, "Our company is having financial problems, so we may be a tough credit to get approved," or, "Please do whatever you can to get the deal done for us." Even when financial problems are obvious, pointing them out before they are discovered will hurt your ability to negotiate effectively. Doing so makes it clear that you're embarrassed or nervous about your company's financial situation. A good negotiator can, and will, use that to his or her advantage.

And be careful about confirming any financial problems pointed out by the lessor. Generally, when you agree with someone, the chances are greater you'll begin to take his or her side—to see the other person's point of view. And that will invariably weaken your mental fortitude, and you'll unconsciously be inclined to concede to a lessor's demands for increased deal security or a higher lease rate. By not openly agreeing with someone's statement, even though you recognize the problem, you're better able to keep a proper negotiating perspective.

There's another reason to avoid confirming the severity of business risks: When you don't offer any confirmation, businesspeople are inclined to ignore, or lessen, those risks in an effort to make profits. Leasing company management is often preoccupied with near-term profits, something that drives it to rationalize risks. If you support its fears, you'll lessen your chances for a better deal.

Here's What to Do: Don't Confirm Problems

Keep your negotiating leverage high by:

- Only giving a lessor the financial information it specifically asks for.
- Not readily volunteering information about any company financial problems. Let those problems be discovered in the ordinary course of a lessor's credit investigation. When you volunteer information about financial problems, it's likely you're defensive, and a lessor representative will try to use that against you.
- Never confirming the severity of any company financial risk. Simply acknowledge the facts as they are.
- Simply listening when a lessor representative talks about the financial risks of dealing with your company—unless, of course, he or she is incorrect.
- Stating affirmatively that, in your opinion, any financial problems don't appear to be that bad and, if those problems do in fact exist, that your company is making a major effort to correct them.
- Matter-of-factly confirming financial problems that you feel must be acknowledged.
- Not second-guessing a lessor on financial risks. That is, don't anticipate how risky your lease situation is for a lessor. More likely than not, unless you worked for the lessor, you could not properly assess what its real concerns are. Most lessees overestimate the risk to a lessor and are easily talked into paying more than necessary. For example, some lessors finance equipment on the strength of its inherent resale value, not on the financial strength of the lessee. In that case, a lessee's financial problems are secondary. If a lessor knows that you think otherwise, you'll be charged a higher-than-necessary lease rate.

Avoid Asking the Lessor to Find and Supply the Equipment You Need

Permitting lessors to supply your equipment gives them an opportunity to overcharge you. When a leasing company buys equipment from its selected supplier, or deals directly with your suggested supplier, it may negotiate an undisclosed purchase discount. If you're unaware of the price discount, your apparent lease interest rate will be much less than what you're actually being charged. See Chapter 2 for a discussion of hidden discount problems.

Lessees that ask lessors to "source" equipment for them clearly signal that they don't know what they're doing or that they're indifferent to the lease interest charge. Making such a request is a negotiating mistake.

Here's What to Do: Find Your Own Equipment

Use these techniques to avoid weakening your negotiating position:

- Never ask whether a lessor can source the equipment you need from any of its suppliers.
- If you want to let the lessor source the equipment through its suppliers to see whether it can get you a better deal, always get price quotes from your own equipment suppliers. By doing so, there's less chance that the lessor will profit from a hidden price discount. (Note: In fairness to lessors, a few have volume purchase discount arrangements from which you can benefit, but you must independently verify the price you're offered to ensure that there are no hidden profits.)

Avoid Doing Anything on a Handshake

Telling someone whom you don't know that you're honest can hurt you in a negotiation, particularly if he or she is not. Unfortunately, in today's no-holds-barred business world, honest people, those who never bluff, are viewed as naive. And saying that you're naive opens the door for someone to attempt to take advantage of you.

And if you're honest, be careful. It's a fact that many honest people tend to think that everyone is honest. Having that belief may blind you to your opponent's dishonesty. This is not to say that you have to be dishonest to protect yourself but only that you're better able to identify dishonest manipulation if you don't assume that your opponent is honest.

Here's What to Do: Never Offer That You're Honest

If you're an honest person, maintain a negotiation mystique by:

- Never making a point of telling someone how honest you are. If you feel a pressing need to tell someone that you're honest, be honest with yourself about the real motivation behind that need. You may find, for example, that you're trying to project an image of what a good person you are, something that has little consequence in a business negotiation. If you're a decent person, let your actions show it.

- Never telling your opponent that you think he or she is honest in an effort to get a confirming reaction. Let his or her actions tell you over time.

- Avoiding statements like, "I do everything on a handshake." A devious negotiator will abuse your honesty.

- Never making statements like, "I trust you people," or, "I deal only with people I trust." Naive people make statements like this. In the beginning of a relationship, trusting someone is often a subjective decision, a guess based on what you think rather than on facts. Such statements can let your opponent know that outwitting you may only require an appearance of honesty and a smile. A trusting person may not, for example, review a lease document as carefully as he or she should, giving a lessor the incentive to load it with lessee traps.

- Always being careful if someone plays to your honesty. He or she may be setting you up to be manipulated.

- Getting everything in a deal in writing. Lease transactions are extremely complex; issues can easily be misunderstood or twisted. And promises are easily forgotten. If you don't understand what's written, ask for a clarification; otherwise, you may be outnegotiated. For example, devious negotiators often use statements like, "Gee, I'm sorry. We really intended that to mean . . ."

Avoid Asking the Lessor for Assistance

Some lessees, particularly inexperienced ones, request help from lessors in evaluating financing offers. They ask, for example, the lessor's salesperson to compute the inherent lease interest rate in a deal. A lessor knows that, if you're unfamiliar with leasing basics, you probably won't catch sophisticated traps—and may jump at the opportunity to build some in. Asking for help can be an open invitation to a lessor to take advantage of your situation.

Here's an example of what can happen: A practice used by some computer lease salespeople, when asked to compute the lease simple interest rate, was to take the prospective lessee through the rate computation using an incorrect financial calculator setting, one that would result in a rate computation lower than it actually was. For instance, if you were quoted a monthly, in advance, lease rate, the representative would run the calculations using a monthly, in arrears, setting—something rarely detected.

Statements like, "You probably know more about these types of deals than I do," "Would you please explain the best way to make our lease-versus-purchase analysis?" or, "This is the first deal I have done, so don't be too tough," give the same kind of message. Such statements tell the lessor that you're unsure of yourself, too trusting, and probably easy to take advantage of.

Here's What to Do: Don't Ask for the Lessor's Help

No matter how self-conscious you are about your lack of knowledge or inexperience:

- Never rely on your opponent for assistance.
- Never assume that a lease salesperson will give you a break by telling him or her to, in effect, go easy on you. If you're unsure of yourself, spend a weekend reading a good lease handbook. Learn the technical lingo. Regardless of how little experience or knowledge you have, don't confess it to a lessor. Keep the lessor guessing. It will be less likely to attempt to get away with something clever. Negotiating is a game of bluffing. Those who bluff the best get the most.

Avoid Indicating That You Have Little Time or Interest

At times, overworked people, and people who do only what's necessary to keep their jobs, skip over details. If a lessor negotiator suspects you're either *overworked* or a *slacker,* he or she may try to slip something by you.

Statements like, "My boss only cares about getting the financing arranged," "I am very busy and have little time to spend on this deal," or, "I'm loaded with work," tell someone that you may overlook details.

People like this often have little patience with complex document provisions. And they're easily convinced not to concern themselves with lease agreement boilerplate, provisions that allegedly contain industry-standard conditions and obligations.

People who do only what's necessary to keep their jobs are easy marks for lessor negotiators. Typically, such people use any excuse to pass on responsibility to someone else. Statements like, "I never read our leases. I leave it to the lawyers," or, "I am a lawyer, so I'll leave the business issues in the lease documents to the businesspeople," give these types of people away. If you're such a person, at least don't tell the lessor.

And be careful about making these types of statements to look important. They can create more deal problems than necessary. Experienced negotiators know, for example, that people who make such statements often don't communicate well with members of their negotiating team and important points fall through the cracks. The fact that you as a businessperson, for example, won't read the lease provides the lessor with an opportunity to slip a complex business issue by your lawyer. A lawyer with a similar inclination can cause problems for the businesspeople.

People covering up inexperience or knowledge insecurities also make these types of statements. If a negotiator suspects you of doing that, you are more likely to be barraged with slick double-talk in hopes that maintaining your image takes precedence over getting the best deal.

Here's What to Do:
Don't Project Insecurities

Follow these tips to maintain a solid negotiating image:

- Don't make statements to cover up insecurities or appear important.
- Learn to think honestly about why you want to say something before you say it. If you're uncomfortable about lack of knowledge or experience, get some expert help. The cost of outside consulting services can often be less than the price you'll pay if you miss a financial trap.
- Even if you don't read lease documents, or take the time to understand the business issues, never tell the lessor that fact.

Avoid Giving Compliments

Compliments at the start of a negotiation can give you away. Statements like, "I've heard a lot of good things about your company," or, "I've heard that your company is very reputable," are frequently made by people enamored with an upcoming business relationship. All too often, this love-at-first-sight attitude is unwarranted and indicates a negotiation blind spot.

People who make statements like this early in a business relationship are typically those who want to be liked, want to appear to be nice, or need approval. These needs can compromise an objective and effective approach to getting the best possible deal. For example, people who need to be liked tend not to push hard for concessions if their opponent starts to get angry.

There is nothing wrong with any of these personal inclinations, but a business negotiation is not the place to satisfy, or project, them. If you do, an experienced negotiator will make an effort to use these inclinations to manipulate you.

Here's What to Do:
Be All Business

To ensure that you don't project information about yourself that the other side can use:

- Be all business, particularly at the beginning of a negotiation. Maintain an arm's-length distance.

- Don't let your opponents know that you favor them or their company for any reason.

- Suspend any positive belief you have about an opponent or his or her company. It may prevent you from seeing that you're being taken for a financial ride. For example, if you think someone's ethical, you'll be less alert for trickery. A belief that someone you don't know will be ethical often results from a personal need to believe that the person is ethical. A strong personal need, not based in fact, will get in your way in a negotiation.

Avoid Appearing Too Reasonable

It's a mistake to appear reasonable, or fair, early in a business negotiation. If your opposition thinks that you may not be reasonable, it will be more likely to stretch to give you a better deal.

Statements like, "I am not concerned about the upgrade rate if you can assure me that you'll be fair," or, "I know that you have to make a fair profit," will work against you. An experienced lease negotiator can keep his or her opponent off guard by appearing unfair or unreasonable.

Here's What to Do: Don't Appear Too Reasonable

To avoid weakening your negotiating image:

- Don't volunteer that you're a fair or reasonable person. Ask for what you want and let the other party stand up for himself or herself.
- If you're an empathic person, don't project it. Negotiators know that empathic people tend to be swayed easily by logic and fairness arguments.
- If a negotiator tries to determine how empathetic you are early in a negotiation by, for example, asking whether you can see his or her point of view on a particular issue, don't take the bait. Simply say that you hear the person's point and will take it into consideration in your negotiations, nothing more.

Here's How to Handle an Initial Lessor Telephone Call

As discussed in the preceding two sections, what you say to a lessor can make a difference in your ability to outwit your opponent. In face-to-face meetings, people tend to be more aware of what they're saying. For some reason, they're less aware in telephone conversations, particularly early ones. So to avoid weakening your negotiating position, you must be extremely aware of the effect of what you're about to say to a lessor representative in every telephone conversation. Lessor representatives know how to listen for clues that can help them outmaneuver you.

To get an idea of how easy it is to provide a lessor with clues that can hurt your negotiating ability, let's examine a typical telephone dialogue early in the lease process. As you will see, a careless approach can lead to trouble, whereas with a little restraint and awareness, it's easy to maintain, or enhance, a good negotiating posture.

Handling a Call—The Wrong Way

Here's the wrong way to handle a telephone call to a prospective lessor. As you read through the caller's statements, feel the impressions that this prospective lessee is creating for you:

1. Hi, Dick. This is Pete at Union Air Corporation. We haven't done business before, but you were highly recommended to us. A friend of mine told me you have the best rates in town.

2. I just found out from the boss that we need to get 20 forklift trucks by next week.
3. We're behind in our production schedule. And we must lease the trucks because our capital acquisition budget is zero for the rest of this year.
4. What is your best rate? And how fast can you get a lease document over to have it signed?
5. By the way, make sure you give me your lowest lease rate. We don't have time to shop lease rates with other lessors, OK?
6. And be prepared to negotiate quickly. Talk to you soon. Bye.

In my role as a lessor, I have received many calls like this. They're music to a lease-marketing person's ears. The caller, in effect, is handing the leasing company a blank check.

What the caller has done in this example may appear obvious to you. But all too often, it's not obvious to the person making the call. Let's examine what the lessor is being told. Here's the impression created by the caller:

1. He wants to be the lessor's friend, hoping that the lessor will help him out of his problem; hence, the compliments.
2. He has little time to put together the equipment financing, and it's unlikely he'll get competitive bids. If he doesn't shop the lessor market, he will have no basis for determining whether the rate offered is a low market rate.
3. He must lease because his company has no money available to purchase the forklifts. In addition, the equipment is important to the profits of the business. The company is behind in its production schedule, and a hefty lease rate can easily be rationalized.
4. He's ready to sign the lease and will probably pay little attention to the terms and conditions of the lease documentation.
5. He's confirmed that his company won't seek competitive bids and may have no idea what current market rates are.
6. He wants to get a lease document signed. It's clear that his priority is getting the deal done, not getting the best rate. It's likely that if he's told he has absolutely the lowest rate that can be offered, he would be inclined to talk himself into believing it.

Very simply, since this prospective lessee has stated that he has no money to purchase the equipment, no time to shop lease rates, and therefore probably no time to negotiate fairly for himself, he's done our job for us. Pete has told us that he is neither experienced nor self-confident. Chances are good that if we offer a lease rate that looks fair, even if it's above-market, he'll go for it. Seem unlikely? You'd be surprised how often this happens.

What else might the lessor do with a caller like this? Certainly, it could offer to order the forklifts Pete needs from a vendor with which the lessor deals, providing another profit opportunity by negotiating an undisclosed purchase price discount.

Handling a Call—The Right Way

Now let's take the same situation and look at the best way to handle a call to a prospective lessor. Put yourself in the lessor's position and see what a different impression you get if you are approached in the following manner:

1. Hi, Dick. This is Pete at Union Air Corporation. We would like to acquire twenty forklift trucks, preferably to take delivery next week. But if we don't, it won't be the end of the world.
2. We're considering leasing the trucks rather than purchasing them. However, we are going to keep our options open.
3. Give me your best lease rate quote. We will be calling several other companies this afternoon, and we are going to take the lowest offer.
4. I am not going to give anyone the chance to rebid, so sharpen your pencil and do the best you can.
5. By the way, I will be supplying to you later today our form lease document. This is the one we want to use on this transaction. And since the dollars involved are low, we don't want to negotiate it. Talk to you soon. Bye.

This approach would tell a lessor that:

1. Although the equipment could be put to immediate use, the company's not under any delivery time pressure.
2. The company will lease, but only if the deal is right.
3. It will be a competitive bid situation.
4. The lessor's initial offer should be its lowest because there won't be a second opportunity to quote.
5. The lessee is experienced, requiring the lessor to use the lessee's form lease. It's unlikely that this prospective lessee will fall for any lessor tricks.

In this case, Pete creates the impression that he is not only self-confident but also a hard-nosed businessperson. He sounds like an experienced lessee negotiator, one who is unlikely to fall for any lessor tricks. In this case, the lessor's initial offer will invariably be more lessee-favorable than in the case of the first call.

Make Sure Your Team Knows Your Strategy

Before you begin discussions with any lessor, it's important that you discuss the approach you intend to take with everyone who may be involved in your lease transaction. If you don't, there's a good chance that someone may inadvertently damage your negotiating posture. For example, if your lawyer or accountant discloses that your department does not have funds allocated to purchase equipment, all the care you used in talking to a lessor representative to avoid giving clues that could weaken your negotiating position will be wasted.

Here's What to Do: Have a Unified Front

To ensure that your team offers a unified negotiating front to your lessor opponent:

- Organize a team meeting to discuss every aspect of your equipment needs, concerns, and areas that, if known, could provide a lessor with a negotiating edge. For example, go over your strategy in approaching the lessor marketplace, such as whether you'll use a competitive bid approach or whether lease brokers will be permitted to submit bids. Chapter 4 will be of help in doing this.

- Make sure that everyone knows the type of statements, as discussed earlier in this chapter, that will provide a lessor with a negotiating edge.

- Get the benefit of everyone's lease experience and knowledge as they may relate to your upcoming lease financing.

- Make sure that everyone involved knows what must be done, when it must be done, and his or her specific job responsibilities.

- Agree together on a deal timetable that works for your company, considering any risks.

- Put together a confidential, written summary of your meeting as a guide for everyone to follow.

Chapter 4

Establishing Solid Negotiation Objectives

A Negotiation Plan Sets the Stage to Win

The way you personally conduct yourself early in the lease-financing process establishes how you'll be perceived as a negotiator by your opponent. If you appear disorganized, your opponent will feel more inclined to try to slip something by you. If you're on top of every issue, he or she will think twice before attempting to do so. Organized people project an image of strength, disorganized ones an image of weakness. The weaker you appear, the less effective you'll be as a negotiator.

In addition, a negotiator able to respond decisively and immediately as issues arise gains respect, credibility—and power. He or she, in effect, becomes the deal maker. People are more willing to compromise with a deal maker, knowing (or at least believing) that he or she has the ability to conclude the transaction. On the other hand, negotiators who must continually defer issue decisions because, for example, they have to "pass it by management" quickly make it clear that they have little power. Their opponents are rarely willing to stretch for an immediate compromise when an on-the-spot decision cannot be made.

In order to set a professional tone that will keep your opponent off guard, you must be prepared to respond firmly and knowledgeably to every issue as it arises. To do this, you must know exactly what you want and what you'll concede before you start talking to a leasing company. In other words, you have to know what your overall company negotiation objectives will be. And there is only one way to do this: by coming to the negotiating table armed with an internal deal objectives mandate supported by every company member with an interest in the deal's outcome.

What's the best way to determine your company's lease negotiation objectives? Start by assessing your business, financial, tax, accounting, and legal needs—and build a consensus of what is, and is not, important to the various individuals who will have a say in the lease negotiation. Remember, negotiating is like going on a trip: If you don't know where you want to go, you'll never know whether you've reached your destination. And in addition, without knowing what you hope to achieve, it's impossible to make the necessary compromises to keep your deal on track. If you know what you must have, you know what you have to trade with to get it.

Get Internal Support

For the reasons just mentioned, a negotiator must know what will be minimally acceptable to his or her client company before discussions start. Negotiators who don't make the effort to learn in advance what will be acceptable risk their effectiveness. There is nothing worse than walking away from the negotiating table having stated that the deal is off unless you get a certain concession only to return with hat in hand because management wouldn't back you up. And even more upsetting is believing that you've successfully negotiated a favorable lease only to find out, for example, from your accountants at the end of the fiscal year that the structure you used adversely impacts your company's financial statements and that, with minor changes during the negotiation process, you could have avoided the problem.

Often the difficult part of getting prenegotiation internal support is convincing the various department executives, each with different objectives, to agree in advance to what may be the necessary compromises. The effort, however, is worth it. Having a unified front ensures maximum effectiveness. For example, a $1.00 purchase option may be very desirable to your manufacturing manager but may not be so desirable to your financial executive or your tax adviser. A finance lease containing a $1.00 purchase right must be reported in a company's financial statements as, in effect, an asset purchase, with the rent liability basically treated as a long-term debt liability item on the balance sheet. And for federal income tax purposes, it must be treated as a conditional sale transaction, requiring the asset to be depreciated rather than the rent payments' being expensed. In the case of a small-dollar lease transaction, the treatment may be irrelevant. That may not be the case, however, if the lease involves millions of dollars of equipment. If its treatment is not irrelevant, the advantage of being able to acquire the equipment for a low price may be outweighed by the adverse tax and financial reporting implications. The point here is to know in advance what effect every important lease issue decision will have on all concerned and the level of acceptability for any potential compromises.

Internal support is important for another reason: When a leasing company knows that all levels of your management are fully behind your position, it's less likely to waste your time with clever tactics in an effort to call your bluff. In addition, since leasing companies always hope to build a long-range relationship, knowing that your management supports your positions can eliminate tactics that might jeopardize their chances of participating in future business.

Identify the Key Business Areas to Address

To establish proper deal objectives, you first have to identify the issue areas that are critical in your lease financing. Some will be obvious. Many, to the less experienced, won't be. In addition, you must always maintain a proper perspective: If the deal is small, negotiating certain typically critical issues may be a waste of time. In other words, you must know when to compromise, even if you feel you're being run over.

Generally speaking, the smaller the lease, the less you should concern yourself about having to make unfavorable concessions—something too many negotiators lose sight of. For example, attempting to shave another .5% off an annual lease interest rate on a $4,000, five-year lease is rarely worth the time spent, particularly if it causes the negotiations to collapse or runs up negotiating fees. On a monthly basis, paying the additional .5% in lease interest in this case amounts to about another $1 in rent, or $60 over the term of the lease. (The monthly, in advance, rent charge for a five-year lease on a $4,000 item of equipment at an 11% lease simple interest rate is $86.96. At a 10.5% interest rate, the monthly rent is $85.98.) Of course, if you're negotiating a master lease for a series of future small transactions, the time spent cutting the rate down may very well be justified.

What should you consider in setting up your negotiation objectives? At a minimum, a negotiator should assess a transaction from the following perspectives:

- Income tax
- Accounting
- Overall financial implications
- Cash flow
- Cash leveraging
- Down payment requirements
- Collateral requirements
- Financial guarantees
- Financial statement reporting
- Operations
- Market image
- Bank borrowing restrictions
- Potential equipment disposition profits

- Equipment use flexibility
- Competitive needs
- Equipment vendor purchase discounts
- Early termination possibilities and penalties
- Possible end-of-lease continued equipment use needs
- Potential end-of-lease market value
- General business needs

As suggested earlier, to assess the implications and relative importance of a lease financing, you must take time to discuss with, and ensure the understanding of, those individuals whose area of operation could be affected or who have the final say on the deal negotiated. The best approach that I've found when dealing with a large upcoming lease is to have everyone who may be affected or interested meet with me and discuss all needs and concerns, as well as potential compromises. At the meeting, I assist in identifying in the details of, and getting agreement on, the overall negotiation objectives; that is, what concessions we must have or we will walk away from the transaction (often referred to as deal points) and what issues can be compromised. In a group, issues, needs, and concerns, as well as compromise positions, are inevitably brought to the surface that no one individually would have considered. A group session quickly puts a transaction in the proper negotiation perspective. It's not unusual, for example, to find that a request that someone would have characterized as a deal point was based on misinformation or lack of understanding and that, once fully informed, the person is willing to consider a compromise.

Those of you who haven't used a group-meeting approach for setting negotiation objectives will find, as everyone becomes more familiar with various needs and issues, that meetings on future lease financings will get shorter. And eventually, except for unusual issues or financings, all that may be necessary is to circulate an issue consensus memorandum to the interested parties for comments. The advantage of a meeting, however, is that you're assured of getting the answers and information you need in a timely manner.

In the case of a small-dollar lease financing, a meeting is often not warranted unless you anticipate that you'll be doing more such transactions in the near future, in which case it may be useful in setting, and getting a consensus on, your overall small-transaction objectives. It's always advisable, however, to circulate to all interested parties a deal objective memorandum and checklist, so concerns and needs may be identified.

I can't emphasize enough that, before you start negotiating, you must know the sensitivity of all potential points of disagreement as well as your negotiating fallback positions.

Determine Your Specific Deal Priorities

The simplest way to define your specific negotiation objectives is to put together an issue discussion checklist either to use in your internal strategy meeting or, if you decide a meeting is not necessary, to circulate among relevant parties. The list should cover all possible issue areas that may impact each segment of your company's business. As I mentioned earlier, I always prefer a group meeting: Everyone gets the benefit of everyone else's experience and expertise, resulting in a multidisciplinary assessment of what your upcoming lease negotiation objectives should be.

Whether you have a meeting or not, I've found it extremely effective in establishing overall objectives to have each individual involved rate the level of importance of each item to determine which points can be compromised and what concessions you have to trade with to get what you absolutely must have.

You can use the following "Negotiation Objectives Checklist" as a guide in developing company-specific negotiation objectives. As you become more familiar with your overall company's needs, this checklist will evolve to fit them more specifically. Before you use this list, you might consider reviewing a typical lease agreement you've signed to see what other items you should add that may have implications for your company. If you don't have a lease, you can benefit by going over any basic equipment lease form. If none is handy, my equipment leasing forms book, entitled *The Complete Book of Equipment Leasing Agreements, Forms, Worksheets, and Checklists* (published by AMACOM), will provide you with the type of forms that you can use as a review guide. Once you've got your issue checklist together, have everyone rate each item on a scale of one to 10, with one being most important and 10 the least important. For example:

> 1–4 = *deal point:* No compromise accepted. This request must be granted or the deal is off.
>
> 5–8 = *compromise considered:* Depends on what is given in return.
>
> 9–10 = *throwaway issue:* The issue is not worth arguing about but, after appropriate resistance, can be conceded to show good-faith negotiating.

To give you an idea of how the process works, let's go through my issue discussion checklist, item by item. I've included the typical brief explanation I give to the negotiating team during our priority-rating meeting to facilitate your use of the checklist in a meeting. The checklist without comments has been included in the Appendix.

Negotiation Objectives Checklist

Negotiation Objectives With Priority Rating

✓ 1. Lessor must not be a broker.

Author's Comment. Dealing with a leasing company acting solely as a financial intermediary adds risk: Since such a company lacks the money to purchase and lease your equipment, you have little assurance that the deal it offers is valid or possible. I prefer not to deal with brokers unless there's a distinct advantage and then only if they have market credibility and a readily verifiable and solid success performance history.

✓ 2. Lessor must provide financial statements.

Author's Comment. If the lessor isn't financially strong, it may not have the funds necessary to pay your equipment vendor when the equipment arrives. In addition, there's a greater likelihood of a future lessor bankruptcy, which may create problems if it occurs during your lease term. Getting a financial statement is also a good way of determining whether a lessor claiming to be a principal funding source, rather than a broker, is telling the truth. If the company's financial statements are weak, chances are you're dealing with a broker.

✓ 3. Lessor must put up a performance bond.

Author's Comment. I rarely ask a lessor to put up a performance bond, but you may want to consider it when dealing with a lease broker or financially weak lessor. The bond guarantees that you'll get monetary damages in the bond amount if the lessor doesn't perform. I avoid dealing with leasing companies if I think I would need a performance bond because of the time lost if they can't deliver as promised.

✓ 4. Lessor must submit a written bid.

Author's Comment. I never rely on verbal offers. Misunderstandings and mistakes are likely. In addition, although technically you can enforce certain verbal promises in a court of law if a lessor doesn't deliver as promised, the time and money involved in attempting to do so are rarely worth it. As far as I'm concerned, this always gets a rating of "one."
    a) Bid must be firm.

Author's Comment. When dealing directly with a principal lessor, I expect the offer to be firm, subject generally only to a credit check and reasonably mutually acceptable lease documentation. In situations when it may be desirable to deal with a lease broker, I am willing to go along with a best-effort offer, a nonfirm offer, provided the broker has an excellent reputation and adheres to a strict performance timetable. Some reputable brokers can deliver very cost-effective lease financing but, particularly in multimillion-dollar transactions, are not willing to guarantee that they can do so by making their offer firm. If you have a firm offer, and the leasing company doesn't perform, it's liable for all damages incurred as a result of its failure.

✓ 5. Lessor must accept all lessee business requests as an award condition.

Author's Comment. I insist that the lessor agree, in writing, and as a condition of being given a lease-financing award, to every important lessee business request. Typically, I ask that the lessor rewrite its lease offer, if necessary, and incorporate every concession it is willing to make. Then I have the lessee accept the award by so indicating in a statement at the end of the lessor's offering letter. A form of lessor offer, with the appropriate accepting statement, is included in Chapter 6.

✓ 6. Lessor must hold the lease rate firm for three months.

Author's Comment. I always require that a lessor's offer be firm for a specified period of time—long enough to cover delivery of the equipment, including any possible delays, and to negotiate the lease documents comfortably. Typically, three months is sufficient if the equipment is immediately available from the vendor. If equipment is to be delivered in the future, of course, the commitment must be appropriately extended.

✓ 7. Lessor must pay all transaction expenses.

    a) If deal goes through
    b) If deal collapses
        (1) For any reason
        (2) Due to lessor's failure

Author's Comment. Requiring the lessor to pay for all expenses connected with a lease financing, such as legal and investment banking fees, can reduce your cost of financing. Of course, if the lessor incorporates the estimated transaction expenses in computing its rent charge, in effect the lessee is paying them indirectly, with interest, through relatively higher rent charges to the extent that they have been accurately estimated. However, if the financing does not close, the lessor, not the lessee, is out of pocket up to the amount that the lessor has agreed to pay. Sophisticated lessees are often willing to assume identified transaction expenses if they decide not to pursue the financing after the lessor has been given the award but not if the lessor fails to deliver the financing on the terms and conditions offered. If you're considering a large lease financing, particularly if it's an underwritten leveraged lease transaction, the issue of who pays what expenses is worth careful consideration.

✓ 8. Lessor must offer ±15% equipment cost latitude without penalty.

Author's Comment. When asking for financing on equipment that's not immediately available, or before the final configuration is settled on, it's good practice to require the lessor to provide an equipment cost leeway to cover possible cost changes—particularly increases. For example, if a lessor offers to finance a $1 million computer system at a specified lease rate, a cost increase to $1.1 million may give it an opportunity to walk away unless you accept a higher lease rate. A cost decrease, on the other hand, generally doesn't create such a lessor opportunity. However, if there is a penalty for not using all the funds held available—in the form, for example, of a nonutilization fee—a lower acquisition cost will increase financing costs.

✓ 9. There must be no commitment fee.

Author's Comment. A commitment fee adds to the cost of financing and must be factored into your lease-versus-purchase analysis. If it is, and leasing is still cost-effective, paying a commitment fee should not be a problem, unless there's a possibility the equipment may not be leased. Generally, I do not recommend that a commitment fee be paid unless the lessor is being asked to provide a firm lease rate commitment in excess of six months from the award date.

✓ 10. There must be no nonutilization fee.

Author's Comment. A nonutilization fee is payable if the total cost committed to by the lessor is not used. For example, if the lessor has committed to a $500,000 lease financing and the equipment turns out to cost $350,000 because, for example, of a vendor price reduction, a nonutilization fee would impose a payment penalty based on the unused commitment fund amount. I generally recommend avoiding nonutilization fee commitments, but if there is little chance that the price will drop or that management will decide against leasing, providing such a fee to a lessor willing to make a long-term commitment is an acceptable risk.

✓ 11. Lessor must accept the lessee's form of lease.

Author's Comment. Sophisticated lessees are drafting their own in-house lease agreements and requiring lessors to accept them as a condition of being awarded the lease financing. Taking this approach can substantially reduce the time and expense of documenting an equipment financing. It also virtually eliminates the possibility of business oversights, document mistakes, and lessor traps.

✓ 12. Master lease is required.

Author's Comment. A master lease is a two-part lease, containing a main, or "boilerplate," portion and a "schedule." The main portion contains all terms and conditions that generally apply to any lease financing, such as insurance and maintenance requirements. The schedule portion contains those terms and conditions that apply to the specifics of a particular transaction, such as rental rate and lease term. Typically, the schedule is one or two pages, while the main portion is substantially longer, generally in a large transaction anywhere from 20 to 100 typewritten pages. When a master lease form is used, the boilerplate is negotiated once, and a lessee can finance future equipment without major document review or negotiation by simply executing a new lease schedule, which then becomes a lease in and of itself by incorporating by reference the terms and conditions of the boilerplate portion.

✓ 13. Lessor must submit its form lease with its bid.

Author's Comment. If you don't have an in-house form lease, it's advisable to require lessors to submit their form lease for review along with their bid. This makes it easier to negotiate changes as a condition of a lease award.

✓ 14. Operating lease characterization is required (for accounting purposes).

Author's Comment. Although it's difficult to structure most long-term leases as operating leases for accounting purposes, it's often advantageous to attempt to do so. An operating lease has less of an adverse impact on a company's financial reporting. The time to advise a lessor of your desire is when requesting quotes on an upcoming lease financing.

✓ 15. Lessor must be a tax lessor.

Author's Comment. A tax lessor indirectly passes equipment ownership tax benefits through to the lessee in the form of relatively lower rent charges. Typically, lessors able to use, and provide lessee credit for, available ownership tax benefits are the most rate-aggressive. Nontax lessors, such as money-over lessors, are less rate-aggressive, typically computing their lease rates based on a markup over their borrowing rate.

✓ 16. Single-investor lease structure is required.

Author's Comment. A single-investor lessor uses 100% of its own cash to pay for the equipment purchase, as opposed to, for example, a leveraged lease lessor, which might only put up 20% of the purchase funds, borrowing the rest from a third-party lender. Fewer financing participants generally means faster closing and less negotiating time and expense.

✓ 17. Leveraged lease structure is required.

Author's Comment. Although a leveraged lease typically takes more time to put together because of the increased complexities, it can provide a cheaper lease rate and is worth considering on transactions in excess of $1 million.

✓ 18. Lowest rental rate should be obtained.

Author's Comment. In certain circumstances, the lowest rent may not be a primary objective. For example, other business needs, such as upgrade financing rights and lease flexibility, may be more important.

✓ 19. Lease term should be as long as possible.

Author's Comment. The longer the lease term, the lower the relative rent payment dollar amount—but typically, the higher the interest charge. In certain situations, cash flow, not interest cost, may be a primary consideration.

✓ 20. Lease term should be as short as possible.

Author's Comment. The shorter the lease term, the higher the relative rent payment dollar amount—but typically, the lower the interest cost. Companies with equipment obsolescence concerns or short-term needs often consider short lease terms a priority.

✓ 21. No interim rent should be required.

Author's Comment. Paying interim rent adds to the cost of a lease financing. However, as long as it's factored into the leasing decision, theoretically, I don't have a problem with the concept. The difficulty is that, typically, the interim term can't be reasonably projected and you must assume a worst-case scenario. I generally prefer to limit the amount of guesswork in a lease financing.

✓ 22. There should be no rent payment obligation until the vendor is paid.

Author's Comment. Once you accept equipment for lease under a typical finance lease, you're obligated to pay rent for the entire term, without off-set for any reason, including a lease violation by the lessor. In many situa-tions, equipment is sold on a net 30-day basis, meaning that the lessor does not have to pay the vendor until 30 days after you accept the equipment for lease. If the lessor fails to pay as required, you may still be technically ob-ligated to pay all the rent due, even if the equipment is repossessed for nonpayment. To avoid potential problems, sophisticated lessees require vendor payment as a condition to any long-term rent obligation.

✓ 23. Rent may be paid by regular check.

Author's Comment. Leases often require rent to be paid in immediately available funds. Technically, that means cash or the equivalent, such as cer-tified check, bank check, or funds wire transfer. Most lessors overlook this requirement and allow payment by check. As a general rule, I request spe-cific language permitting payment by regular check to avoid potential problems because, for example, of a lessor's change of mind.

✓ 24. Rent should be expressed as a percentage of equipment cost (automatic adjustment for cost changes).

Author's Comment. Some leases state rent in absolute dollars, such as $1,500 per month. If the rent is negotiated before the equipment arrives, and if the purchase price changes, the lease has to be amended to reflect the new rent charge. To avoid having to spend time and money entering into a lease amend-ment, I always recommend that the rent charge be expressed as a percentage, such as 2.4%, of equipment cost. This way the rent is automatically adjusted for equipment dollar cost changes, and no lease amendment is necessary.

✓ 25. Lease term must start on a specific monthly date.

Author's Comment. Companies that lease equipment often request that all lease terms start on the same date, such as the first of the month, so it's administratively easier to process rent payments. Doing so, however, may require the use of interim rent periods, running from the date the equip-ment goes on lease, if other than the first of a month, through the end of the acceptance month.

✓ 26. There should be a fixed-price renewal option.

Author's Comment. The right to renew a lease for an agreed-upon fixed rate locks in what you have to pay in the event the equipment is needed beyond the original lease term. For obvious reasons, fixing a renewal rate before signing a lease guarantees that you won't pay too high a rate if the lease must be renewed. As explained in Chapter 2, however, care must be taken in structuring such a renewal to avoid jeopardizing, for income tax purposes, the characterization of the lease as a true tax lease, rather than as an installment sale, so anticipated income tax benefits are not lost. Very simply, the right to renew cannot be so low that, over the renewal term, the lessee has the use of the equipment for substantially all of its useful life for a nominal rent payment. For example, if a lessee could renew a five-year lease on a computer for one dollar a year for ten years, the IRS would undoubtedly take the position that the lessee, rather than the lessor, was in effect the equipment owner and that the lessor was an equipment lender. The result would be that the lessor would lose the right to claim the equipment ownership tax benefits (those benefits only being available to the lessee), and the lessee would lose the right to deduct the rent charges.

✓ 27. There should be a fair market renewal option.

Author's Comment.   You should always have the right to renew a lease, even though you do not, or your management does not, believe that you will need to do so. Without such a right, if the equipment is needed, the lessor can dictate any renewal charge. A fair market value renewal right, although not fixing a specific renewal rent, does at least guarantee that not more than the reasonable market rate can be charged—and it does not jeopardize the characterization of a lease for income tax purposes.

✓ 28. There should be no automatic renewal provision.

Author's Comment.   Some lessors insert clever renewal provisions that state that the lease is automatically renewed if the lessee does not notify them within a certain period of time before the end of the lease term of its intent to end the lease. The notice "windows" are generally narrow, requiring, for example, that the lessee state in writing no sooner than 120 days, and no later than 30 days, before the end of the lease that it does not wish to renew. If the lessee forgets to do so, the lease is deemed renewed for, typically, one year. Automatic renewal provisions are dangerous: They're easy to overlook. When representing a lessee, I refuse to permit a lessor to incorporate such a provision in a lease.

✓ 29. There should be a fixed-price purchase option.

Author's Comment.   Fixed-price purchase options put a limit on the cost of buying lease equipment from a lessor. It's always wise to have such an option. As explained in Chapter 2, however, such options are treated in the same manner as fixed-price renewal options, and care must be taken not to have them so low that they jeopardize the characterization of the lease as a true tax lease for income tax purposes.

✓30. There should be a fair market purchase option.

Author's Comment. A fair market value purchase option, like a fair market value renewal option, will not jeopardize the tax characterization of a lease as a true lease for income tax purposes, and having one ensures that the equipment can be purchased from the lessor for a market-reasonable amount in the event it is desirable to do so at the end of the lease term.

✓ 31. Lessor should have no right to require the lessee to purchase at lease end.

Author's Comment. Some lessors incorporate what is referred to as a "put"—a right to force the lessee to purchase leased equipment for a stated price at the end of the lease term. Doing so guarantees the lessor its economic return. Puts should be permitted only when the lessor is providing other significant benefits and then only on the advice of tax counsel, inasmuch as their presence can jeopardize the tax nature of the lease.

✓ 32. There should be an early lease termination option:

  a) Beginning at lease term start
  b) Beginning after one year

Author's Comment. It's always a good idea to have the right to end a lease early in the event the equipment becomes obsolete or surplus to your needs. Although an early termination option can be expensive to exercise, having one costs nothing. Typically, an early termination right starts after one year, although some start as soon as the lease term starts. From a lessor standpoint, when the right to exercise is effective is generally of little concern, inasmuch as the termination payment required keeps the lessor economically whole regardless of the date of exercise. I usually request that the right to exercise begin as soon as the lease term begins.

✓ 33. Lessor must supply early termination and casualty schedules with its bid.

Author's Comment. Most leasing companies don't supply casualty values or termination values until all lease issues have been negotiated and the lease document is ready for finalization. Because these values can be arbitrary, and it's easy for a lessor to slip in an unfair penalty cushion, I require termination and casualty value schedules to be submitted along with the lessor's lease offer. This gives everyone on the lessee's side a chance to review them by, for example, comparing them with those submitted by other lessors.

✓ 34. Early lease termination should be permitted without penalty.

Author's Comment. Ideally, any lessee should have the right to terminate a lease at any time during the lease term without penalty. Unfortunately, such a right is rarely available when leasing equipment for a long term. If a lessor freely offers such a right with little, if any, termination penalty, make sure you have competitive quotes. It's likely the rent will be far above market to make up for the added risk of getting the equipment back in a short period of time.

✓ 35. There should be a right to sublease.

Author's Comment. Having the ability to sublease can provide a way to lower the cost of equipment that is still subject to lease but is no longer needed.

✓ 36. There should be a right to sublease without lessor consent.

Author's Comment. Not having to ask for the lessor's permission to sublet is best.

✓ 37. Lease default should not be permitted without prior written notice from the lessor.

Author's Comment. Requiring the lessor to notify a lessee in writing prior to a lease agreement default's becoming effective, with a reasonable cure period after notice, prevents the lessee's oversights from creating lease defaults.

✓ 38. Lessee should have the right to upgrade financing.

Author's Comment. Certain types of equipment, such as data-processing systems, often require upgrades to increase capacity or efficiency. Having a lessor committed, at a predetermined lease rate, to provide the upgrade financing is often cost-effective.

✓ 39. Lessor should cooperate in upgrade financing.

Author's Comment. In certain situations, you may not want the lessor to provide upgrade financing, but because the upgrade will be attached to the lessor's equipment, its consent will be needed. A provision requiring the lessor to cooperate by providing the necessary paperwork is a good idea.

✓ 40. Lessee should have the right to self-insure equipment.

Author's Comment. Leases typically require lessees to insure the leased equipment. To avoid paying an insurance premium, some ask for the right to self-insure—assuming the payment responsibility for any loss or damage relating to the equipment. Some lessors will agree to this, provided the lessee is creditworthy.

✓ 41. Lessee should have the right to self-maintain equipment.

Author's Comment. Leases generally require that the lessee maintain the equipment in good operating condition. At times, they require that the lessee contract with a third-party maintenance company to ensure that the equipment will be properly taken care of and that, when it comes off lease, it will in fact be in first-rate condition. Third-party maintenance is often expensive and, at times, may not be available—which can result in a technical lease default. If you can properly handle necessary maintenance, the right to self-maintain can provide cost savings. A fallback is to negotiate the right to self-maintain the equipment in the event a third-party maintenance contract is not reasonably available.

✓ 42. Lessor must pass through all manufacturer warranties.

Author's Comment. Some equipment manufacturer warranties can be enforced only by the equipment owner—the lessor in a lease situation. If you have the ultimate equipment condition responsibility under a lease, you must contractually have the lessor pass its rights to enforce all warranties directly through to your company.

✓ 43. Lessor can make no lease assignment without the lessee's consent.

Author's Comment. Most leases permit a lessor to assign some or all of its interest in a lease to any third party—and many do. As a result, you could end up having to deal with someone with whom you are not happy. To avoid this, it's advisable to have a provision that prevents your lessor from making such an assignment.

✓ **44. Lessor can assign its lease interest for security purposes only.**

Author's Comment. Permitting the lessor to assign its lease interest to an equipment lender as security for an equipment purchase loan is often an acceptable compromise if a lessor resists any general limits on its assignment rights. In a security interest assignment, the lessor remains the owner, and unless the third-party loan is not paid, the lender never enters the picture. Insisting that rent payment be made directly to a third-party lender in the case of such an assignment, something usually required by the lender, ensures that the third-party loan will be paid.

✓ **45. Lease may not be assigned to:**

a) A lessee line bank
b) A lessee competitor

Author's Comment. A lessor should not be permitted under any circumstances to assign any interest in your lease to any of your bank lenders (doing so can reduce your company's borrowing capability) or, for obvious reasons, to any competitor.

✓ **46. No lessee income tax indemnities should be required.**

Author's Comment. In the past, lessors have required that lessees indemnify them for any loss of equipment ownership tax benefits, regardless of who caused the loss. In today's market, lessees rarely have to agree to any such indemnity—and I don't recommend doing so.

✓ **47. Lessor income tax indemnifications should be required only for lessee's acts or omissions.**

Author's Comment. If you have to agree to indemnify a lessor for loss of equipment ownership income tax benefits, only do so for losses that result from your company's acts or omissions.

✓ **48. Lessor must pay all equipment costs (sales taxes, installation, etc.).**

Author's Comment. Very often, lessees prefer that a lessor pay all costs connected with the leased equipment, such as sales taxes, insurance, and installation. If you want a lessor to do so, this must be spelled out in your lease; otherwise, it may refuse. If a lessor does agree to pay all equipment costs, however, your lease rent will be based on the added cost, with the result that you'll be paying lease interest on these costs.

✓ 49. There should be no lessee end-of-lease equipment redelivery cost.

Author's Comment.   End-of-lease redelivery provisions can be onerous, with some requiring that the equipment be delivered at your expense anywhere in the world the lessor designates. Limiting your redelivery expense and distance obligation is good idea.

✓ 50. End-of-lease equipment return should take place at the lessee's site.

Author's Comment.   The best end-of-lease redelivery provision lets a lessee deliver the equipment to the lessor at the lessee's site.

Once everyone has rated each issue, compute the group average for each item and then go over the results to make sure each group member agrees on the level of importance that will be attributed to each negotiation point. Very often, once the group sees the average rating, it may decide that a particular item deserves a different rating. For example, if it turns out that item 21 on the checklist ("No interim rent. . . ") has a group average rating of three, people may feel it should not be a deal point if a lease offer is otherwise quite favorable and agree to change the rating to, say, six.

The rating exercise will cause everyone to think as a group about what is best. Expect a lively discussion as you bring together different needs and viewpoints. It will pay negotiating dividends.

An Example of How the Objective-Setting Process Works

Here's an example of how the process works from one of my recent priority-rating meetings. You'll see how the various points of view and needs came together on a particular issue.

Some months ago, I was representing a major airline in its lease acquisition of a Boeing 737 aircraft. We had called a meeting of the department heads whom we felt would be affected by the lease. The following people were present:

> *Operations:* Peter G.
> *Finance:* Tim P.
> *Maintenance:* Robert Y.
> *Legal:* Harris H.
> *Contracting:* Terry W.
> *Lease administration:* Pam T.

The discussion that went on regarding the issue of whether the lessor must commit to using the airline's form of lease agreement went like this:

Dick Contino: The next item on our checklist is whether we are going to require as a condition of a lease award that the leasing company agree to use our in-house form of lease agreement rather than theirs. Let's take a preliminary reading on how each of you would rate this on our scale of one to 10. As we've done before, in our first pass, don't give me the reason you came to your particular rating conclusion. After we see where everyone stands, we will then discuss how each of you arrived at your rating, and then, once everyone has had the opportunity to give his or her reason and we've discussed those reasons, we'll let each of you rate the item one last time before we move on to the next item. Peter, why don't you start us off this morning?

Peter G. (operations): I'd give it a 7.

Tim P. (finance): A 6.

Robert Y. (maintenance): I think I'd go with an 8.

Terry W. (contracting): Definitely a 5.

Pam T. (lease administration): A 7.

Harris H. (legal): I agree with Terry but would up it by one.

Dick Contino: OK, our rating priority average is a 6.5. [This was determined by adding 7 + 6 + 8 + 5 + 7 + 6 = 39 and dividing the result by 6.] Would anyone like to make a comment? So far, this means that we will push hard for getting the lessor to use our form lease, but we will be willing to accept its form if we can't get agreement.

Harris H. (legal): As far as I'm concerned, this is definitely a deal point. If the lessor won't agree to using our form of lease, we shouldn't do business with it. I don't have the time to go over what is probably a lease agreement filled with hidden traps. And even if I did, I'm concerned that I might miss something. These people are always trying to put something over on us. Let's insist on using the form Dick provided us. It's one that has all the lessor projections necessary and, in addition, gives us the legal protections and business flexibility we want.

Peter G. (operations): Harris, I appreciate your concerns, but I need the lowest rental rate, and if that means accepting doing business with a lessor that won't accept our form of lease, I would agree to do so. I know that, between you and Dick, you can negotiate what we need to have in their agreement.

Dick Contino: You both have a point, but I believe in today's market, with lessors scrambling for business, we can get the lowest rate and force them to accept our form of lease. Peter, when must the financing be in place?

Peter G. (operations): I need the plane yesterday.

Dick Contino: We can use the lessor's form, but I think it will add another month to our lease negotiations. There may be substantial revisions. The form I'm suggesting we use is already in Harris's computer, and it would take little time to handle any lessor-negotiated revisions.

Tim P. (finance): The lowest rate is a prime concern to me as well. But I think, considering the problems we've had with our line banks in pursuing the amount of lease financing we have, I'd prefer to use our in-house form. I've passed it by our main banker, and she thinks it's fine. And if we use the lessor's lease, we may lose time getting it reviewed.

Terry W. (contracting): Harris and I can live with whatever you feel is best. Naturally, it would make our lives easier to start to use the same form lease for all our lease deals, but if it gets in the way of the lowest rate, we'll live with it.

Dick Contino: OK, if there are no other comments, let's quickly rate this issue again.

Peter G. (operations): A 4. [Formerly, Peter rated it a 7.]

Tim P. (finance): A 2. [Formerly, Tim rated it a 6.]

Robert Y. (maintenance): A 4. [Formerly, Robert rated it an 8.]

Terry W. (contracting): A 5. [No change in rating.]

Pam T. (lease administration): A 2. [Formerly, Pam rated it a 7.]

Harris H. (legal): One.

Dick Contino: The rating priority average is now a 3. This means that we will insist on using our form lease, and if the lessor won't go along with it, we'll kill the deal and move on to on another lessor. If everyone's satisfied, let's move on to the next item on our priority checklist.

As you can see from the issue discussion dynamics, having all interested parties in the same room has solid benefits. It saves you time in coming to a consensus about your negotiation objectives, and it allows you to go into your negotiation knowing that you have full support for the positions you're taking. In addition, everyone has been able to reconsider their needs based on what is generally good for the company, something that will benefit all.

What's Next?

Once you organize your negotiation objectives, it's time to sit down and write a request for lease quotes (sometimes called an "RFQ" or a "bid letter")—a letter to the lessor outlining your business, financial, tax, accounting, and sometimes legal needs. The RFQ must cover every issue the lessor must address in preparing its lease bid and, in addition, should set the conditions under which a lease award will be made. Properly written, your RFQ will make the lessor's responses easy to analyze.

After you receive lessor bids, you have to analyze each bid to determine which offer is best for your company. And once you've made an award, you have to negotiate and document the terms and conditions under which you will lease the equipment from the lessor.

The following chapters will take you step by step through each of these stages so you're able to get the best possible lease deal.

Chapter 5

Using the Bid Request to Outnegotiate a Lessor

The Proposal Negotiation— Where Your Deal Is Made

Your ability to negotiate effectively in any situation depends on your bargaining leverage. Obviously, the greater your leverage, the more likely you'll get what you ask for. What many people fail to understand is that a party's bargaining leverage depends not only on his or her negotiating persuasiveness but also on the particular stage in a deal's process, something I refer to as process leverage. Therefore, to maximize your negotiating ability, not only must you understand the essence of effective negotiating, but you must be able to identify those periods during the deal process when your inherent leverage is highest.

In a lease situation, a prospective lessee generally has the highest process leverage during the period before a lease award is made, referred to as the proposal stage, because to get the financing award, a prospective lessor knows that it must meet all lease offer requests or at least be able to offer attractive alternatives. On the other hand, once a lease agreement has been signed, the lessor has the greater deal leverage. If, for example, a lessee then discovers an overlooked request, getting it incorporated is solely up to the lessor's generosity. The test of a good lease negotiator is therefore one of both tactical skills and process leverage awareness. And if you take full advantage of your process leverage during the proposal stage, you can get concessions that otherwise would be unavailable. The purpose of this chapter is to show you just how to do that.

Gaining Control by Setting Bid Guidelines

How you handle the process of getting lessor bids is critical. Simply calling prospective lessors, telling them the details of your upcoming financing, and asking them to send offers is not the right approach. There is only one way to ensure that you not only get what you want but get it quickly: by putting together a comprehensively written set of bidding guidelines (commonly referred to as a "request for quotes," or simply an "RFQ") and sending it to your prospective leasing companies. Your RFQ should outline the financing deal you want. In addition, it should contain a deal timetable indicating, for example, when bids are due and when your award decision will be made. A well-thought-out RFQ will force lessors to organize their bid responses so they can be quickly and simply evaluated.

Preparing and circulating a well-thought-out and comprehensive written RFQ, sometimes also called a bid letter, can be time-consuming, but it's a work investment that will pay off, particularly if you intend to shop the lessor marketplace for competitive quotes. It ensures that all leasing company offers are uniform and thus readily comparable. Without a strict set of bidding guidelines, the lessor responses will vary, making it difficult, if not impossible, to evaluate simply. An RFQ side benefit is that its preparation forces everyone on your team to focus on what is needed, so there are no oversights. A good RFQ is the most effective negotiation tool a prospective lessee can use, regardless of its particular format, whether it's a formal, legal-looking deal proposal or a well-written business letter.

A professional-looking RFQ has an added benefit: It will enhance your negotiating image, something that can help you win points in a tough negotiation. A concise and comprehensive RFQ signals that you're an experienced lease negotiator. And people who look as if they know what they're doing have more negotiating leverage.

A Request for Quotes Overview

What should an RFQ cover? Very simply, it should cover every key business, financial, legal, tax, and accounting requirement important to your lease financing. For example, the RFQ should identify the lease structure desired, such as a two-, three-, or five-year lease term. And it should encourage the lessor to offer benefits or structures not requested that may enhance the financing. Finally, it should also lay the groundwork for lessor concessions, such as an agreement to use your lease document form. Very simply, an effective RFQ should raise, and be used to settle, all important financing and contractual issues.

In addition to describing the type of financing you want, your RFQ must provide enough information so the lessor can formulate the best possible lease offer. For example, if your equipment vendor has offered a

90-day payment grace period following delivery, letting the lessor know that may enable it to price its offer more aggressively. In such a case, becoming the equipment owner for income tax purposes prior to any equipment cash investment can enhance a lessor's yield and lower the rent offer correspondingly. For details of how this works, see a technical leasing book, such as my *Handbook of Equipment Leasing—A Deal Maker's Guide*, second edition (published by AMACOM).

Here's a basic overview of the issue areas that should be considered in writing your RFQ:

- The equipment types and the manufacturer
- The number of equipment units that will be involved
- The equipment's aggregate and per-unit cost
- Any favorable vendor payment terms
- When the equipment delivery is anticipated
- The lease type desired; that is, net financial lease or service lease
- The lease term and any renewal periods desired
- The rental payment mode; that is, monthly, quarterly, semiannually, or annually in advance or in arrears
- The extent of any acceptable tax indemnifications
- Whether the equipment will be self-insured
- What options are required
- A request for appropriate casualty and termination values
- Who will have the responsibility for the transaction's fees and expenses
- Whether a tax ruling is necessary or desirable
- Whether it is acceptable for a favorable tax ruling to be a prerequisite to execute the lease documents
- Whether a favorable tax ruling should relieve any tax indemnification obligations assumed
- The deadline for the submission of lease quotations
- When the transaction will be awarded
- Whether underwriting bids are acceptable
- If underwriting proposals are permitted, whether the bids may be on a "firm" or "best-effort" basis
- Potential equity participants and lenders that may be unacceptable if the transaction is to be underwritten

Picking the Right Bidding Request Format

An RFQ can take the form of a conversational letter or a formal, stylized deal proposal. The formal deal sheet format, often looking as if it was written by a lawyer, gives the impression that the requesting company knows the leasing game. It sets a solid negotiating tone. But it may not always be the best choice. For example, in small deals, where the lessor's profit is low, its overly complex nature or formal tone may discourage bidding. On the other hand, in multimillion-dollar lease financings, it may be more appropriate to use a formal request approach, in which the structured deal memorandum will enhance your bargaining ability by projecting a more sophisticated image.

Regardless of the format you use, your RFQ must always:

- Define the financing and business structure you want
- Request commitments on all issues considered important
- Provide only the deal information necessary to compute an aggressive lease offer
- Avoid stating anything that could weaken your negotiating position

What to Avoid: An Ineffective Request for Quotes

Let's start by taking a look at a letter a client of mine received a few years ago as an example of what not to do. The dates, telephone numbers, names, and addresses have been changed, but everything else remains unchanged, including writing errors.

Sunny Day Company
34 Orchard Street
White Plains, New York 10604
(914) 991-8900

May 2, 19XX

Ms. Shelly Prisel, Marketing Vice President
Blitz Leasing Corporation
1245 Funding Drive
Glen Cove, New York 11542

Dear Shelly:

This is to confirm our conversation this afternoon. I was relieved to get in touch with today! We're in a hurry to put together the financing on our new computer system.

The parent company has insisted we update the automation in our department now. As I mentioned, my boss just informed me that we have no capital budget room to purchase any additional computer equipment this year. We need to get a Matrix Sentex Payroll Processing System on board this month to get our payroll administrative problems straightened out. It should cost somewhere between $200,000 and $250,000.

Frankly, I'm not sure what the best arrangement is for us under a lease financing and am relying on you to keep me out of trouble. We have been more than pleased with what you've provided in the past.

I need you to give me your best lease rate as soon as possible, within three days, because our equipment has a setup deadline of three weeks. We're getting it shipped in tomorrow. If you can't get a letter off to me with your offer, just call it in. If I am not here, please give the rent quote to my secretary.

Incidentally, I would really like to take you up on your offer for dinner at the Palace. I hear the meals are outstanding. How about tomorrow, so we can discuss the progress you're making for us?

Also, I tried our bank today and found they're not offering any lease financing until September. So, I guess you're it. We need a favor, so pull out the stops to get me an aggressive rate.

Sincerely,

Dave Fastrack
Assistant Manager

DF: II

Here are some comments on Dave's letter:

- Dave has made a number of serious negotiating mistakes. The tone of his letter is unprofessional and shows he's begging. And he's confirmed, if Mary doesn't already know, that he probably doesn't know what he's doing.
- Dave's letter indicates that he thinks Mary will be fair and not take advantage of the spot he and his company are in. But chances are excellent that Mary will.
- Dave has painted himself into a corner by telling Mary that he has no funds for equipment purchasing, he isn't getting competitive bids, and the equipment is being delivered shortly. He has put Mary in negotiating control.
- He has omitted important lease requests, such as purchase, renewal, and termination options.
- The equipment specifics at this late date are sketchy.
- He's willing to take a verbal quote, increasing his chances of being manipulated once he makes the award.

- He's given Mary an opportunity to increase her negotiating leverage by decreasing his lead time. She can, for example, delay dinner and thus delay submitting her offer, using a need-more-information excuse.
- The only thing Dave can count on is dinner and he'll pay dearly for it.

Writing an Effective Request for Quotes

Now that you've seen what not to do, let's look at the right approach. To provide a comprehensive overview of an effective RFQ, let's start by examining in detail a formal RFQ, one that might be used in, say, a $3 million lease financing. If you know how to write a large-ticket RFQ, it's easy to write a small-ticket or middle-market transaction RFQ. Once we've done that, we'll examine two less formal letter approaches that can be used.

A Formal Request for Quotes

The RFQ examined in this section has been included in the Appendix, without comments for your ease of use. Before you read any further, it may be helpful to scan it quickly for an overview.

The RFQ is divided into five parts: the general financing request, the request introduction, the proposal guidelines, the equipment specifics, and the deal timetable.

The General Financing Request

The general financing request section is as follows:

Request for Quotations to Lease Equipment April 12, 19XX

SunBird Corporation is issuing this Request for Quotations (RFQ) to obtain equipment lease bids from prospective lessors. This RFQ is not an offer to contract. SunBird Corporation will not be obligated to lease the specified equipment until a mutually satisfactory written lease has been executed by all parties.

This portion of the RFQ merely identifies who you are (in this case, SunBird Corporation) and what you want (an equipment lease). It also clearly states that this RFQ should not be interpreted as an offer to contract but rather is merely an exploratory request. Although it's unlikely that anyone could interpret the RFQ as an offer to contract, enabling the lessor to bind SunBird Corporation to a deal by responding, most lawyers like to make this fact absolutely clear to avoid any possibility of an argument. It's a good idea to date the RFQ for easy future reference, particularly if it must be amended after it's issued.

The Request Introduction

The request introduction section is as follows:

A. Proposal Request—General

> In accordance with the terms and conditions specified below, SunBird Corporation wishes to receive proposals from equipment leasing companies (Lessors) to provide lease financing for certain data-processing equipment.
>
> In the evaluation of each proposal, SunBird Corporation will rely on all written and verbal representations made by each prospective Lessor, and each representation will be incorporated into any and all formal agreements between the parties.
>
> No Lessor receiving this RFQ is authorized to act for, or on behalf of, SunBird Corporation prior to the receipt of written acceptance by SunBird Corporation of a satisfactory lease proposal and then only in accordance with the specific terms, if any, of the acceptance.

The purpose of the request introduction is to let each prospective lessor know that it will be held accountable for everything it tells you, whether verbally or in writing, and that you not only intend to rely on what is stated but will also include it in the written deal. You want to make it clear that the lessor will be held to any promises made to induce you to enter into a lease. Salespeople have been known to make promises that are conveniently forgotten or twisted when the financing is documented.

This section also prohibits any lessor, prior to the lease award, from acting as your representative for any reason. This is particularly important if your RFQ ends up in the hands of a lessor that intends to broker the transaction. Brokers have been known, upon receipt of an RFQ, to start shopping for lease investors or lenders, claiming improperly that they have been authorized to represent the prospective lessee. Without authorization, investors and lenders typically won't review broker submissions.

The RFQ makes it clear that, if and when an award is given, the leasing company may only act specifically in accordance with the terms and conditions of the award. Although statements of this nature can't guarantee that your company won't be held accountable for improper actions or representations by a lessor, they can set the tone you need in order to keep a lessor under control. For example, it's not unheard of for lessors to misrepresent the terms of a deal to a lease-investor to get a financing commitment, hoping to talk the prospective lessee into accepting less than it wants at the last minute.

The Proposal Guidelines

The lessor proposal guidelines are as follows:

B. Proposal Guidelines

> 1. Your proposal must be submitted in writing and follow the guidelines in this RFQ. If not, it will be rejected.

Even if the financing you're considering is small, insisting that a lessor submit its proposal in writing is good business practice. It prevents mistakes, eliminates common misunderstandings, and lessens the opportunity for any intentional deal manipulation by a lessor. All too often, lessors, in spite of your deal requirements, submit unresponsive proposals, either because they are careless or because they can't offer what you want. Telling each that an unresponsive proposal may be rejected helps ensure that lessors make every effort to respond carefully to your requests.

> 2. All RFQ requirements must be addressed. Specifically identify any requirements that cannot be satisfied.

Requiring that the lessor indicate specifically any requirement that it is unable to meet will make your evaluation of its offer much easier. It also helps ensure that any issue you want addressed is not overlooked, either by you or by a lessor.

> 3. If you can offer any additional benefits not requested in this RFQ, identify them as "Additional Benefits" and state them in a separate section at the end of your proposal.

It's not unusual for a creative and competitive lessor to attempt to win your business by offering more than you've asked for. Once again, to make your proposal evaluation process easy so you can compare "apples to apples" require that any such additional benefit be listed in a separate section to allow you to readily identify it.

> 4. You must notify SunBird Corporation no later than the Lessor Proposal Intent Notification Due date specified in the Timetable in section D if you intend to submit a proposal in response to this RFQ.

Requiring each lessor intending to respond to notify you of its interest in doing so within, say, a week after receiving your RFQ will ensure that you have adequate time to get a good cross section of market offers. The key in any lease negotiation is to maintain sufficient lead time before your equipment is delivered to comfortably negotiate your lease needs. If, for example, your RFQ is sent to six leasing companies with a three-week proposal submission deadline, receiving only one response on the due date would require you to send additional RFQs to other lessors. If you knew earlier that only one prospective lessor would be responding, you could send additional RFQs out sooner, thereby preventing a substantial loss of lead time.

> 5. SunBird Corporation may, without liability and at its sole discretion, amend or rescind this RFQ prior to the lease award. In such event, each Lessor offering to submit a proposal will be supplied, as the case may be, with an RFQ amendment or a notification of our intent not to proceed.

Although, generally speaking, a prospective lessee has no liability to leasing companies receiving its RFQ, this type of statement is prudent to include.

> 6. Your proposal will be considered confidential, and none of the contents will be disclosed to a competing Lessor.

Lessors are always concerned that innovative techniques that may make them uniquely competitive in a given situation may be disclosed to a competitor in an effort to get the best deal. A comforted lessor may go all out, knowing that its approach will be protected.

In certain situations, you may not want to include this type of statement because it may be better to be able to disclose to each competitor any unique offer by one lessor. Doing so may assist in promoting a very aggressive offer. The fair way to handle such a disclosure is at a bidders' meeting, where all proposing lessors are invited to attend to ask questions and hear about what others have offered, on an anonymous basis, and then given an equal opportunity to revise their offer if they wish.

A bidders' meeting has other benefits. In complex deals, it's often easiest to accumulate and address questions that will inevitably arise in a group meeting with all potential lessors present. And having everyone in the same room for a preaward question-and-answer session heightens the competition.

> 7. You shall be responsible for all costs incurred in connection with the preparation of your proposal and any contract(s) in response to this RFQ.

Although, again, it's unlikely that a prospective lessee would have any responsibility for expenses related to the preparation of a lease proposal, statements of this nature make it clear that such costs are a lessor's responsibility. A lessee client of mine once had a problem when a lower-level, inexperienced individual inadvertently agreed to pay a submitting lessor, prior to any lease award, for an expert to appraise the equipment so a more aggressive bid could be submitted. The lessee hadn't used an RFQ in this particular situation and, to avoid any possible embarrassment, paid the expense.

> 8. Your proposal must be signed by a duly authorized representative of your company.

From time to time, a proposal is submitted, inadvertently or intentionally, signed by someone not having appropriate legal authority to bind the lessor, such as a sales representative who is not a corporate officer. Avoid the potential for a problem by making it clear what you expect.

> 9. Your proposal must be submitted in triplicate and remain in effect at least until the lessor proposal commitment cutoff date specified in the Timetable in section D.

Asking for the number of review copies that you'll need can save time. Stating how long you need the lessor's offer held open is extremely important. Make sure it's effective for the time necessary to review all proposals, with a cushion to cover unexpected delays.

> 10. Your proposal should be accompanied by (a) a copy of your most recent annual report or financial statements or appropriate bank references with account officer name and telephone number; (b) a description of any material litigation in which you are currently involved; and (c) a statement of any potential conflict of interest, and plan to avoid it, as a result of an award.

This request, particularly in a multimillion-dollar financing, is important. The financial and bank information will allow you to identify financially weak lessors or lease brokers, in the event you deem it advisable to avoid dealing with them. In addition, it may not be advisable to use even a financially strong lessor if it is a defendant in a major lawsuit that could seriously impair its financial condition.

You may also choose not to deal with lessors that have a conflict of interest, such as a lessor owned in part by a competitor of your company. Under a lease arrangement, a lessor has access to financial or other information that you may not want known to a competitor.

> 11. SunBird Corporation intends to announce its award decision no later than the Award Announcement date specified in the Timetable in section D.

Stating when you intend to make the award decision will prevent annoying and repeated telephone calls from anxious and aggressive sales representatives trying to find out the award status.

---

12. Any questions concerning this RFQ should be sent in writing to:

SunBird Corporation
1823 Third Avenue
New York, New York 11020
Attn. John Peterson

Telephone no.: (212) 754-2367

Any questions and answers that we feel would be of assistance to all Lessors submitting proposals will be promptly distributed to each.

Providing for a write-in question-and-answer procedure is another good way to keep telephone call work interruptions to a minimum. And it assures all prospective lessors that they will fairly receive any information that could be of assistance. Putting everything in writing also keeps misunderstandings to a minimum.

---

13. SunBird Corporation may enter simultaneously in negotiations with more than one Lessor and make an award to one or more without prior notification to others with which we are negotiating.

This simply states your policy in approaching the lease negotiations. It also reinforces the competitive intent.

---

14. Any information supplied to you in this RFQ by SunBird Corporation or otherwise by any representative in connection with this RFQ is confidential and may not be disclosed or used except in connection with the preparation of your proposal. If you must release any such information to any person or entity for the purpose of preparing your proposal, you must obtain an agreement prior to releasing the information that it will be treated as confidential by such person or entity and will not be disclosed except in connection with the preparation of your proposal.

Requiring prospective lessors to keep the deal details confidential, releasing them to third parties only if necessary to prepare a bid, is good business practice. You want to avoid information falling into the hands of competitors or others having no need to know about your activities.

---

15. If you are a selected Lessor, prior to our making the award, you will be supplied with a copy of our form lease document(s) for your review. Your response to the acceptability of the document provisions, with exceptions noted in writing, will be a condition precedent to any award.

Requiring the use of your in-house form lease agreement as a condition of a lease award will save time and money and avoid mistakes and lessor document traps. And making the selected lessor respond in writing with agreement exceptions will enable you to set the attorney drafting and negotiating ground rules.

The Equipment Specifics

The RFQ equipment specifics are as follows:

C. Equipment Lease Requirements

---

1. Equipment Description, Cost, and Trade-In

a. The equipment will consist of electronic data-processing equipment (Equipment) acquired from the following designated vendor(s):

Vendor	Equipment Description	Cost
StarByte Computer Corp. Buffalo, NY	(1) Model 423 Computer	$1,850,000
	(7) Model 3 Remote Ctrs.	$ 350,000
Micro Tech, Inc. New York, NY	Material Tracking System	$ 150,000
	Installation	$ 120,000
	TOTAL	$2,470,000

(i) The final cost of the Equipment may vary as much as +(10)% or – (20)%, and your financing offer must permit this leeway without penalty.

b. If you can provide more advantageous financing by supplying equipment you own, have access to, or can acquire through volume discount arrangements with a vendor, please provide the specifics in the "Additional Benefits" section. If you intend to offer to provide any used equipment, the serial number(s), current location(s), and owner(s) must be stated in your proposal.

(i) Any equipment you offer to supply must be delivered to SunBird Corporation at 937 Secour Drive, Buffalo, New York 11342 no later than the Anticipated Equipment Delivery date specified in the Timetable in Section D and be ready for acceptance no later than the specified Anticipated Equipment Acceptance date. You must provide a firm delivery date commitment with contractual assurances and remedies for failure to meet such date, which should be stated in your proposal.

c. The Equipment will replace equipment under an existing lease of computer equipment, and SunBird Corporation would like you to propose an additional financing arrangement that would incorporate the buyout of that lease. The specifics of the existing lease are as follows

Lessor: AmerLease Corp.

Lease term: 7 years

Lease start date: March 1, 19XX

Lease end date: February 28, 19XX

Monthly rent: $21,324, in advance

Lease termination amount as of August 31, 19XX: $397,000

Equipment: Micro Tech, Inc., XTRA Material Tracking Computer System

Original equipment cost: $1,253,000

Right to sublease: yes

Purchase option: fair market

Renewal option: year-to-year, 90 days' prior notice, fair market

(i) If you can provide any other arrangement that would be beneficial, such as subleasing the existing equipment to another lessee, please so indicate.

This provision supplies each bidding lessor with the basics about the equipment SunBird wants to lease as well as equipment currently under lease with another lessor that will be replaced. At times, it makes sense to have a new lessor pay the replaced equipment termination penalty and incorporate it into the new financing. A word of caution: Wrapping a termination penalty into a new equipment financing can be very expensive and should generally be considered only if the new lease rate is below your company's borrowing rate or there are borrowing problems.

Allowing a proposing lessor to supply equipment you need can produce cost savings if, for example, it has a volume purchase discount arrangement with an appropriate equipment vendor that exceeds your offer discount and the lessor is willing to pass some or all of its discount to you. Lessors that specialize in, for example, computer equipment often make such general arrangements with computer suppliers to increase deal profits.

Here's how a lessor discount benefit would work: Assume that the best equipment purchase discount you can get from your vendor is 15%. A lessor specializing in the equipment you need may have a general 22% purchase discount available because of its high-dollar lease purchases. The increased discount can result in a rent savings since the actual rent dollar amount is based on equipment cost. The lower the cost, the lower the dollar rent.

Letting a lessor know that you'll consider used equipment can also lower rent charges simply because of lower purchase costs. Some lessors, for example, warehouse, for resale or re-lease, equipment that has been returned by their lessees. But be careful. Lessors have been known to induce lessees into giving them the award by falsely claiming to have acceptable used equipment and then, after the award, claiming the equipment was sold. Requiring that the lessor identify the equipment so it can be inspected before an award usually prevents your being taken in by this ploy.

---

2. Estimated Delivery and Acceptance Date

It is anticipated that the Equipment will be delivered and accepted for lease no later than the Anticipated Equipment Delivery and Anticipated Equipment Acceptance date(s) specified in the Timetable in section D.

You must specify when equipment is expected to arrive so the lessor knows when the lease will start, something critical to determining rent. For example, in calculating transaction rent, a lessor must know when it will become the equipment owner and thus when equipment ownership tax benefits will be available for transaction pricing purposes. Lessor pricing calculations are beyond the scope of this book, so if you want further detail about how a lessor makes its calculations, I recommend purchasing a technical lease-financing book containing lessor pricing models, such as my *Handbook of Equipment Leasing—A Deal Maker's Guide*, second edition (published by AMACOM).

---

3. Equipment Payment

    The Equipment must be paid for by the Lessor no later than thirty (30) days following acceptance for lease.

In order to avoid any embarrassing problems, such as having the equipment repossessed for nonpayment, have the lessor commit to pay your equipment vendor in a timely manner, certainly no later than the end of the payment grace period permitted by the supplier. If the lessor is purchasing from its supplier, require that the lessor disclose the payment arrangement and provide evidence of payment so you know the equipment has been paid for.

As discussed in Chapter 4, it's advisable to specify in your lease agreement that your rent payment obligation will not begin until the equipment vendor is paid in full. This should be stated, as indicated below, in both your lease term (item 5) and rent (item 6) request sections, so there is no misunderstanding or room for a lessor's lawyer to argue anything less.

---

4. Equipment Location

    The Equipment will initially be accepted for lease at our manufacturing plant located at 937 Secour Drive, Buffalo, New York. We must have the right to move the equipment to any location in the United States without the prior consent of the Lessor but upon providing thirty (30) days' prior written notice.

You must inform the lessor where the leased equipment will be located so it can make any necessary state, county, and sometimes federal notice filings to avoid successful claims against its equipment by any of your other creditors.

Many lessor-written lease agreements specify that the equipment may not be moved to a new location without the prior written consent of the lessor and then only on 60 days' prior written notice. If you need to move the equipment, having to get the lessor's consent can delay the process. Generally, a lessor will waive the consent requirement as long as you agree to give adequate prior written notice.

---

5. Primary Lease Term

Your proposal must provide offers to lease the Equipment for Primary Lease Terms of five (5) and seven (7) years. The Primary Lease Terms must run from the later of the Equipment acceptance for lease or payment in full by the Lessor for the Equipment.

It's always good business practice to request several lease term quotes since some lessors will offer more aggressive rates on, say, a five-year term than on a seven-year term. And I recommend doing this even if company management insists on leasing, say, for seven years because a significantly lower cost may dictate reconsidering that position. For example, it may be more cost-effective when leasing equipment that has a high obsolescence risk to have a five-year term with a right to renew for two additional years at a capped fixed rate, such as 15% of the primary term rent.

Your lease term obligation, as suggested above, should be conditional upon the payment of the equipment vendor in full, on or before the equipment purchase price due date. And the lessor should be required to provide you with evidence of payment no later than five business days after payment is due. Nonpayment should give rise to a lease default, which, in turn, should give rise to remedies against the lessor.

---

6. Primary Term Rents

Rent payments must be quoted on a monthly, in advance, and quarterly, in arrears, basis.
The rent payments must be expressed as a percentage of Equipment Cost and be on a consecutive, level basis. The nominal lease interest rate must be provided for each rent quote.
SunBird Corporation shall not be obligated for payment of rent until the Equipment vendor has been paid in full.

It's advisable to ask for several rent periodicity quotes because a lessor, through its use of tax or other benefits, may be able to offer more aggressive rates, say, quarterly in arrears rather than monthly in advance. And there is only one way to find out: Ask.

Rent should be quoted as a percentage of equipment cost, rather than a fixed dollar amount, so it's easy to recompute without a lease amendment if the cost changes. In addition, having the lessor specify the lease interest rate (often referred to as the nominal lease interest rate) for each quote allows you to determine an offer's aggressiveness quickly.

Once again, this provision contains a reminder that SunBird won't incur rent obligations until the vendor has been paid.

---

7. Interim Lease Term

   No Interim Lease Term will be permitted that requires payment of interim rent.

8. Interim Rents

   No Interim Lease Term rent payments will acceptable.

In this case, SunBird has elected not to consider lease offers containing interim rent. However, as mentioned in Chapter 2, there may be some situations in which an interim period is acceptable, in which case the preceding two subsections would be appropriately modified.

---

9. Options

   a. SunBird Corporation must have the option to renew the term of the lease year-to-year for a total of three (3) years, on a fair market value basis. Offers providing for a fixed-price renewal will also be considered. Any fixed-price offers should be included in an "Additional Benefits" section at the end of the Lessor's proposal.

   b. Lessee must have the right to purchase the Equipment at the end of the Primary Lease Term and each Renewal Term for its then fair market value. Offers providing for the right to purchase for a fixed percentage of Equipment Cost will be given favorable consideration and should be included in an "Additional Benefits" section at the end of the Lessor's offer.

c. SunBird Corporation must have the right, beginning as of the end of the first year of the Primary Lease Term, to terminate the lease prior to the end of the Primary Lease Term, or any Renewal Term, in the event the Equipment becomes obsolete or surplus to SunBird Corporation's needs.

(i) In the event of an early termination, SunBird Corporation shall have the right to arrange for the sale or re-lease of the Equipment. Any proceeds from the sale, or anticipated proceeds from the lease, of the Equipment shall reduce any termination penalty payment required.

(ii) A schedule of early termination values must be included with your proposal.

d. SunBird Corporation must have the right to upgrade the Equipment, by adding equipment or replacing components, at any time during the term of the lease, and the Lessor must provide financing for such upgrade for a term coterminous with the term remaining during the upgrade period at a financing rate that will not exceed the Lessor's transaction nominal after-tax yield.

A prospective lessee should insist on maximum flexibility by requesting every available lease option. A detailed discussion of these options can be found in Chapters 6 and 7. And when asking for the right to terminate your lease early, always insist that a termination value schedule be included with the lessor's offer. Keep in mind that if you don't ask for an option, chances are good it won't be offered.

10. Insurance

   The Equipment shall be self-insured.

If you want to self-insure your leased equipment, something a lessor may have difficulty granting, the request should be made in your RFQ when negotiating leverage is greatest. If self-insurance isn't important, but you have other special insurance needs or simply want to make clear the type of insurance you will be purchasing, this should be specified in your RFQ.

---

11. Casualty Value Schedule

A schedule of casualty values, expressed as a percentage of Equipment Cost, for both the Primary Lease Term and any Renewal Term(s) must be submitted with your proposal.

It's important that you receive a copy of the lessor's casualty value payment schedule when its offer is submitted. Such payments are sometimes arbitrarily increased to build in extra profits in the event the equipment is destroyed. One way to keep lessors honest is to review and compare these payment schedules before the award is made. The casualty amounts will be of particular concern to a company asking to self-insure.

---

12. Transaction Fees

Lessee will not pay financing commitment or nonutilization fees.

If you don't want to pay any fees, such as commitment or nonutilization fees, it should be so stated in your RFQ.

---

13. Accounting Classification

Preference will be given to a lease that qualifies as an operating lease under the applicable accounting guidelines.

A lease qualifying as an operating lease for accounting purposes is often preferable but is difficult to structure in long-term lease arrangements. The best time to consider the possibility is at the initial stage, so the preference request should be made in the RFQ, when the bidding lessors have the greatest incentive to meet your company's needs.

---

14. Single-Source Preference

Preference will be given to Lessors that intend to provide 100% of the funds necessary to purchase the Equipment over those that intend to leverage the purchase with third-party debt. Your proposal must disclose your intent.

(a) In the event you determine it would be advantageous to propose a leveraged lease-financing structure, it should be submitted assuming a long-term debt interest rate of 6.75% per annum. In addition, the following terms will apply:

(i) Our investment banker, Chicago First Corporation, will be responsible for securing the third-party leveraged lease debt at a rate satisfactory to SunBird Corporation, within our sole discretion.

(ii) You must provide assurance that the lease will qualify as a true lease for federal income tax purposes under the current tax rules and guidelines.

(iii) You must state whether your proposal is on a best-effort or firm basis; preference will be given to proposals on a firm basis.

(iv) At the time of submission of your proposal, you must be prepared to identify all lease participants (with contact name and telephone number), including each identified equity and debt participant, so they may be called immediately for verification in the event you are the successful bidder.

Specifying the investment structure not only shows that you're a sophisticated lessee, something that will enhance your negotiating position, but helps ensure that the offer you get will contain few deal surprises after the award. The advantages and disadvantages of the various lease investment structures are discussed in Chapter 1. Being able to talk directly to all lease participants will ensure that your deal has not been misrepresented to anyone by the lessor.

---

15. Broker Disclosure

We will give a preference to lease offers from principal funding sources that do not intend to resell or broker the

> transaction. In the event that you do not intend to act as a principal and purchase the equipment for your own account, you must disclose that in your proposal.

Use this provision if your preference is to deal with principal lessors, but you are willing to entertain offers that will be brokered.

> 16. Expenses
>
> Lessor shall be responsible for payment of all fees and expenses of the transaction, other than the Lessee's own direct legal fees in connection with documenting the lease transaction, including fees and expenses incurred in connection with the arranging, or documentation, of the Equipment lease.

Requiring that the lessor assume all transaction expenses is preferable. And making sure you know who is paying what expenses before making an award is critical.

The Deal Timetable

A deal timetable is essential to ensure that your financing is completed in a timely manner. And the timetable should be updated as needed. Here's the one SunBird Corporation included in its RFQ:

D. Timetable

> SunBird Corporation will adhere to the following time schedule in connection with evaluating submitted proposals, making the award decision, and negotiating the equipment lease document(s):

Action	Date
Lessor Proposal Intent Notifications Due	_____
Lessor Proposals Due	_____
Lessor Proposal Commitment Cutoff	_____

Lessor Notification of Initial Qualification	_____
Form Lease Document(s) Sent to Qualified Lessor(s)	_____
Lessor Response to Form Lease Document(s)	_____
Lessor(s) Selection	_____
Award Announcement	_____
Lease Negotiations—Start	_____
Lease Signing	_____
Anticipated Equipment Delivery	_____
Anticipated Equipment Acceptance for Lease	_____

An explanation of the action categories is as follows:

- *Lessor proposal intent notifications due:* the date when each leasing company receiving the RFQ must indicate its willingness to submit a lease offer. Typically, I recommend setting a date one week following the delivery of the RFQ to prospective bidders.
- *Lessor proposals due:* the date when all lessor proposals are due. Set a date that will provide adequate lead time to have the transaction rebid, get the equipment delivered and operationally accepted, and cover any unforeseen delays.
- *Lessor proposal commitment cutoff:* the date through which the lessor must keep its proposal available for acceptance by the lessee. I recommend setting a date that will provide adequate time to review all proposals, with a margin for comfort.
- *Lessor notification of initial qualification:* the date when the lessee will make the preliminary lease award, subject to acceptance of the lessee's form lease documents. Set a date with which you're comfortable.
- *Form lease document(s) sent to qualified lessor(s):* the date when the lessee's form lease documents will be sent to the initially selected lessor(s) for review and comments. The date is typically one shortly following the lessor notification of initial qualification date.
- *Lessor response to form lease document(s):* the date when the initially selected lessor(s) must submit comments to the lessee's form lease documents. Typically, I recommend giving each lessor two weeks to review the form lease agreement and respond.
- *Lessor(s) selection:* the date on which you will make the final winning lessor(s) selection. Set a date that will give you adequate time to review with your lawyers the lessors' form lease agreement responses.

In certain situations, it may be a good negotiation approach to select three lessors specifying a first-place, second-place, and third-place award and si-

multaneously telling all three that if negotiations break down with the first-place lessor, you will immediately begin negotiations with the second-place lessor and similarly, if necessary, with the third-place lessor.

- *Award announcement:* the date when all lessors will be notified of your lessor selection decision. Typically, I recommend setting a date one to two business days after the lessor(s) selection date.
- *Lease negotiations start:* the date when negotiations will begin with the winning lessor. I usually recommend setting a date three to five business days following the award announcement date.
- *Lease signing:* the date when you expect all lease negotiations to be concluded and the lease documents to be signed by all parties. The date you set will depend on the complexity of the lease financing. A simple transaction can be documented in one week, whereas a complex leveraged lease transaction may take three months. Seek the advice of experienced legal counsel in setting this date.
- *Anticipated equipment delivery:* the date when the equipment is anticipated to arrive on the lessee's premises.
- *Anticipated equipment acceptance for lease:* the date when the lessee expects to accept the equipment for lease. This date should allow sufficient time to ensure that the delivered equipment is operationally acceptable.

A Less Formal Request for Quotes

In certain situations, as mentioned earlier, a less formal RFQ will do the necessary job. For example, in a $100,000 lease financing, there are fewer issues and negotiating risks. Here's how Dave Fastrack should have written his letter RFQ:

Sunny Day Company
34 Orchard Street
White Plains, New York 10604
(914) 991-8900

May 2, 19XX

Ms. Shelly Prisel, Marketing Vice President
Blitz Leasing Corporation
1245 Funding Drive
Glen Cove, New York 11542

Dear Shelly:

We are planning to take delivery on a Matrix Sentex computer system during the last week of May and are interested in having you submit a lease financing quote

---

for our internal purchase/lease evaluation. We will not accept a brokered transaction and are looking to you to be the actual lessor. Please submit the quote in writing no later than May 5, 19XX.

The equipment cost is anticipated to be $215,000. We need some leeway in your bid, however, to cover a cost variance of 15% up or down. The actual system configuration is a Model 3 Excel Payroll Processing System, sold by Matrix Computer Company. I've enclosed a copy of our vendor equipment purchase order confirmation detailing the equipment specifics. The vendor expects payment in full on the date we accept the equipment for lease.

We would like to see monthly, in advance, and quarterly, in arrears, quotes for three-year and five-year lease terms. We want a 10% purchase option and the right to renew the lease for successive one-year terms, the first-term renewal rent not to exceed 25% of the original term rent and the remaining renewals at a rent equal to the fair market rental value. We would also like the right to terminate the lease before the end of the basic term and ask that you submit a schedule of termination values beginning at the end of the first year. Incidentally, we also would like you to submit your casualty value schedule along with your quote.

If you have any thoughts about other structures or options that may be beneficial, please include them in your response.

Our decision will be made by May 10, 19XX. The lease must be signed no later than May 15, 19XX.

If you have any questions, my direct line is (914) 991-8795.

Sincerely,

Dave Fastertrack
Assistant Manager

BT: II

The preceding letter, although still informal, tells the leasing company what is needed. It states the equipment specifics as well as the lease terms that Sunny Day Company is looking for. And it tells when the bids are due and when the decision will be made.It also does not indicate that a lease is the only alternative. To keep negotiating leverage highest, you must leave the door open to a purchase possibility, at least as far as the leasing company is concerned.

An Informal Deal Sheet Approach

If your company leases a high volume of equipment each year, you might consider putting together a deal sheet format that you can fill out and attach to a simple lease request cover letter.

Here's a suggested format. If you decide to use a similar format, use the Lessee Proposal Stage Checklist at the end of this chapter to ensure that you've covered all issues of importance in your deal.

Sunny Day Company
34 Orchard Street
White Plains, New York 10604
(914) 991-8900

May 2, 19XX

Ms. Shelly Prisel, Marketing Vice President
Blitz Leasing Corporation
1245 Funding Drive
Glen Cove, New York 11542

Dear Shelly:

We are planning to take delivery on the equipment specified on the attached term sheet during the last week of May. We would be interested in receiving a lease-financing quote to determine whether leasing is the best alternative for us. Please submit a written quote no later than May 5, 19XX.

If you have any thoughts about other structures or options that may be beneficial, please include them in your response. Incidentally, we will not accept a brokered transaction and are looking to you to be the actual lessor.

Our decision will be made by May 10, 19XX.

The lease must be signed no later than May 15, 19XX.

If you have any questions, my direct line is (914) 991-8795.

Sincerely,

Ben Thoughtful
Assistant Manager

BT: ll

Sunny Day Company
Term Sheet
May 2, 19XX

Equipment	Matrix Sentex Computer System, Model 3 with Excel Payroll Package.
Equipment cost	$215,000, ±15%.
Vendor	Matrix Computer Company.
Delivery date	May 29, 19XX.

Lease term(s)	3- and 5-year.
Rent quote	Monthly, in advance, and quarterly, in arrears.
Purchase option	10% of equipment cost.
Renewal option	Year to year for three years. Maximum first year, 25% of primary rent; thereafter, year-to-year fair market rental value.
Early termination right	Anytime after first year of base lease term.
	Attach schedule to proposal.
Bid due date	May 5, 19XX.
Award date	May 10, 19XX.

Special provisions:
1. Transaction must be single-investor, nonbrokered.
2. Lease must qualify as operating lease for accounting purposes.
3. Net finance lease is required.
4. Our master lease must be used in the form enclosed. Please identify with proposal any provisions that are not acceptable.
5. Casualty value schedule must be sent with your quote.

Saving Time With a Summary Response Sheet

Every leasing company's offer will have a different format. Digging through each one can take work. To simplify your job, you can include with your RFQ a Summary Response Sheet for the lessor to complete and return with its proposal. The sheet should list, in an orderly and clear fashion, every key review item so a quick look will tell you whether the proposal is in the ballpark.

The Summary Response Sheet must be tailored to your company, and I suggest using the Lessee Stage Proposal Checklist to identify what should be included for your particular needs. Here's an example of what I'm suggesting:

Proposal Summary Response Sheet

Leasing company information:

Name: _____

Address: _____

_____

Deal contact: _____

Telephone no.: (___)_____

Equipment cost (±15%): _____

Lease Term	Lease Rate Factor (as a % of cost)	Payment Mode (e.g.) (monthly, in arrears)	Interest Rate (nominal)
3 years	_____	_____	_____
5 years	_____	_____	_____

Purchase option (check one):
_____ FMV _____ Fixed price (___% of equipment cost)

Renewal option (check one):
_____ FRV, for ____ years, every ____ year(s)

Early termination option (check one):
____ Not available ____ Available, beginning the __ year of the lease
term

Fixed Price:
____ % of primary rent, every ____ year[s]

Schedule of values attached? (___ yes ____ no)

Upgrade financing option? (___ yes ____ no)

State future lease rate determination basis if upgrade financing not fixed at award (e.g., adjustment so lessor can maintain nominal after-tax yield, pretax yield): _____

Casualty schedule attached? (___ yes ____ no)

Transaction structure (check one):
_____ Single investor _____ Leveraged lease

Lessor offer (check one):
_____ Brokered (___ best effort ____ firm)
_____ Principal lessor

Lessor financial statement attached? (___ yes ____ no)

It should be apparent that using a Proposal Summary Response Sheet will enable you to make a preliminary determination. As a general rule, I keep the Proposal Summary Response Sheet brief, only identifying key hurdle items. For example, if the lowest lease rent possible is a company's objective, it's easy to eliminate nonaggressive offers. In situations in which companies annually process many lease transactions, I often suggest greater detail, which allows them to use the sheet as a definitive deal evaluation and organization spreadsheet. Personally, I always prefer to use it only to provide a preliminary overview.

Handling an Overlooked RFQ Point

If you discover you've left an important request out of your RFQ after you've sent it out, immediately call each lessor and tell it that you'll be sending out an amended RFQ. Follow up each telephone call with a letter confirming your telephone conservation, preferably sent by fax, unless the amended RFQ can be promptly prepared and sent by either E-mail, facsimile, or overnight delivery to all lessors.

The omitted point or points should be incorporated into a complete, amended, and dated RFQ rather than simply put alone in a letter, so there's less chance of a misunderstanding or an unresponsive proposal resulting, for example, from your letter's being separated from the original RFQ. A bid not incorporating your amendment must be revised if it otherwise looks good, resulting in the loss of valuable lead time.

If you discover the oversight after you've made the lease award, promptly notify the winning lessor and negotiate a revision to the letter of award (typically, a countersigned copy of the lessor's proposal letter). A sophisticated lessor may suggest that the missing item or items simply be incorporated into your deal when the lease is negotiated, hoping to increase its negotiating leverage as your delivery lead time decreases. So be careful. Avoid the lessor's tactic by insisting that it agree to a revised award letter.

Getting the Deal You Want

Now you have the information necessary to put together an effective RFQ. Every minute spent putting together a solid written request for quotes letter will save you hours of negotiation hassles and disappointments. And it will put you in control of the financing process.

Remember, the objective of a lessor-beating RFQ is to outline your business needs and legal requirements carefully, as suggested throughout this chapter. By covering every issue critical to your company's needs and financing objectives—and getting a lessor commitment on those issues before a lease award is made—your finance negotiations will be far simpler and less costly. Use the checklist in the following section to ensure that nothing has been overlooked. And never forget, your greatest bargaining leverage is during the proposal stage, before you've made a lease award. Take full advantage of it.

A Lessee Proposal Stage Checklist

The following are the issues that a prospective lessee should address in considering its negotiation objectives and in preparing its request for bids letter.

Equipment Description

- What type of equipment will be involved?
- What is the manufacturer?
- What is the model?
- How many units will be involved?

Equipment Cost

- What is the total cost involved?
- What is the cost per item?
- Is the cost per item fixed?
    - If not, what is the probable cost escalation?

Equipment Payment

- When must the equipment be paid for?
- Must the entire purchase price be paid at once?

Equipment Delivery

- What is the anticipated delivery date?
- How long should the lessor's lease commitment run past the anticipated delivery date?

Equipment Location

- Where will the equipment be located?
    - At the lease inception
    - During the lease term

Equipment Lease

- What type of lease is desired?
    - Net finance lease
    - Service lease
    - Other

Lease Period

- How long must the lease term run?
- Will an interim lease period be acceptable?
    - If so, what is the latest point in time at which the primary term must begin?
- How long a renewal period is desired?
- How will the renewal right be structured (for example, five one-year periods, one five-year period)?

Rent Program

- When should the rent be payable?
  - Annually
  - Semiannually
  - Quarterly
  - Monthly
  - Other

- Should the payments be "in advance" or "in arrears"?
- If there is an interim period, how should the interim rent be structured?
  - Based on the primary rent (for example, the daily equivalent of the primary rent)
  - Based on the long-term debt interest rate
  - Other

- If there will be a renewal period, how should the renewal rent be structured?
  - Fixed
  - Fair rental value

Options

- What type of options are desired?
  - Fair market value purchase right
  - Fixed-price purchase right
  - Fair market rental value renewal right
  - Fixed-priced renewal right
  - Right of first refusal
  - Termination right
  - Upgrade financing right
  - Other

- Is a right of first refusal specifically unacceptable?

Casualty and Termination Values

- If a termination right is required, will the termination value be a primary consideration in the lease decision?
- Must the termination and casualty values be submitted at the time of the lessor's proposal?

Maintenance and Repair

- Who will have the equipment maintenance and repair obligations?
  Are third-party maintenance contract requirements acceptable?

Tax Indemnifications

- What tax indemnifications, if any, will be acceptable?

Insurance

- Is the right of self-insurance desired?

Taxes

- What taxes will be assumed?
  - Sales
  - Rental
  - Other

Transaction Expenses

- What expenses other than the lessee's legal fees, if any, will be assumed if the transaction is completed? (Usually, this is only a concern in underwritten transactions.)
  - Counsel fees for any lenders and their representatives
  - Acceptance and annual fees of any lender representative (trust arrangement)
  - Counsel fees for the lessor-investors and any representative
  - Counsel fees for the lessor-investor's representative (trust arrangement)
  - IRS private ruling letter fees
  - Documentation expenses
  - Debt placement fees
  - Other
- What expenses, if any, will be assumed if the transaction collapses?

Tax Ruling

- Is an IRS private letter ruling necessary or desirable?
- Can a favorable letter ruling be a prerequisite to any obligations to the lessor under the lease, such as a nonutilization fee?
- Should a private letter ruling relieve any tax indemnification obligations to the lessor?

Submission Date

- What is the latest date on which a lessor proposal may be submitted?

Award Date

- On what date will the transaction be awarded?

Type of Proposals

- Is a leveraged lease or single source preferred?
- Is an underwritten transaction acceptable? If so:
    - Will "best-effort" as well as "firm" proposals be accepted?
    - If "best-effort" proposals are acceptable, how long after the awards will the underwriter have to firm up the prospective lessor-investors and any lenders?

Prospective Equity and Debt Participants—Underwritten Transaction

- Are any prospective lessor-investors or lenders not to be approached?

Chapter 6

Evaluating the Lessor's Offer

A Key Step: Evaluating the Lessor's Offer

After preparing and sending out a request for lease quotes, the next step in your lease-financing process will be to carefully evaluate each lessor response—the lessor's lease proposal. This is a critical part of the proposal stage negotiation. It is your first opportunity to narrow the lessor field down to those offering the best deal. In addition, after reviewing the proposals, you may see a need to request changes or additions and ask for a rebid. And once you select a lessor, the proposal will become the basis for the later deal documentation.

Even if you've done your request for quotes (RFQ) job right, chances are good that you'll receive responses that don't follow your RFQ directions or are confusing, vague, or misleading. If you get an unresponsive proposal that looks interesting, don't go a step further with it until the lessor has delivered a clear, revised offer—in writing.

To evaluate a lessor's proposal effectively, you have to know what to look for. For example, you must make sure that, after the lease award, the lessor will have little, if any, room for rate increases or other manipulation. Let's now explore how to evaluate and negotiate a lessor's lease proposal to get the best possible deal.

Offer Negotiation Objectives

As discussed in Chapter 5, because the major terms are decided and the lessor or underwriter is selected during the proposal stage, this period is one of the most important in a lease financing. For a lessee, this is a period when it typically has the greatest bargaining leverage, particularly if

---

Sample Lessor Proposal

Northstar Leasing, Inc.
3100 Lealand Avenue, Suite 3344
White Plains, NY 10604
(914) 987-8700

February 25, 19XX

Union Carbon, Inc.
2200 West Street, Suite 200
Chicago, Illinois 60607

Attn.: R. Peters

Gentlemen:

In accordance with your request for proposals dated March 15, 19XX, Northstar is pleased to propose our plan for the lease of your on-order computer equipment.

Based on an acquisition cost of $806,374.00, Northstar lease rates are as follows, as a percentage of acquisition cost:

- If the equipment is purchased during the first nine months of 19XX:
  5-year rate: 2.103%
  7-year rate: 1.67%

- If the equipment is purchased during the last three months of 19XX:
  5-year rate: 2.14%
  7-year rate: 1.69%

The above lease rates are based on a debt interest rate of 8.5%. In addition, they are subject to a satisfactory credit review of Union Carbon and are subject to documentation.

Please call if you have any questions on any of the above or if any points require clarification.

Very truly yours,

Mike Sivilli
Vice President

---

more than one lessor is involved in the bidding. And this is the time when a lessee should press for the tough concessions. Once the lease award has been made, circumstances change, and the winning bidder is in the stronger negotiating position.

From the lessor's perspective, the proposal stage negotiating strategy is to get a prospective lessee to "sign off" on a proposal letter quickly, giving less time to lessee negotiators to think and possibly come up with problem requests. Once lease documentation has begun, particularly if there are near-term equipment deliveries, a prospective lessor's negotiating position is further improved. Pressure has increased to get the financing in place so the vendor can be paid when the equipment arrives, and there is less time to look for another lessor if deal problems arise. In addition, once an award has been made, prospective lessees are psychologically more reluctant to start over with new people.

A Proposal Overview

Stated simply, the proposal letter outlines the lease "deal" offered by the lessor. Typically, it won't address every possible issue, but it will set the basic framework of the lessor's commitment. If you don't use a comprehensive RFQ, chances increase that you won't be offered everything you'll want—or should have. Always keep in mind when negotiating a lease proposal that the lessor's offer objective is to provide only what's absolutely necessary to get an award. And if they can get away with it, many lessors will try to entice you into an award with nothing more than a low rent offer. On page 152 is an example of such a lessor proposal we received in response to a detailed RFQ from one of my clients. Only the names have been changed.

For many lessees, this proposal would seem satisfactory. What about you? In this case, the leasing company, Northstar, had been sent the RFQ below. See what you think after reading it. Names and other pertinent information have been changed to ensure anonymity.

Request for Lease of Computer Equipment Union Carbon, Inc.

Prior to the award of this transaction to a prospective bidder, no recipient of this Request for Proposal is authorized to act for, or on behalf of, UNION CARBON, INC., in connection with the placement of any interest in the proposed lease.

UNION CARBON, INC. (Lessee), is requesting proposals from lessors (Lessor) for a long-term net finance lease (Lease) of certain computer equipment in accordance with the terms and conditions more fully described below.

Lessee requests that Lessor adhere to the following guidelines and conditions. However, should a Lessor wish to provide a lease proposal that, in Lessor's opinion, is more favorable than permitted under the specifications set forth below, Lessor may submit, concurrently with the proposal herein requested, other proposals in sufficient detail to define how the alternative proposal(s) may be more advantageous to Lessee.

1. Equipment Description and Cost Latitude
   a. The Equipment will consist of new electronic data-processing equipment from DataMix Corporation, as follows:

Item #	Model & Description	Quantity	Unit Price	Total Price
1	B 7301 8.0 MHz processor	1	$100,000	$ 100,000.00
2	System 3 hardware automation package	1	$800,000	$ 800,000.00
3	System 3 software	1	$ 6,039	$ 6,039.00
	Total list price:			$ 906,039.00
	Less 11% discount:			$ 99,664.29
	Net price:			$ 806,374.71

   b. It is requested that the proposals provide a latitude of ±10% with respect to the final Equipment Cost.

  2. Estimated Acceptance and Settlement Date

It is further anticipated that the Equipment will be delivered and accepted by Lessee no later than August 15, 19XX, but it's possible that delivery and acceptance may be delayed until September of 19XX. It is further expected that payment for the Equipment will be required no sooner than 90 days following acceptance.

  3. Location of Equipment

The Equipment will be located in Springfield, Massachusetts.

  4. Term
   a. Proposals should be submitted based on initial lease terms of five and seven years.
   b. The initial term shall run from the date of Equipment acceptance by Lessee.

  5. Rentals
   a. Rentals should be quoted on both a monthly, in advance, and semiannually, in arrears, basis.
   b. Although it is anticipated that the Equipment will be delivered and accepted on or before August 31, 19XX, there is a remote possibility that the schedule will not be met. As a result, two rental quotations should be made (assuming there would be a rental rate difference): one for acceptance on or before August 31, 19XX, and the second for acceptance after August 31, 19XX.
   c. Rentals shall be consecutive, level payments, expressed as a percentage of Equipment Cost.
   d. No interim rental payments will be acceptable.
   e. The nominal per annum lease interest rate must be stated for each rental quotation.

  6. Equity

Proposals (i) in which Lessor will be the sole principal investor for 100% of the cost of the Equipment and (ii) that are on a firm basis will be given priority consideration. Any other proposal should specify the specific terms and conditions of the variance.

  7. Extended Term Rentals

Lessee must have an option to extend the Lease from year to year for a total of at least five years on a fair market rental basis.

8. Early Termination

    a. Lessee must have the right to terminate the Lease prior to the end of the initial lease term in the event the Equipment becomes obsolete or surplus to Lessee's need. The proceeds of any sale or re-leasing following such termination are to be applied toward the reduction of any termination premium required.

    b. The right to terminate early shall be exercisable beginning as of the end of the initial lease term.

    c. A schedule of termination values, if any, must be submitted at the time the proposal is submitted.

9. Purchase Option

Lessee must have the right to purchase the Equipment at the end of any extended term of the lease for the Equipment's then fair market value.

10. Upgrade Right

Lessee must have the right to upgrade any or all of the Equipment at any time. The principal upgrading terms and conditions must be outlined.

11. Other Terms

Other significant terms and conditions should be specified.

12. Approval

Lessee reserves the right to approve any and all aspects of each proposal.

13. Form Documents Supplied

Lessor's form lease documents must accompany the proposal.

14. Documentation Fees and Expenses

Lessee will pay only its own counsel fees.

Submission

All proposals must be received no later than March 20, 19XX, and should be sent to:

Union Carbon, Inc.
2200 West Street, Suite 200
Chicago, Illinois 60607
Attn.: R. Peters

In the event any questions arise, Mr. Peters can be reached at (312) 234-7879.

As you can see, Northstar ignored every RFQ guideline—except, of course, the rent request. As it turned out, the approach was clever. The rental rates offered were below-market and got the deal manager's attention. As a result, Union Carbon decided not to throw out the proposal as unresponsive. This is what Northstar was apparently counting on. And its tactic almost paid off because Union Carbon's financial vice president, Mr. Peters, was aggressively looking for the lowest lease rate, and he decided to keep Northstar in the running. He called Northstar to pursue the offer, but when it preferred not to discuss details over the telephone and asked for a meeting, he decided to give me a call to ask me to attend with him.

Based on what he told me, I surmised that Northstar's low rent offer was a tactic to get an exclusive dialogue going with Union Carbon and suggested that we immediately have a conference call with Northstar's representative to see if I could determine whether the offer was in fact legitimate. During the call, it became clear that they were using a lowball rate ploy: offering rates that would get Union Carbon's attention but ones that Northstar had every intention of increasing. The Northstar representative was generally evasive. For example, when we asked about termination options, we were told that a meeting was necessary to go over the entire package. I then suggested that Northstar respond specifically to each item—giving it two days to do so. Two days went by, and Union Carbon received nothing. Mr. Peters called Northstar, but the representative was unavailable and never returned the call. The moral of this story: A 15-minute phone call saved the expense and time of sitting through what would have been a useless meeting with Northstar.

Reviewing the Lessor's Offer in Detail

Writing lease proposals has become an art. They're often carefully worded to look clear and unambiguous yet contain loopholes for the lessor to increase rates or gain other advantages. The less experienced lessee is particularly at risk, all too often making incorrect assumptions about what a lessor is offering in its rush to get the financing done. The good news is that most lessor proposals are relatively short, typically two to four pages in length, so a careful business and legal review can be accomplished quickly.

The first step in reviewing the lessor's proposal is to make sure each RFQ item has been clearly and adequately addressed. If you receive a poorly written or unresponsive proposal, such as the one in the preceding section, it's likely that the lessor has one purpose in mind: to get an award, while leaving room to negotiate advantages. If there's something you don't understand in a lessor's proposal, get clarification—in writing.

To give you a solid basis for reviewing and evaluating a lessor offer, we're going to examine, in the next section, common provisions lessors use in their proposals and look at some of the ways a lessor will attempt to trick you with clever language. The provisions we'll be discussing have been taken from actual proposals. The names of the leasing companies and any other participants, however, have been changed. The selected provisions are presented in the order in which they usually appear in a proposal.

Before we begin our detailed examination, let's take a quick general look at two typical lessor proposals, one a nonunderwritten, single-investor lease offer and the other an underwritten leveraged lease-financing offer. Typically, although an underwritten leveraged lease proposal will be more complex than a nonunderwritten lease proposal, both types contain the same basic elements.

Sample Letter: Nonunderwritten Proposal

Northstar Leasing, Inc.
3100 Lealand Avenue, Suite 3344
White Plains, New York 10604
(914) 987-8700

February 25, 19XX

Union Carbon, Inc.
2200 West Street, Suite 200
Chicago, Illinois 60607

Attn.: R. Peters

Gentlemen:

Northstar Leasing Company (NLC) offers to purchase and lease to Union Carbon, Inc. (Union), newly manufactured forklift trucks on the following terms and conditions:

1. Equipment Description:	The equipment shall consist of four (4) new special-service forklift trucks, model no. RZ-7, manufactured by Diamond International Corp.
2. Equipment Cost:	Approximately $100,000.
3. Delivery and Payment:	Delivery of the Equipment is anticipated on June 12, 19XX, but in no event shall it be later than August 1, 19XX. NLC shall pay for the Equipment on delivery and acceptance.
4. Lease Term:	Eight years, beginning on delivery and acceptance of the Equipment.
5. Rental Program:	Union shall remit 32 consecutive, level, quarterly, in advance payments, each equal to 4.4000% of Equipment Cost.
6. Options:	At the conclusion of the Lease Term, Union may (with at least 120 days' prior written notice):
	a. Buy the Equipment for an amount equal to its then fair market value.
	b. Renew the Lease with respect to the Equipment for its then fair rental value.
7. Tax Benefits:	The rent is calculated based on the assumption that NLC will be entitled to:
	a. Three-year MACRS depreciation on the full Equipment Cost, 200% declining balance switching to straight-line, and

	b. A corporate income tax of 34%.
8. Fixed Expenses:	This is a net financial lease proposal, and all fixed expenses—such as insurance, maintenance, and personal property taxes—shall be for the account of Union.

If the foregoing is satisfactory to you, please indicate your acceptance of this offer by signing the duplicate copy of this letter in the space provided therefor and returning it directly to the undersigned.

This offer is subject to the execution of mutually satisfactory lease documentation and expires as of the close of business on March 15, 19XX.

Very truly yours,

Northstar Leasing Company

By _____
            Vice President

Accepted and Agreed to on this

_____ day of _____, 19XX

Union Carbon, Inc.

By _____

Its _____

Sample Letter: Underwritten Proposal

Northstar Leasing, Inc.
3100 Lealand Avenue, Suite 3344
White Plains, New York 10604
(914) 987-8700

February 25, 19XX

Union Carbon, Inc.
2200 West Street, Suite 200
Chicago, Illinois 60607

Attn.: R. Peters

Gentlemen:

Northstar Leasing Company (NLC), on behalf of its nominees, proposes to use its best efforts to arrange a lease for one new corporate aircraft for use by Union Carbon, Inc. (Union), under the following terms and conditions:

Lessor:	The Lessor will be a commercial bank or trust company acting as owner trustee (Owner Trustee) pursuant to one or more owners' trusts (Trust) for the benefit of one or more commercial banks

	or other corporate investors (Owner Participant). The Trust shall acquire the Equipment and lease it to the Lessee.
Lessee:	The Lessee shall be Union Carbon, Inc.
Equipment:	One new Foker SZ-77 aircraft.
Cost:	For the purposes of this proposal, a total cost of $12 million, ±5%, has been assumed.
Delivery Date:	Delivery of the Equipment is anticipated as of September 1, 19XX; however, it shall be no later than November 1, 19XX.
Interim Lease Term:	An Interim Lease Term shall extend from the Delivery Date until the Commencement Date. For purposes of this proposal, the Commencement Date is assumed to be December 1, 19XX.
Interim Rent:	The Lessee shall pay Interim Rent equal to interest-only on the total cost of the Equipment at an interest rate equal to the Long-Term Debt Interest Rate.
Primary Lease Term:	The Primary Lease Term shall be ten years from the Commencement Date.
Primary Rent:	From the Commencement Date, the Lessee shall make 20 consecutive, level, semiannual payments, in advance, each equal to 2.2000% of Equipment Cost.
Debt Financing:	An investment banker acceptable to NLC and the Lessee shall arrange for the private placement of secured notes or similar instruments (Indebtedness) to be issued by the Lessor for a principal amount equal to 80% of total Equipment Cost to certain institutional investors (Lenders), which may be represented by an indenture trustee or agent bank (Agent). This proposal assumes that the Indebtedness shall be amortized in semiannual payments of principal and interest at an 8% per annum interest rate (Long-Term Debt Interest Rate), payable in arrears over the term of the Lease. In the event that the Long-Term Debt Interest Rate varies from that assumed, the rent shall be adjusted upward or downward, so that the Owner Participant's after-tax yield and after-tax cash flow will be maintained. The Indebtedness shall be secured by an assignment of the Lease and a security interest in the Equipment but otherwise shall be without recourse to the Owner Participant and the Lessor.
Insurance:	The Lessee may self-insure the Equipment.
Purchase and Renewal Options:	At the end of the Primary Term, the Lessee may (with 180 days' written notice prior to the end of the term): 1. Renew the Lease on the Equipment for its then fair market rental value for one two-year period.

2. Buy the Equipment for an equivalent price and under similar conditions as rendered by a third party approached by the Lessor and agreed to by the Lessor prior to the sale to that third party.

If the Lessee does not elect to exercise any of the above options, the Lessee shall return the Equipment to the Lessor at the end of the term at a mutually agreeable location.

Termination Option: At any time during the Primary Lease Term, on or after two years from the Commencement Date, the Lessee may (with 180 days' prior written notice) terminate the Lease in the event the Equipment becomes obsolete or surplus to its needs, on paying a mutually agreed on termination value.

Fixed Expenses: This is a net financial lease proposal with all fixed expenses—such as maintenance, insurance, and taxes (other than net income taxes)—for the account of the Lessee.

Expenses of Transaction: NLC shall pay all transaction expenses, including:

1. fees and disbursements of special counsel for the Agent and the Lenders;

2. acceptance and annual fees and expenses of the Agent;

3. fees and disbursements of special counsel for the Owner Trustee and the Trustor;

4. acceptance and annual fees and expenses of the Owner Trustee;

5. fees and disbursements in connection with obtaining a ruling from the Internal Revenue Service;

6. expenses of documentation, including printing and reproduction; and

7. fees and disbursements in connection with the private placement of the Indebtedness.

If the transaction is not consummated for any reason, the Lessee shall pay all of the above fees and expenses.

Nonutilization Fee: Once NLC has obtained equity investor commitments satisfactory to the Lessee, the Lessee shall be liable to NLC for a Nonutilization Fee equal to 0.5% of the Equipment Cost in the event it does not lease the Equipment in accordance with the intent of this proposal.

Commitment Fee: A Commitment Fee of 0.5% per annum shall be paid by the Lessee on the outstanding equity investor commitment. The fee shall accrue as of the date investor commitments satisfactory to Union, have been obtained, shall run up to the Commencement Date, and shall be payable pro rata

	on a monthly, in arrears, basis.
Tax Assumptions:	The Rent is calculated based on the assumptions that:

1. the organization created by the Trust will be treated as a partnership for federal income tax purposes;

2. the Lessor will be entitled to seven-year MACRS deprecation on 100% of the Equipment Cost, 200% declining balance switching to straight-line;

3. the Lessor will be entitled to deduct interest in the Indebtedness under Section 163 of the Internal Revenue Code;

4. the Lessor will be entitled to amortize the transaction expenses over the Interim and Primary Lease Terms using a straight-line method;

5. the effective federal income tax rate of the Owner Participant is 34%; and

6. the Lessor will not recognize any income from the transaction other than from Lessee rental, termination value, stipulation value, and indemnity payments to the Lessor.

Tax Ruling: The Lessor plans to obtain an Internal Revenue Tax Service ruling with respect to the tax assumptions stated above. The Lessee shall agree to indemnify for the tax assumptions above. Such indemnity shall remain in effect until a favorable ruling has been obtained.

If the foregoing proposal is satisfactory to you, please indicate your acceptance by signing the duplicate copy of this letter in the space provided therefor and returning it directly to the undersigned.

This offer expires at the close of business on March 20, 19XX, and is subject to the approval of the Owner Participant's Board of Directors and mutually satisfactory lease documentation.

Very truly yours,

Northstar Leasing Company

By _____
      Vice President

Accepted and Agreed to on this

_____ day of _____, 19XX

Union Carbon, Inc.

By _____

Its _____

Proposal Issues to Address

As suggested earlier, in reviewing a lessor proposal, there are two primary considerations: First, you have to make sure the lessor offer addresses every important transaction aspect—such as rent, insurance, and lease options—and second, you must identify any clever loopholes, hidden traps or potential for problems, which, for example, would allow the lessor an opening to increase the lease rent unfairly. To do this, you must:

- Insist that all proposals be in writing.
- Make sure all issues have been properly addressed.
- Have the lessor rewrite any vague or ambiguous provision in an amended proposal.
- Eliminate proposal language that has potential for clever lessor maneuvers.

Eliminating potential lessor loopholes is often the most difficult task. In most cases, it requires technical knowledge and experience. Fortunately, the potential for loophole maneuvering is limited to certain deal aspects common to all lease financing. These are discussed below, so even if you lack lease experience, you'll know what to look for and when, possibly, you need expert assistance.

The best way to show you how to assess a lessor's offer is to examine, step by step, an actual proposal. We're going to use as a discussion base the two proposals in the prior section. For your convenience, the applicable provisions are repeated below in the context of the analysis discussion.

Are You Dealing With a Principal or a Broker?

For the reasons discussed in Chapter 1, dealing with a lease broker has some advantages and some disadvantages, so this is an issue you'll want to address carefully. For a prospective lessee, the choice among the different variations often represents a question of delivery date and price. If you have a near-term equipment delivery, it's typically advisable to limit your consideration to lessor principals, because dealing directly with the lease investor lessens the risk that the financing cannot be done within the short time frame. If there is plenty of time, the best approach may be to pursue a syndicated leveraged lease transaction, in which a lease underwriter brings together multiple debt and equity investors to provide the necessary funding. In the latter case, although the transaction will certainly be more involved, it may provide the best rental rate. You are referred to Exhibit 3-1 for some assistance in evaluating your deal lead time.

All too often, a lessor acting as a broker won't disclose its intent for fear of being excluded from the bidding process. Fortunately, most broker-acting lessors won't actively claim that they are principals to avoid being sued if they can't find a lease investor, but some may mislead you into thinking they are principals through cleverly misleading proposal language.

You must be particularly careful in today's lessor market because the distinction between brokers and principals is not as clear as in the past. For example, it's not uncommon for principal lessors to broker part, or all, of the lease transaction to a third-party investor or for a traditional lease underwriter to invest some of its own funds in an equipment lease.

So if you don't want to deal with a traditional broker, or to have a unknown investment partner added by the lessor, you must determine who is going to make the lease investment—the company submitting the proposal or a yet unknown participant that the offeror intends to identify after the lease award. If you're dealing with a reputable leasing company, the proposal language will generally be clear. But if you're dealing with a nervous or devious lease broker, it may not be obvious.

**Sample Provision: Underwritten
Proposal Funding Offer**

Northstar Leasing Company (NLC), on behalf of its nominees, proposes to use its best efforts to arrange a lease for one new corporate aircraft for use by Union Carbon, Inc. (Union), under the following terms and conditions:

Lessor:

The Lessor will be a commercial bank or trust company acting as owner trustee (Owner Trustee) pursuant to one or more owners' trusts (Trust) for the benefit of one or more commercial banks or other corporate investors (Owner Participant). The Trust shall acquire the Equipment and lease it to the Lessee.

A leasing company typically defines its intended investment commitment directly in one of two areas—in the introductory paragraph or in the "Lessor" section of the proposal. Let's take a look at the funding provision in our sample underwritten proposal.

The lessor's intent is clear. The proposal states that:

- Northstar is acting on behalf of "nominees," not on behalf of itself.
- The financing proposal is a "best-efforts" offer, a qualification used in underwritten, or brokered, offers.
- The "Lessor" will be a trust acting on behalf of one or more commercial banks or corporate investors.

Let's now compare this with the introductory section of our sample nonunderwritten proposal:

Sample Provision: Nonunderwritten Proposal Funding Offer

Northstar Leasing Company (NLC) offers to purchase and lease to Union Carbon, Inc. (Union), newly manufactured fork-lift trucks on the following terms and conditions:

The intent of Northstar in this case is also clear. It states flatly that it is offering to "purchase and lease to Union Carbon, Inc.," the specified equipment. Unfortunately, many proposals are not as clear, either intentionally or because of carelessness. Those are the offers you must quickly identify. Let's take a look at some misleading provisions taken from actual proposals to get a feel for what to look for.

Sample Provision: Misleading Funding Offer

Lessor:
GASU Leasing Company, its affiliates, assigns, or nominees.

At first glance, it may appear that the lessor is acting as a principal, offering to put up the funds necessary to purchase the equipment for lease to the lessee. However, upon closer examination, it becomes clear that this provision can be cleverly misleading. The provision states that the lessor could be one of GASU's "affiliates, assigns, or nominees." So GASU has the option of transferring the financing, in whole or in part, to a currently unknown third party. In other words, GASU has the right to act as broker.

It's conceivable that all GASU intended was to reserve the right to assign a security interest in the equipment and lease in the event it borrowed a portion of the equipment investment funds from a third-party lender. If so, GASU is simply guilty of sloppy proposal writing and should have provided for such a right in a "Debt" section.

If GASU did intend to cover a third-party lender assignment, it made an additional mistake. Technically speaking, a lender would not be considered a "lessor" even though it would acquire many of the lessor's substantive rights as security for the equipment loan—something discussed in greater detail in the following chapter. There is one more possibility:

GASU was considering bringing in a lessor investment partner. If so, the provision should be more specific, as you'll see shortly.

As a general rule, when you have an ambiguity, even though a later provision seems to clear it up, it's always advisable to have the proposal rewritten so nothing is left to chance. For example, if GASU has no intention of brokering the lease, it should be required to rewrite the provision as follows:

Sample Provision: Misleading Funding Offer Revised

Lessor:

GASU Leasing Company or any of its subsidiaries.

As you can see, the language creating the ambiguity was removed, and *affiliates* was changed to *subsidiaries* to avoid the possibility that GASU considers companies with which it does business, lease investors, to be affiliated with it because of, say, a long-term business relationship.

If GASU wants the right to bring in a lessor investment partner, the provision should be rewritten as follows:

**Sample Provision: Funding Offer
With Investment Partner Right**

Lessor:

GASU Leasing Company or any of its subsidiaries. GASU may elect not to be the sole lease investor, in which case GASU shall request the participation of a third-party lease investor. Notwithstanding the election, GASU shall be primarily obligated to invest the entire equipment cost as lessor.

If you're willing to let GASU elect to broker the lease to a third party, the provision would be clearer if written as follows:

Sample Provision: Funding Offer With Broker Right

Lessor:

GASU Leasing Company or any of its subsidiaries. In the event GASU elects not to act as sole principal lessor, it may act as underwriter and bring in the necessary equity and debt participants.

If GASU will act solely as broker, the provision should be written as follows:

Sample Provision: Broker-Only Offer

Lessor:

GASU Leasing Company, as broker, will provide an owner-lessor, not later than 15 days following the Award Date, that will supply the funds necessary to purchase the Equipment and lease it to Lessee, under the terms and conditions set forth in this proposal.

Here's a provision that looks similar to the preceding one, but it's one that can get you into trouble:

Sample Provision: Potentially Misleading Broker Funding Offer

Lessor:

GASU Leasing Company has an owner-lessor that will provide the necessary lease investment funds.

In this case, it's clear that GASU intends to act as a broker. However, as is the case with most brokers using this provision, it's unlikely that GASU has at the proposal stage a committed lessor-investor. Why? Because investors rarely make firm investment commitments until after a lease award. So what's going on? GASU is undoubtedly attempting to make the prospective lessee comfortable with its broker approach.

Some brokers will take a chance and claim that they have investors lined up, even when they don't, because they know that most prospective lessees will believe them and not press further. They also know that, if they are asked for a specific name, most lessees will take any reasonable excuse why it can't be disclosed, such as that they've been required by the investor to keep it confidential until an award is made.

Is the Offer Firm?

Typically, a lease underwriter will state in the first paragraph of its proposal whether the offer is made on a "best-efforts" basis or a "firm" basis. There are risks and advantages to each, as explained in this subsection.

A best-efforts proposal is one in which the leasing company offers nothing more than to try to arrange the lease financing on the stated terms and conditions. There are no performance guarantees, and the underwriter is generally not liable to the prospective lessee if it cannot perform.

Sample Provision: Best-Efforts Offer

GASU Leasing Company is pleased to respond to your request for lease quotations and proposes to use its best efforts to arrange an equipment lease according to the terms and conditions set forth in this proposal.

A firm underwritten bid is simply that: The underwriter states that it can deliver the financing under the proposed terms and conditions. In effect, the underwriter guarantees that it will find the necessary lessor debt and equity participants willing to provide the financing as offered.

Sample Provision: Firm Offer

GASU Leasing Company is pleased to respond to your request for lease quotations and proposes to arrange, on a firm-commitment basis, an equipment lease for XYZ, Inc., according to the terms and conditions set forth in this proposal.

From the prospective lessee's viewpoint, whether to go with a best-efforts or firm offer is often a trade-off between lead time loss and price. Underwriters will often offer a better price on a best-efforts bid because they'll stretch to get a better deal when they're not financially guaranteeing their performance. The best-efforts offer, however, has a downside for a prospective lessee: a potential for loss of lead time. If the underwriter cannot, after having been awarded the deal, rapidly find a lessor, valuable documentation time is lost. In fact, if the underwriter takes an extended period to market the deal, the possibility becomes greater that no lessor will accept the deal. The reason: Prospective lessor-investors become suspicious when a transaction has been around the marketplace for a while and may refuse to consider it for that reason alone.

If you decide to take a best-efforts offer, make the award conditioned on the underwriter's meeting a performance timetable. If the schedule is not met, and you can't afford to lose time, seriously consider beginning negotiations with another lessor.

If you want a firm offer, make sure that the provision designating the lessor is clear, one in which the leasing company unequivocally commits to act as principal lessor. If you're willing to consider an underwriter because it claims to have a lease investor already committed, don't make the award until the name of the investor has been disclosed and you've talked to an investor representative to confirm the commitment, or make the award contingent upon disclosure and confirmation within, say, two business days. If there is going to be a problem, the time to find out is when the remaining bidders are still in the picture.

Watch Out For: Broker Firm-Offer Risks

A word of caution about firm underwritten offers. As you now know, all lease-financing offers, even directly from principal lessors, are generally qualified. And the qualifications water down the leasing commitment. In the case of an underwritten offer, there is an additional risk: If the underwriter doesn't have the financial strength to make the lease investment, and it can't find the necessary investors or lenders, its firm commitment is meaningless.

Here's What to Do: Check Financial Strength

Carefully investigate the financial condition of a lease underwriter offering a firm bid. If it doesn't have the financial capacity to make the lease investment, the fact that the offer is firm is of no value.

Has the Lessee Been Properly Named?

Although this is rarely a problem, make sure the lease offer correctly identifies the entity you want to be on the lease as lessee. It's not unusual, for example, for a company to seek lease offers on behalf of a subsidiary and not make it clear that it will not provide credit support. For example, a proposal may name Union Carbon, Inc., as the lessee when in fact Union Carbon, Inc., plans to have Union Carbon Development, Inc., a subsidiary, as the lessee. If the lessor bases its credit approval on Union Carbon, Inc.'s, financial statements, it may refuse to accept the subsidiary as the lessee. If the mistake is not discovered until the last minute, there may not be enough time to solve the problem by, for example, getting the necessary board of director approval for a parent-company guarantee.

The lessee entity is identified in a special "Lessee" section or in the proposal introduction. Here's how it appears in our sample underwritten proposal:

**Sample Provision: Underwritten Proposal
Lessee Identification**

Lessee:
The Lessee shall be Union Carbon, Inc.

In the nonunderwritten proposal, the lessee identification is equally clear:

**Sample Provision: NonunderwrittenProposal
Lessee Identification**

Northstar Leasing Company (NLC) offers to purchase and lease to Union Carbon, Inc. (Union), newly manufactured fork-lift trucks on the following terms and conditions:

There is another reason you must ensure that the lessee entity has been properly and fully identified: A lessor may purposely use a misleading identification in an effort to win the award and provide a basis for later increasing the lease rate. Assume that Union wanted its subsidiary, Union Carbon Development, Inc., to act as lessee. An unscrupulous lessor might identify the lessee entity as follows:

Sample Provision: Misleading Lessee Identification

February 25, 19XX

Union Carbon, Inc.
2200 West Street, Suite 200
Chicago, Illinois 60607
Attn.: R. Peters

Gentlemen:
Northstar Leasing Company (NLC) offers to purchase and lease to Union newly manufactured forklift trucks on the following terms and conditions:

Here, the letter is addressed to Union Carbon, Inc., but the lessee is identified only as "Union." A deal manger in a hurry might overlook the sloppiness, particularly if the lease rate offered was attractive. If the lessor was in fact trying to outsmart Union, the lease agreement would arrive with Union Carbon, Inc., named as lessee. And when Union points out the mistake, the lessor representative would act surprised and say that he or she has to go back to management for approval. The representative would then suggest that, in the interim, the document be negotiated. At the last minute, the representative would apologetically claim that the approval was based on the parent company's credit, but with a "slight" rate increase, the lessor could put the subsidiary, Union Carbon Development, Inc., on as lessee.

Although, typically, this is not an area in which a leasing company will attempt to trick a prospective lessee, it does happen. Here's another example of how a devious lessor attempted to use the bait-and-switch tactic:

Sample Provision: Another Misleading Lessee Identification

February 25, 19XX

Union Carbon, Inc.
2200 West Street, Suite 200
Chicago, Illinois 60607
Attn.: R. Peters

Gentlemen:
Northstar Leasing Company (NLC) offers lease financing for four newly manufactured forklift trucks on the following terms and conditions:

Here, the proposal is addressed to the parent company, but as you can see, the introduction says nothing about which entity would be the named lessee. And a project manager in a rush to get the financing closed could easily assume that Northstar was willing to have the subsidiary as lessee.

Has the Equipment Been Fully Identified?

The lessor's proposal should detail the equipment covered by its offer. Provisions that don't pin down the equipment specifics can create problems. For example, a vague equipment description may allow the lessor an opportunity to claim, properly or improperly, that it had assumed a different manufacturer or system makeup in setting its lease rent. Although a lessor providing an offer on generally described equipment, such as four trucks, may not legally be able to argue its way out of the financing, having a right to sue is of little use when you're facing a near-term equipment delivery. The simplest way to avoid problems is to require the lessor to attach a schedule to its proposal describing the equipment exactly as on your vendor's purchase order.

Another important point: If some or all of the equipment you want financed will be used, as opposed to new, this should be stated in the proposal. If it isn't, the lessor may claim that the offer was only for new equipment and that, although it will finance the used portion, the lease rate on those items must be increased to offset the lower potential resale or re-lease profits. And some lessors will not finance used equipment. You don't want to wait until the last minute to find that out.

Here's a good approach:

Sample Provision: A Good Equipment Description

Equipment:

One new Cartex B6702 Data Processing Central Processing Unit and three Model 213 Cartex Monochrome Monitors. The Monitors may be new or used.

Now let's take a look at an actual proposal provision that did create problems for a lessee:

Sample Provision: A Problem Equipment Description

Equipment:

One newly manufactured pickup truck with a cost of $19,700.

At first glance, the preceding provision might appear adequate. But if you're dealing with a devious lessor, or one that made an honest mistake, if neither the lease proposal nor the lease agreement identified the truck in any greater detail, and you have no record of sending the lessor a copy of your specific purchase order with truck details, such as model number and manufacturer, you could be in trouble. Upon receiving the details, the lessor could claim that it assumed the truck was a Ford, rather than, in your case, a Dodge, and that rent must be increased to offset a lower end-of-lease residual value.

Here's a suggested solution:

Sample Provision: Equipment Description Revised

Equipment:
One new pickup truck manufactured by Ford Motor Company, model no. 2300, with a purchase cost of $19,700 and the following options added:

- Air-conditioning
- Special off-road engine package
- Model no. 10 tailgate lift
- Fusion metal truck bed cover

This approach would also work:

Equipment:
One new pickup truck manufactured by Ford Motor Company, model no. 2300, with a purchase cost of $19,700, as more specifically detailed in the vendor's purchase order, attached as Exhibit A to this proposal.

Here's another example of a proposal equipment description that caused problems and left the door open for a rent increase:

**Sample Provision: Another Problem
Equipment Description**

Equipment:
One IBM Model 6700 computer and associated equipment.

The term *associated equipment* is vague, leaving room for a lessor manipulation. As in the earlier example, when the equipment arrived for lease, the lessor claimed that the rent must be increased inasmuch as it had assumed that the associated equipment was IBM equipment and not, as in this case, equipment made by another manufacturer. And in addition, it had assumed that the associated equipment was different than anticipated.

What About Equipment Cost?

The lessor's proposal should specify the total equipment cost, with leeway for cost changes. Cost leeway is particularly important if a lessor is inclined to put a limit on, or "cap," the amount of money it commits to a transaction. For example, a leasing company may agree to lease an oil tanker expected to cost $40 million. Without a cost cap, it may have to invest more than $40 million if there is an unexpected cost escalation. With a cap, the same cost escalation would allow the lessor to walk away, or increase rates, at its whim.

Cost decreases can also be a problem. If the lessor imposes a fee for the failure to use all the committed funds, commonly referred to as a nonutilization fee, if the purchase price drops, the lessee will have to pay an unused funds penalty. The fee would add to the effective cost of leasing. The solution for a lessee is to negotiate a downward cost cushion.

Let's take a look at some cost provisions.

Sample Provision: Nonunderwritten Proposal Equipment Cost

Equipment Cost:
Approximately $100,000.

This cost provision can be misleading. Prospective lessees often assume that *approximately* means that the lessor has little, if any, concern about final equipment cost. Unfortunately, this is rarely the case. If the final cost were $101,000, the lessor would probably say nothing. But what if the cost were $115,000? In this situation, the lessor might walk away, claiming that the cost exceeded its approval limit. Or it might ask for a rate increase. As a general rule, when a lessor internally approves a lease deal, its finance committee caps the allowable investment not to exceed typically an additional 5% to 10% of the proposed purchase price. In this example, and if the investment excess amount was capped at 10%, the lessor's finance committee would have approved a maximum financing of $110,000 [$100,000 + (10% X $100,000)].

Here's a better approach for a lessee:

Sample Provision: Underwritten Proposal Equipment Cost

Equipment Cost:

For the purposes of this proposal, a total cost of $12 million, ±5%, has been assumed.

As you can see, a firm equipment cost, with leeway for increases and decreases, has been specified.

A word of caution: If you want the lessor to pay for equipment-related costs, such as transportation and installation charges, make sure that the "Equipment Cost" provision incorporates these additional charges.

Sample Provision: Additional Equipment-Related Charges

Equipment Cost:

For the purposes of this proposal, a total cost of $12 million, ±5%, has been assumed. Equipment Cost shall be deemed to include the Equipment purchase price as set forth on the vendor's invoice and, if so elected by Lessee, all equipment transportation charges and the cost of installing the equipment on Lessee's site.

What Are the Equipment Delivery and Acceptance Terms?

When equipment is to be delivered and accepted for lease is a key proposal issue. A lessor will generally limit how long it will hold funds available. In some cases, a proposal identifies a delivery date but not a funding cutoff date. This can create confusion and risk for a lessee. For example, a lessor may argue that it's not obligated to provide financing—at least, at the proposed rental rate—if the equipment arrives late. And this is generally fair. A lessor uses the anticipated equipment acceptance date to calculate the rent amount. The later the date, the greater the risk that money-market debt fluctuations will adversely affect the lessor's economic return. To reduce this risk, lessors often use funding cutoff dates—dates beyond which they no longer are obligated to provide the lease financing.

A specific funding cutoff date removes any ambiguity from a lessor's funding commitment. You should insist on having one in every proposal to cover reasonable delivery delays. How far out the commitment will run is a matter of negotiation. Typically, two to three months beyond anticipated delivery is readily acceptable to a leasing company.

Here's what you should avoid:

Sample Provision: Problem Equipment Delivery and Acceptance

Equipment Delivery and Acceptance Date:
September 1, 19XX.

If the lessor has not incorporated a specific a funding cutoff date in a separate section of its proposal, the foregoing provision could limit the lessor's funding obligation up to and including September 1, 19XX.

The following provision is an improvement:

**Sample Provision: Equipment Delivery
and Acceptance Revised**

Equipment Delivery and Acceptance Date:
Delivery of the Equipment is anticipated as of September 1, 19XX; however, it shall be no later than November 1, 19XX.

This approach builds in a cushion for delivery delays, holding the lessor to the outside date of November 1, 19XX.

But here's an even better way to handle this issue:

Sample Provision: Clear Funding Time Commitment

Delivery and Commitment Dates:
Delivery and acceptance of the Equipment for lease is anticipated on or before September 1, 19XX, but in no event shall it be later than November 1, 19XX, at which time the lessor's obligation to purchase and lease Equipment pursuant to the terms and conditions of this proposal shall terminate.

If there is an outside possibility that your equipment delivery will be delayed beyond a cutoff date on which the lessor insists, suggest an extended commitment at a fair rent increase. In this way, if the cutoff date is passed, at least you have financing.

Here's a suggestion:

Sample Provision: Extended Funding Commitment

Delivery and Commitment Dates:

Delivery and acceptance of the Equipment for lease is anticipated on or before September 1, 19XX, but in no event shall it be later than November 1, 19XX, at which time the lessor's obligation to purchase and lease Equipment pursuant to the terms and conditions of this proposal shall terminate—provided, however, Lessor shall purchase and lease the Equipment to Lessee under the terms and conditions contained herein if accepted for lease no later than February 1, 19XX, at a rental rate computed by increasing the Rent's simple interest rate by 0.025% per annum.

There's one more point to consider: Some prospective lessees want the lessor's purchase obligation specifically stated in both the proposal letter and the lease agreement. Although implicit in a leasing company's statement of an offer to lease specified equipment is the obligation to purchase it, nothing forces the leasing company to pay in a timely manner. A late payment may jeopardize a good vendor relationship and create an equipment repossession risk. To handle this concern, some lessees insist on a specific vendor payment obligation.

Sample Provision: Vendor Payment Obligation

Delivery and Payment:

Delivery of the Equipment is anticipated on June 12, 19XX, but in no event shall it be later than August 1, 19XX. Lessor shall pay the Equipment vendor in full for the Equipment no later than two business days following the receipt from Lessee of evidence of Equipment acceptance under the Lease.

As you will note, the clause is similar to the "Delivery and Payment" clause contained in the sample nonunderwritten lease proposal, but it goes a step further—clearly stating when the lessor must pay the equipment vendor *in full* shortly following acceptance. A similar clause should be inserted in the lease agreement.

Here's a proposal provision combination that allowed a leasing company to successfully and unfairly argue a rent increase:

Sample Provisions: Delivery and Equipment Payment

Delivery: Second Calendar Quarter.

Equipment Payment: Third Calendar Quarter.

In this particular case, the equipment didn't arrive until the third calendar quarter, when it was promptly accepted for lease. The lessor took the position that its lease rate was based on delivery and start of the lease in the second calendar quarter and that, since delivery was in the third quarter, it lost certain anticipated (and undisclosed) benefits. Therefore, the rent had to be adjusted upward "slightly" to compensate for the loss. The lessee was inexperienced and accepted what in fact was a fallacious statement. Strictly speaking, the proposal was conditioned on a second-quarter delivery. The fact that there was no real economic loss may have been irrelevant: The lessee had not complied with the conditions of the proposal. The problem could have been avoided if the delivery provision had simply been deleted and the phrase *Acceptance and* had been inserted in between *Equipment* and *Payment*.

Ambiguous delivery and funding provisions don't always work against the lessee. Here's one that got a lessor in trouble:

Sample Provision: A Lessor Delivery and Funding Mistake

Delivery/Commitment Termination:

Delivery under the lease will be completed prior to July 1, 19XX, and if such delivery is not completed, Lessor's commitment will terminate.

In this case, the lessor had priced its lease rent based on the equipment's going on lease on or before July 1, 19XX. A common mistake is to assume that equipment will be accepted on the date it's delivered. As it turned out, the equipment met the delivery requirement but, because of operational problems, was not accepted by the lessee until October 2. The lessor argued for an increase in rent as a result of the delay. The lessee argued successfully that the proposal language merely required delivery, and not acceptance, on or before July 1. The lessor should have used the phrase *acceptance for lease* instead of the word *delivery*.

**Sample Provision: Correcting the Lessor's
Delivery and Funding Mistake**

Acceptance/CommitmentTermination:

Equipment acceptance under the lease will be completed prior to July 1, 19XX, and if the Equipment is not accepted for lease on or before such date, Lessor's commitment will terminate.

What Is the Period of Use?

Clearly, the proposal letter must specify the equipment's term of use. It's not unusual for there to be two lease terms: an interim term and a primary term. The interim term covers the period of time from when the equipment is accepted for lease up to the start of the primary, or main, term. Interim periods are commonly used when many items of equipment are involved and deliveries are scattered over many months. By consolidating the start of the primary lease terms to, for example, calendar quarters, the rent payment and processing mechanics are simplified. An interim term may, however, be imposed even if only one item of equipment is involved, to increase the lessor's economic return through additional rent income.

Sample Provision: Underwritten Proposal Interim Term

Interim Lease Term:

The Interim Lease Term shall extend from the Delivery Date until the Commencement Date. For purposes of this proposal, the Commencement Date is assumed to be December 1, 19XX.

This is straightforward. It's anticipated that the equipment will be delivered and accepted for lease before December 1, and if so, there will be an interim term, or stub period, running from the acceptance date up to December 1, the start of the primary term.

Although the existence of an interim term doesn't necessarily mean that an interim rent will be payable, typically they go hand in hand. Interim rent is discussed in the following subsection. It's helpful to keep in mind that if you need to use an interim term approach to consolidate rent payment dates administratively, a lessor may be willing to provide it without imposing an interim rent.

Example: The Interim Technique for Rent Consolidation

Company B wants to lease 120 trucks from Company A. The trucks will be delivered over a 12-month period at a rate of 10 trucks a month. Company B wants to pay rent quarterly, in arrears. Company A proposes this solution:

1. There shall be four primary lease terms, starting as follows:
   a. First primary term: April 1, 19XX
   b. Second primary term: July 1, 19XX
   c. Third primary term: October 1, 19XX
   d. Fourth primary term: January 1, 19XX

2. All trucks delivered and accepted for lease in the calendar quarter preceding the nearest primary term start date shall be on interim lease until the start date, at which time the primary term shall begin for such trucks.

Without the interim arrangement, Company A could end up with as many as 120 different primary lease term start dates and, thus, 120 different rental payment dates.

Whether there is an interim term or not, the proposal must spell out the equipment's primary period of use requested by the prospective lessee.

**Sample Provision: Underwritten Proposal
Primary Lease Term**

Primary Lease Term:
The Primary Lease Term shall be 10 years from the Commencement Date.

In our situation, December 1 is designated as the commencement date, the arbitrary date on which the primary term begins. When there is no interim term, the primary term begins on the date the equipment is accepted for lease.

What Rent Payments Are Proposed?

One of the most important proposal points to cover is the lease rent: how much is due and when it is to be paid. And to avoid lease amendments in the event of cost changes, as discussed in Chapter 5, the rent should be expressed as a percentage of equipment cost rather than as a fixed dollar amount.

Sample Provision: Nonunderwritten Rent Provision

Rental Program:

Union shall remit 32 consecutive, level, quarterly, in advance payments, each equal to 4.4000% of Equipment Cost.

This provision is straightforward and incorporates the rent-as-a-percentage-of equipment-cost concept. It does not, however, specify the lease simple interest rate, something that, although not critical, can save you time in your proposal review.

Here's how I like to see rent quoted. In the following provision, lease term and rent are incorporated into the same paragraph.

Sample Provision: Simple Interest Rate Quoted

Lease Rent and Term:

Primary Lease Term: 5 years.

Primary Lease Rent: Sixty (60) consecutive, monthly, in advance payments, each equal to 2.041% of Equipment Cost.

Annual Simple Interest: 8.581%.

Watch out for the following approach:

Sample Provision: Ambiguous Rents

Lease Rent:

If the equipment is purchased during the fourth quarter of 19XX, the monthly lease rate factor (monthly rent = lease rate factor X Equipment Cost) for a three-year lease is 3.12211%.

What's missing? The lessor failed to indicate whether the rent was payable in advance or in arrears and, in addition, did not state the lease simple interest rate. This was intentional. In this situation, the lessee assumed that the rent was payable monthly in arrears, providing a lower lease financing cost than if it had been in advance. If the lessor had stated the lease simple interest rate, the lessee would have been able to determine that it had made an incorrect assumption. The difference between an advance and an arrears payment would be as follows:

	Annual in Arrears	**Annual in Advance**
	Simple Interest	Simple Interest
3 years:	7.749%	8.213%
Difference in annual simple interest lease rate = 0.464%.		

Unfortunately, the lessee learned about the incorrect assumption when the lease agreement arrived, too late to shop for another financing offer.

Watch for Interim Rent Traps

In reviewing your rent provision, watch out for any interim rent traps. As explained earlier, interim rent can add to the effective cost of your lease financing and must be factored into your cost analysis. In our sample underwritten proposal, it's easy to spot. Sometimes, it's not so clearly identified.

Sample Provision: Underwritten Proposal Interim Rent

Interim Rent:

The Lessee shall pay Interim Rent equal to interest-only on the total cost of the Equipment at an interest rate equal to the Long-Term Debt Interest Rate.

Rental Adjustments Can Be Trouble

You can see from our sample underwritten proposal ("Debt Financing" section) that the leveraged lease rent is based, in part, on the interest rate on funds borrowed to pay a portion of the equipment purchase price. Leveraged lease proposals, therefore, typically contain a rent adjustment provision that permits a lessor to adjust rents if the debt rate assumed in calculating the lease rents changes.

Example: The Need for a Rent Adjustment Clause

Company B proposes to lease to Company A a $1 million material-handling system. The transaction will be leveraged with 80% debt at an assumed interest rate of 6% per annum. The terms are as follows:

Lease term   10 years
Loan term   10 years
Annual rent $120,000
Annual debt service (level in arrears)
($8,000 at 6%) $108,700

The annual rent will cover the annual debt service by $11,300 ($120,000 – $108,700). Assume that, when Company B goes into the debt market, the best available annual interest rate is 10%. The annual debt service, assuming level payments, will be approximately $130,200. In this case, not only will the increased debt service expense erode the lessor's return, but the lessor will have to invest an additional $10,200 a year ($130,200 – $120,000) to make up for the shortfall.

The rental adjustment clause, enabling the lessor to be protected against an increased interest rate, is typically incorporated in the "Debt Financing" section of a leveraged lease proposal. The following rent adjustment provision is from our sample underwritten proposal:

**Sample Provision: Underwritten
Proposal Rent Adjustment**

Debt Financing:

An investment banker acceptable to NLC and the Lessee shall arrange for the private placement of secured notes or similar instruments (Indebtedness) to be issued by the Lessor for a principal amount equal to 80% of total Equipment Cost to certain institutional investors (Lenders), which may be represented by an indenture trustee or agent bank (Agent). This proposal assumes that the Indebtedness shall be amortized in semiannual payments of principal and interest at an 8% per annum interest rate (Long-Term Debt Interest Rate), payable in arrears over the term of the Lease. In the event that the Long-Term Debt Interest Rate varies from that assumed, the rent shall be adjusted upward or downward, so that the Owner Participant's after-tax yield and after-tax cash flow will be maintained. The Indebtedness shall be secured by an assignment of the Lease and a security interest in the Equipment but otherwise shall be without recourse to the Owner Participant and the Lessor.

The preceding adjustment provision is fair, not only allowing the lessor to protect its return by adjustment upward if the actual debt interest rate is higher than assumed, but also requiring downward rent adjustment if the debt comes in lower than assumed.

A word of caution about the rental adjustments: A prospective lessee should be able to verify independently that any permitted or required rental adjustment has been fairly made. This may require expert help. Some adjustment provisions, for example, provide that the lessor can adjust rents so that its "economic return" is maintained. These are dangerous for a lessee because *economic return* has many meanings, and a lessor could choose any one that provides the most profit. For example, under a general economic return standard, the lessor could adjust rents so its pretax or after-tax yield, pretax or after-tax cash flow, or any other of a number of economic return criteria, or combinations thereof, are maintained. And if the lessee doesn't know the actual criteria, it has no way of verifying whether the adjustment was made fairly. Matters can be even more complicated. A lessor often refuses to disclose certain internal investment criteria necessary to make the rent computations, such as overall corporate income tax rate, claiming—and in many cases, rightly so—that the information is confidential. One solution is get the lessor to agree to give all necessary information to an independent analysis company, such as an accounting firm, which would be called in, if necessary, to verify the adjustment without disclosing the assumptions.

Is Too Much Credit Support Required?

The financial backing behind a lease obligation is often critical to the lessor's willingness to offer lease financing, at times requiring a lessee to provide substantial additional credit support—and in some cases, more than necessary. So it's important that you carefully review—and if necessary, negotiate a reduction of—any such support required.

A lessor may, for example, ask for a full and unconditional guarantee of all lease obligations from a creditworthy entity, such as a parent company or bank. Or it may request support from the equipment supplier, such as a deficiency guarantee that would require the supplier to pay the lessor for any loss if a lease default occurs. Or if available, it may ask for an assignment of a "take or pay" contract between the lessee and one of its customers. In small-business lease transactions, the owner's personal guarantee is often required.

Sample Provision: Credit Support

Guarantee:

All Lessee's lease obligations shall be unconditionally guaranteed by Lessee's parent company, Union Carbon, Inc.

All too often, prospective lessees, particularly those with a financial skeleton in the closet, are mistakenly reluctant to negotiate a reduction or an elimination of the support requested. Those that are willing to ask typically find that a lessor may be receptive to something less, particularly when the lessor knows that it has requested more than necessary.

Will the Owner Structure Cause Delays?

In proposing an underwritten lease transaction, the underwriter may provide that one of a number of different alternative entities will own the equipment—such as a trust, partnership, or special-purpose corporation—depending on the tax, ownership, or liability issues. And at times, in certain nonunderwritten transactions in which, for example, the lessor intends to bring in an investment partner or establish a special-purpose corporation to limit potential liability, an alternative owning structure may be stated. In either event, you will want to consider carefully the timing and mechanical implications of working with an underwriter or a lessor that proposes a complex ownership structure. As a rule of thumb, the more complex the lease transaction elements, the longer it will take to put the financing in place, and the greater the risk of a deal-breaking disagreement among the parties involved.

Some structures can cause problems after the deal is closed. For example, if equipment ownership is not centralized in a multiple-investor situation, the lessee may have to deal individually with each investor throughout the lease if, for instance, consents are necessary to lease agreement variations. The solution is to require that there be a single representative with authority to handle all lessee-related issues. The representative chosen, however, may add to the problem if it's someone who is not familiar with the needs of a lessee. Once again, that should be addressed and incorporated into the lessor's proposal before the award is made.

**Sample Provision: Underwritten
Proposal Ownership Structure**

Lessor:

The Lessor will be a commercial bank or trust company acting as owner trustee (Owner Trustee) pursuant to one or more owners' trusts (Trust) for the benefit of one or more commercial banks or other corporate investors (Owner Participant). The Trust shall acquire the Equipment and lease it to the Lessee.

As you can see, the owner structure can be complex.

What Is the Debt Arrangement?

If a leveraged lease is proposed, the debt arrangement terms and mechanics should be clearly outlined in the proposal letter. Points that you must consider are:

- Who will find the debt
- Who will pay the debt placement fee
- The debt repayment schedule
- The assumed per annum interest charge
- The assumed principal amount as a percentage of equipment cost
- The form of lender representative
- Whether the debt will be recourse or nonrecourse to the lessor

The debt provision found in our sample underwritten proposal was examined from a rent adjustment point of view. Now let's look at it from a debt arrangement perspective.

**Sample Provision: Underwritten
Proposal Debt Assumptions**

Debt Financing:

An investment banker acceptable to NLC and the Lessee shall arrange for the private placement of secured notes or similar instruments (Indebtedness) to be issued by the Lessor for a principal amount equal to 80% of total Equipment Cost to certain institutional investors (Lenders), which may be represented by an indenture trustee or agent bank (Agent). This proposal assumes that the Indebtedness shall be amortized in semiannual payments of principal and interest at an 8% per annum interest rate (Long-Term Debt Interest Rate), payable in arrears over the term of the Lease. In the event that the Long-Term Debt Interest Rate varies from that assumed, the rent shall be adjusted upward or downward, so that the Owner Participant's after-tax yield and after-tax cash flow will be maintained. The Indebtedness shall be secured by an assignment of the Lease and a security interest in the Equipment but otherwise shall be without recourse to the Owner Participant and the Lessor.

This provision, although appearing to address all lessee issues fairly and comprehensively, can still be improved in the following areas:

- *Investment banker:* The choice of investment banker should be solely up to you. The amount of rent payable is directly tied to the debt interest rate: The higher the interest rate, the higher the rent charge; and the lower the rate, the less expensive the lease financing. And the lessor never loses if the provision contains a rent adjustment clause, as our example does. So in this case, the lessor has no financial incentive to get the lowest possible debt interest rate. Its profit is the same regardless of interest cost, and since its primary motivation is closing the lease financing as soon as possible—as opposed, for example, to holding out for the best possible debt interest rate—you may pay more than you have to.
- *Debt structure:* In our sample provision, the lessor states that the debt principal amount is assumed to be 80% of equipment cost. Since the rent adjustment clause provides for adjustment only if the interest rate varies from that assumed in the proposal, 8%, the lessor has no obligation or incentive to accept, say, a 6% interest rate offer from a lender that won't provide the full 80%. Although difficult to negotiate since the lower the debt principal, the higher the required equity investment, it may be worthwhile seeing whether the lessor would agree to some debt leeway, in which a lower-interest debt offer of, say, 75% of equipment cost may be acceptable.
- *Nonrecourse borrowing amount:* The tax rules limit the amount of nonrecourse debt to 80% of equipment cost for the transaction to qualify as a true lease for income tax purposes. In our situation the lessor intends to comply strictly. There is room for variation, even under the existing tax rules—but doing so may be a risk the lessor is unwilling to take.

A suggested provision revision is as follows, *with the revised wording in italics:*

Sample Provision: Underwritten Proposal Debt Assumptions Revised

Debt Financing:

An investment banker acceptable to the Lessee shall arrange for the private placement of secured notes or similar instruments (Indebtedness) to be issued by the Lessor for a principal amount equal to 80% of total Equipment Cost to certain institutional investors (Lenders), which may be represented by an indenture trustee or agent bank (Agent). This proposal assumes that the Indebtedness shall be amortized in semiannual payments of principal and interest at an 8% per annum interest rate (Long-

---

Term Debt Interest Rate), payable in arrears over the term of the Lease. *In the event that the Long-Term Debt* varies from that assumed, the rent shall be adjusted upward or downward, so that the Owner Participant's after-tax yield and after-tax cash flow will be maintained. The Indebtedness shall be secured by an assignment of the Lease and a security interest in the Equipment but otherwise shall be without recourse to the Owner Participant and the Lessor.*

*Here, there is no minimum limit on the debt amount. If a lessor won't agree, try to negotiate a reasonable leeway, such as a minimum of 75% of equipment cost.

Two final comments and one tip about the preceding debt provision: You might want to consider having the right to exclude potential lenders and incorporate the exclusion into the provision. Some potential lenders are notoriously difficult to deal with and should be brought in only as a last resort. In addition, it may not be advisable to have any of your company "line" banks involved, because doing so may create future borrowing restrictions if, for example, your borrowing has hit the banking regulatory limits. Finally, if a debt placement fee has been assumed in pricing the rent, and the lessor or underwriter does not have to pay one because, for example, an investment banker wasn't hired to locate the third-party debt, consider requiring the underwriter to pass that saving on to you, as lessee.

At times, a lessor will set up a debt situation that provides room to manipulate the financing offered. I received the letter on page 188 some years ago that attempted just that. Once again, names have been changed to ensure anonymity.

The proposals accompanying the cover letter didn't incorporate the fact that the rents were subject to adjustment if interest rates changed. So if the cover letter got separated from the proposals, a reader could be misled. The other problem with this particular offer was that, since no interest rate was stated, there was no way of pinning down what "money-market rate" was used in calculating the rent.

Will the Equipment Location Cause Problems?

Where leased equipment will be located should be agreed to by the lessor in the proposal letter. Generally, this issue is of little concern, as long as the equipment is in a place where the laws permit the lessor to claim anticipated tax benefits and make notice filings protecting its property in-

Sample Proposal Cover Letter: Debt Rate Problem

Thunderbolt Leasing Company
2222 Cream Street
New York, New York 10024

November 2, 19XX

RE: Union Shipping Corp.
Mr. R. M. Contino
Contino & Partners
White Plains, New York 16604

Dear Mr. Contino:

We are enclosing the tentative lease proposals covering the lease of an IBM 6700 series computer.

We offer both true lease and finance lease programs, depending on your requirements. All quotations are based on today's money-market rates.

We appreciate the opportunity to present to your client a leasing program and will look forward to discussing this transaction with you at a later date in more detail.

Yours truly,

Bob Friend
Vice President

Enclosures

---

terest, and permit easy repossession if a default occurs. This may exclude use of the equipment outside the laws of the United States. It's particularly important, therefore, if you intend to use, or possibly relocate, the equipment outside the United States to have agreement from the lessor in the proposal. If there will be problems, you don't want to wait until you get the lease agreement to find that out.

A little-recognized fact about equipment locations is that certain locations may enhance a lender's or lease investor's interest in the transaction. For example, if the equipment is to be used in Florida by a division of a California corporation, Florida regional banks may have a high interest in the transaction because of the possibility of doing business with a company to which they normally would not have access.

In our example proposal letters, this location issue has not been addressed. Here's a suggested addition:

Sample Provision: Equipment Location

Equipment Location:
The Equipment shall be located at Lessee's main plant, 222 South Bleaker Street, Buffalo, New York. In the event Lessee desires to relocate the Equipment, it may do so anywhere in the United States, provided Lessor is given 60 days' prior written notice.

The foregoing provides a lessee with flexibility and the lessor with adequate notice in the event that security interest filings are advisable. Although not in this provision, it's not unusual for the lessor to require the lessee to obtain its prior written consent before a relocation. Avoid this if possible. Trying to get a written consent can delay your relocation, and as long as the move is restricted to within the United States, a lessor simply doesn't need that right.

What About the Cost of Equipment Insurance?

Standard in every lease agreement is a requirement that the lessee purchase and maintain during the lease term property damage and liability insurance. At times, the amount required may be excessive, or it may be more cost-effective to self-insure. If either is a concern, the proposal should incorporate what you want.

In our sample proposal letters, insurance is alluded to in the "Fixed Expenses" section, but the terms are not specifically addressed.

**Sample Provision: Nonunderwritten
Proposal Fixed Expenses**

Fixed Expenses:
This is a net financial lease proposal, and all fixed expenses—such as insurance, maintenance, and personal property taxes—shall be for the account of Union.

If you want the right to self-insure, here's a suggested provision to include:

Sample Provision: Right to Self-Insure

Insurance:
The Lessee may self-insure the Equipment.

Have You Got All Necessary Lease Options?

A long-term equipment lease is a major financial commitment, and it's advisable to negotiate maximum contractual flexibility to meet the needs of inevitable business changes. Lessee options can assure that flexibility. For example, say your company has been pursuing for the past two years a corporate expansion program, buying attractive financial service companies. To make travel more cost-effective, last year it entered into a ten-year net finance lease of a corporate jet, at an annual rent of $675,000. Because of a recent economic downturn, your board of directors put the expansion program on hold and asked that you get out of the aircraft lease to cut costs.

You examine the lease and find there is no sublease right or early termination option. Is there anything you can do without obtaining the lessor's agreement? Unfortunately, there is nothing. A typical finance lease contains an unconditional obligation to pay rent for the entire term and no right to cancel or sublease. Approaching the lessor with a request to cancel, particularly in slow economic times, will undoubtedly meet with a resounding "No."

The moral of the story is that, in entering into any lease transaction, it's always best to ask for every conceivable option, even though you don't think they'll be necessary. Options cost nothing to have.

Let's take a look at the options available in our sample proposal letters:

**Sample Provision: Nonunderwritten
Proposal Letter Options**

Options:

At the conclusion of the Lease Term, Union may (with at least 120 days' prior written notice):

   a. Buy the Equipment for an amount equal to its then fair market value.

   b. Renew the Lease with respect to the Equipment for its then fair rental value.

Only two options are offered: a right to purchase and a right to renew. There are other possible lessee options: sublease, early termination, right of first refusal, and upgrade financing options, as well as fixed-price purchase and renewal rights. Although you could wait until your lease arrives to negotiate their inclusion, it's better to have the lessor commit to them before you make your lease award, when your negotiating leverage is the highest.

There is an additional option problem in our sample nonunderwritten proposal. The rights, as they stand, are not clearly defined. For example, there is no standard for determining *fair market value* or *fair rental value*, terms that are subject to individual interpretation. And since more than one item of equipment is involved (four new forklift trucks), there is no way of determining whether the lessee may exercise its right to purchase or renew on an item-by-item basis.

Here are some suggested improvements:

**Sample Provision: Item-by-Item
Purchase/Renewal Option Exercise Right**

Options:

At the conclusion of the Lease Term, Union may (with at least 120 days' prior written notice):

   a. Buy one or more items of Equipment for an amount equal to the Equipment's then fair market value.

   b. Renew the Lease with respect to one or more items of Equipment for the Equipment's then fair rental value.

Lessors often provide that these rights are on an all-or-none basis. As with most lessor positions, this is negotiable. Here's an example of a typical lessor approach:

**Sample Provision: Common Lessor
Purchase Option Exercise Approach**

Purchase Option:

At the expiration of the Primary Lease Term, or any renewal thereof, Lessee shall have the right to purchase all, but not less than all, the Equipment for its then fair market value.

Under this type of provision, if a lessee needs less than all the equipment, the lessor is in a strong negotiating position to get more than fair market value.

In the case of renewal options, some lessors try the following:

Sample Provision: Limited Renewal Term Flexibility

Renewal Option:

At the expiration of the Primary Lease Term, or any renewal thereof, Lessee shall have the option of renewing the Lease with respect to all, but not less than all, of the Equipment on a year-to-year basis at the then fair market rental value—provided, however, that Lessee shall renew the lease for no less than two years.

The foregoing renewal option is not only on an all-or-none basis, but it locks the lessee into a minimum of two years, giving little lease renewal flexibility.

What about our sample underwritten proposal? Well, the purchase and renewal rights are a little more defined, but there are still problems, as you'll see.

**Sample Provision: Underwritten
Proposal Options**

Purchase and Renewal Options:

At the end of the Primary Term, the Lessee may (with 180 days' written notice prior to the end of the term):

    a. Renew the Lease on the Equipment for its then fair market rental value for one two-year period.

    b. Buy the Equipment for an equivalent price and under similar conditions as rendered by a third party approached by the Lessor and agreed to by the Lessor prior to the sale to that third party.

If the Lessee does not elect to exercise any of the above options, the Lessee shall return the Equipment to the Lessor at the end of the term at a mutually agreeable location.

The options included are fair market purchase and renewal rights. Let's take a look at each option.

The Purchase Option

The purchase option has a problem. At first glance, it may appear to be a fair market value option, but on closer examination, you can see that it's a right of first refusal, the lessee having the right to buy the equipment under the same terms as offered by a third party. Does the lessee have a right to buy if the lessor is not "approached" by a third party? What if the third party is someone who is doing the lessor a favor, offering an above-market price? Is the lessor obligated to make an effort to get offers? There are no simple answers to these questions.

Here's a change to the preceding subsection b that makes it more favorable:

Sample Provision: Suggested Purchase Option Revision

    b. Buy the Equipment for an equivalent price and under similar conditions as rendered by a third party approached

> by the Lessor and agreed to by the Lessor prior to the sale to that third party. *The Lessee shall act as Lessor's agent, without commission, to obtain sale or lease bids from creditworthy third parties.*

Another suggestion is to use the approach suggested in subsection A of the nonunderwritten proposal, making it a fair market value purchase right.

Sample Provision: Additional Suggested Purchase Option Revised

Purchase and Renewal Options:

At the end of the Primary Term, the Lessee may (with 180 days' written notice prior to the end of the term):

    a. [Omitted intentionally]

    b. Buy the Equipment for an amount equal to its then fair market value. *"Fair market value" shall be defined to be the average of two equipment appraisals, one submitted by American Appraisal Company and one submitted by SeQan Equipment Appraisers. If either appraisal company is no longer in business when the option is exercised or is otherwise unable to provide an appraisal, then either Lessor or Lessee may elect to have appraisals submitted by two industry-recognized equipment appraisers, one chosen by Lessor and one chosen by Lessee.*

In this revision, a mechanism for determining fair market value has been prescribed. Nothing is left to chance.

The Renewal Option

The renewal option in both the underwritten proposal and the nonunderwritten proposal can be improved. In the case of the nonunderwritten proposal, an approach similar to the purchase options can be taken.

Sample Provision: Nonunderwritten Proposal Renewal Option Revised

Options:

At the conclusion of the Lease Term, Union may (with at least 120 days' prior written notice):

a. [Omitted intentionally]
b. Renew the Lease with respect to the Equipment for its then fair rental value. *"Fair rental value" shall be defined to be the average of two equipment rental appraisals, each for a two-year renewal period, one submitted by American Appraisal Company and one submitted by SeQan Equipment Appraisers. If either appraisal company is no longer in business when the option is exercised or is otherwise unable to provide an appraisal, then either Lessor or Lessee may elect to have appraisals submitted by two industry-recognized equipment appraisers, one chosen by Lessor and one chosen by Lessee.*

A similar change could be made to the renewal option in subsection A of the underwritten proposal.

A Traditional Right of First Refusal. At times, a lessor doesn't want to be obligated to sell the equipment at lease end but is willing to grant a right of first refusal—giving the lessee the opportunity to buy the equipment on the same terms and conditions offered by a third party.

Sample Provision: Right of First Refusal

Right of First Refusal:

At the end of the Primary Lease Term, Lessee shall have the Right of First Refusal to purchase the Equipment for a price and under the terms offered to Lessor by any unrelated third party as to any sale or re-lease of the Equipment.

A right of first refusal has limitations for a lessee because it can't force a sale of the equipment. However, in considering whether to go along with a first-refusal right, keep in mind that there may be an inherent lessee price advantage should the lessor elect to sell. Third parties interested in purchasing, once they learn of the first-refusal right, are often unwilling to stretch for the equipment because the lessee can come in and take advantage of a good deal. Its existence, therefore, often lowers the price someone is willing to offer.

The Termination Option

A termination option, although generally costly to exercise, can be invaluable in enabling you to get out of a lease commitment. Lessors are sometimes reluctant to grant such a right because it limits potential earnings but if pressed will grant it, often with a substantial exercise premium built in.

The sample nonunderwritten proposal does not contain a termination option. The sample underwritten proposal, however, does contain a typical termination option, which—except for three issues, one minor and two major—is reasonable for a lessee.

Sample Provision: Underwritten Proposal Termination Option

Termination Option:

At any time during the Primary Lease Term, on or after 2 years from the Commencement Date, the Lessee may (with 180 days' prior written notice) terminate the Lease in the event the Equipment becomes obsolete or surplus to its needs, upon paying a mutually agreed on termination value.

The option can be exercised if the equipment is deemed to be obsolete or surplus to the lessee's needs. It does not, however, specify that this determination is solely up to the lessee. In addition, the actual termination penalty payment, the termination value, has been left open to mutual agreement.

The following revision would correct these issues:

Sample Provision: Termination Option Revised

Termination Option:

At any time during the Primary Lease Term, on or after 2 years from the Commencement Date, the Lessee may (with 180 days' prior written notice) terminate the Lease in the event the Equipment becomes obsolete or surplus to its needs, *as determined by Lessee within its sole discretion, upon paying the appropriate termination value as specified on Schedule A to this proposal.*

Schedule A should set forth the amount that would have to be paid by the lessee and should include the mechanics of exercise. Keep in mind that termination values can be arbitrarily set and, before the award is made, should be compared against what other lessors offer, possibly reviewed by a leasing expert, and if necessary, negotiated downward.

In addition, the mechanics by which the termination option will be exercised should be incorporated into the proposal.

Sample Provision: Termination Option Exercise Mechanics

On or after the second year of the Primary Term and only at the expiration of each Primary Term year thereafter, Lessee shall have the right, at its option, to terminate the Lease. The Lessee will be required to give Lessor 180 days' prior written notice of its intention to terminate and, during the period from giving notice until the termination date, shall use its best efforts to obtain bids from unaffiliated third parties for the equipment's purchase. On the termination date, Lessee shall sell the Equipment as Lessor's agent for the highest bid received. The total proceeds shall be retained by Lessor, net of any disposition expenses, and Lessee shall pay Lessor the difference, if any, by which the sale proceeds are less than the appropriate termination value indicated on Schedule A attached hereto.

An Option That Can Create Problems: A Put

In some situations, lessors include the right to require a lessee to purchase the equipment at the lease's end, commonly referred to as a "put." If the equipment is not needed, a forced purchase may be unwelcome. However, it may not be all bad. Typically, the put amount is low, enabling the lessee to acquire the equipment at a favorable price, and if it isn't needed, it can be sold without loss to a third party. In addition, the existence of a put can lower the lease term rent payments. But be careful. The existence of a put option can jeopardize the lease's income tax treatment, and tax counsel should be consulted before you agree to its inclusion.

Sample Provision: Put Option

Lessor's Right to Sell:

Lessor may require Lessee, upon 30 days' prior written notice, to purchase any or all of the Equipment for an amount equal to 10% of its purchase cost, in which case Lessee shall pay as additional rent to Lessor on the final day of the Primary Term the appropriate additional rental amount. Upon payment, Lessor shall transfer title to such purchased Equipment, free and clear of all liens and claims.

Here's why a put can lower your dollar rent payments:

Example: The Put Option Rent Benefit

Example Assumptions

- Lease term: 3 years
- Lease per annum simple interest: 8%
- Rent: monthly, in arrears
- Equipment cost: $100,000
- Residual value: $0
- Put: 10% of cost ($10,000)

Rent—Without a Put Option. With no residual value assumed, the lessor will calculate its rent by amortizing $100,000 over three years at an 8% per annum simple interest rate. This results in a monthly rent charge of $3,133.64.

Rent—With a Put Option. In calculating the rent with the put option incorporated, we'll assume, for simplicity of explanation, that the lessor does not need to earn any interest on the put amount payment due at the lease term end. With a put option available, the lessor would amortize only $90,000 over three years at an 8% simple interest rate, resulting in a monthly rent of $2,820.27.

As you can see, the put rent arrangement reduces the monthly rent cash outlay by $313.37, a substantial savings. But there is risk for a lessee. If the lessor elects to exercise the put, the lessee must pay an additional $10,000 at lease end. If the lessor had incorporated the 8% simple interest charge in the put computation, the actual end-of-lease outlay would have been even higher, to cover the interest on the put amount outstanding for three years. And unless the residual value of the equipment exceeds the put payment, you can be sure this right will be exercised. Typically, lessors don't build in puts unless it's highly likely that the equipment will be worthless at lease end.

The Right to Sublease

Having the right to sublease your equipment can increase lease flexibility by enabling you to get someone else to pay the rent on equipment you no longer need. Typically, however, if you're permitted to sublease your equipment, you'll have to remain responsible for the full performance of all original lease obligations during any sublease period. That, however, is a matter of negotiation, and if the sublessee has a solid credit standing, it's possible the lessor may release your company from any continuing lease responsibility.

Here's a suggested provision:

Sample Provision: Right to Sublease

Right to Sublease:

Lessee shall have the right to sublease any or all of the Equipment for a period not to exceed the remaining Lease Term, provided, however, any such sublease shall not release the Lessee from any of the Lease obligations.

What Type of Lease Is Offered?

As discussed in Chapter 1, there are a variety of different lease types, each involving different responsibilities for the lessee and the lessor. Of prime concern for a lessee in considering the lease type offered is the equipment-related expense responsibilities, because they must be taken into account in determining the overall financing costs. For example, many equipment lease transactions involve net finance lease arrangements, under which the lessee must pay all fixed expenses related to the equipment during the lease term, such as maintenance, insurance, and certain taxes.

Here's a typical net finance lease proposal provision:

**Sample Provision: Nonunderwritten
Proposal Expense Responsibility**

Fixed Expenses:

This is a net financial lease proposal with all fixed expenses—such as maintenance, insurance, and taxes (other than net income taxes)—for the account of the Lessee.

This provision means, for example, that the Lessee must directly pay for any equipment sales tax. A lessor may be willing to include it as part of the equipment purchase cost, and if so, a proposal modification is necessary. And it's typically incorporated into the cost provision, as you'll see.

**Sample Provision: Underwritten
Proposal Expense Responsibility**

Cost:

For the purposes of this proposal, a total cost of $12 million, ±5%, has been assumed. For the purposes of this proposal, Cost shall include all equipment sales taxes, transportation, and installation charges.

In our sample provision, the lessor will pay not only the equipment purchase cost but also sales tax, delivery, and installation charges. These charges will be incorporated into the equipment's cost, and the rent will be determined by multiplying the rent factor (in the case of our example underwritten proposal, that would be 4.4000%) times the aggregate lessor investment. For example, if there was a 7% sales tax, a $2,000 delivery charge, and a $10,000 installation charge, the rent payable on a $100,000 item of equipment would be $5,236 ($100,000 + $7,000 + $2,000 + $10,000 = $119,000 x 4.4000% = $5,236).

How Have Transaction Expenses Been Allocated?

Transaction closing expenses can significantly increase a lessee's financing cost and reduce a lessor's profits. It's important, therefore, for a lessee to understand what its transaction expense obligation will be before making the lease award and have it specified in the proposal. In nonleveraged lease transactions, the primary expense is legal fees, and the party incurring the expense usually pays for it. In underwritten leveraged lease transactions, the matter is not as simple: The financing can involve many participants—including equity investors, lenders, an underwriter, and sometimes, trustees—all represented by counsel. And in addition, there can be a variety of other closing expenses, such as:

- Fees and disbursements of counsel for the lenders and their representative
- Acceptance and annual fees of the lender's representative—usually found in a trust arrangement
- Special counsel fees and disbursements for the equity participants and their representative
- Acceptance and annual fees of the equity participant's representative—usually found in a trust arrangement
- Fees and disbursements related to the filing for a private IRS letter ruling
- Documentation expenses, such as reproduction and printing charges
- Fees related to the placement of any third-party debt

If you don't carefully review and agree upon the expense responsibilities before an award, you can be in for an expensive surprise. It's not unusual, for example, for lawyers' fees in a multimillion-dollar leveraged lease financing to be in the $200,000–$500,000 range.

To get a better idea of what to look for, let's examine our sample proposals. The nonleveraged lease proposal says nothing about transaction expenses. It's generally understood that everyone pays their own expenses, basically a lawyer's fee for documenting the lease, but it would be advisable to specify this in the proposal.

Here's one way to do it:

Sample Provision: General Expense Responsibility Allocation

Transaction Expenses:

Each party shall be responsible for its own expenses, including legal fees, documentation cost, and other transaction-related fees and disbursements.

On the other hand, the underwritten leveraged lease proposal addresses transaction expense responsibility in detail.

Sample Provision: Underwritten Proposal Itemized Expense Responsibility Allocation

Expenses of Transaction:

NLC shall pay all transaction expenses, including:

1. Fees and disbursements of special counsel for the Agent and the Lenders
2. Acceptance and annual fees and expenses of the Agent
3. Fees and disbursements of special counsel for the Owner Trustee and the Trustor
4. Acceptance and annual fees and expenses of the Owner Trustee
5. Fees and disbursements in connection with obtaining a ruling from the Internal Revenue Service
6. Expenses of documentation, including printing and reproduction
7. Fees and disbursements in connection with the private placement of the Indebtedness

If the transaction is not consummated for any reason, the Lessee shall pay all of the above fees and expenses.

As you can see, in this case, the underwriter has offered to pay what in fact will be all transaction closing expenses, except for the lessee's legal cost. In an effort to ensure its profit, however, it's not unusual for an underwriter to "cap" these expenses by offering to pay only up to a specified percentage, typically anywhere from .75% to 2.25% of the equipment cost, imposing on the lessee the obligation to pay any excess. Since an underwriter profits by charging the lessor-investors a set fee for bringing them the transaction, the more it can limit its expense responsibility, the less chance closing expenses will erode its profit. In a competitive market, many underwriters are willing, particularly if pushed a little, to assume the entire expense responsibility without a cap.

Example: The Underwriter's Expense Problem

Company A, an underwriter, arranged for Company C and Company D to participate as the equity investors in the leveraged lease financing of one oceangoing tugboat to be leased to Company B. Companies C and D agreed to pay Company A a brokerage fee equal to 2% of the equipment cost for bringing in the transaction. As a condition of the transaction award, Company A had to commit to Company B that Company B would not have to pay any expenses, except its own counsel fees. At the closing, the following costs had been incurred:

Tugboat cost	$6,000,000
Fees for the lender's counsel	20,000
Counsel fees for Companies C and D	50,000
Counsel fees for Company A	2,000
Counsel fees for Company B	35,000
Printing expenses	21,000

What does Company A's profit picture look like?

Company A's "gross" transaction fee is $120,000 (2% x $6 million). All fees and expenses, excluding Company B's counsel fees, total $93,000 ($20,000 + $50,000 + $2,000 + $ 21,000). Therefore, Company A "nets" $27,000 ($120,000 – $93,000). If Company A had a 1% cap, its expense liability would have been limited to $60,000 (1% x $6 million), and it would have made $60,000 ($120,000 – $60,000) instead of $27,000.

An offer by an underwriter to pay all transaction expenses, however, is often not as good as it appears. In calculating the rent offer, it will not only build in room for its underwriting fee but also add a cushion to take care of any transaction expenses it may have to pay. And if possible, it will build in far more than necessary to ensure that its profit is not eroded, leaving it with a very nice profit if expenses are lower than expected. What does this have to do with you as lessee? A lot. As just mentioned, the lessor-investors pay the underwriting fee, and in order for the investor to meet its profit expectation, the rent is increased to cover any transaction expenses, such as the underwriting fee, that must be paid. In effect, therefore, the lessee pays all transaction expenses through the increased rents.

A difficult transaction expense issue, particularly in an underwritten lease situation, is who must pay the expenses if the proposed transaction collapses. Lenders and prospective lessor-investors don't want any responsibility if the financing fails to close, leaving, for instance, only the underwriter and the prospective lessee. Many underwriters attempt to put the failed transaction expense responsibility on the prospective lessee by inserting an appropriate clause in the proposal. Typically, such a clause provides that the prospective lessee must pay all expenses if the transaction is not consummated for any reason whatsoever. This can put a prospective lessee in a dangerous position, particularly if the underwriter's poor performance caused the collapse. The last paragraph of our sample underwritten proposal ("Expenses of Transaction") addresses the collapsed transaction expense responsibility.

Are Any Commitment or Related Fees Required?

At times, lessors impose fees, such as commitment and nonutilization fees, to minimize loss of anticipated profit in the event the lessee fails to lease the agreed-upon equipment or leases less than the anticipated dollar amount committed. As shown in Chapter 2, these fees can be significant and should be carefully considered before you agree to any of them. Our sample nonunderwritten proposal does not incorporate any of these fees. However, our sample underwritten proposal does, providing for both a commitment fee and a nonutilization fee.

**Sample Provisions: Underwritten
Proposal Commitment and Related Fees**

Nonutilization Fee:

Once NLC has obtained equity investor commitments satisfactory to the Lessee, the Lessee shall be liable to NLC for a nonutilization fee equal to 0.5% of the Equipment Cost in the event it does not lease the Equipment in accordance with the intent of this proposal.

Commitment fee:

A commitment fee of 0.5% per annum shall be paid by the Lessee on the outstanding equity investor commitment. The fee shall accrue as of the date investor commitments satisfactory to Union Carbon, Inc., have been obtained, shall run up to the Commencement Date, and shall be payable pro rata on a monthly, in arrears, basis.

These provisions are clear and straightforward. Typically, fees such as these can be negotiated downward or eliminated completely, particularly in a competitive market environment. Although, theoretically, these fees protect against loss of profit, most are arbitrarily set based on what an underwriter or a lessor thinks it can get from a prospective lessee rather than on a mathematically determined measure of the profit that could be lost.

Let's examine some other commitment and nonutilization fee provisions taken from actual lessor proposals. Some can be confusing and must be read carefully.

**Sample Provision: A Confusing
Commitment Fee
Approach**

Commitment Fee:

If this proposal is acceptable to you, the Lessor will require a commitment fee of $16,127.49. This fee would be applied to your first rental payments on a pro rata basis as the line is utilized and would only be refunded to you if this proposed lease transaction is not approved by the Lessor.

In this case, the equipment cost was $806,374.71, making the "commitment fee" equal to 2% of cost. Apparently, the underwriter felt that, by not stating the percentage, it would avoid drawing attention to what in fact was a high-percentage fee. The provision is also confusing, giving an impression that the fee paid will be credited toward the rents due—in effect, an advance rental payment. The provision, however, goes on to say that it would be prorated as "the line is used," making it even more ambiguous.

Here's how the provision should be rewritten if the intent is to require a form of advance rental payment:

**Sample Provision: Commitment
Fee Revised**

Advance Rental:

If this proposal is acceptable to you, the Lessor will require an Advance Rental of $16,127.49. This Advance Rental will be applied toward the Lessee's rentals as and when due. The Advance Rental paid under this section will be refunded in full if this proposed lease transaction is not approved by the Lessor.

Now, the point is clear.

Here's another confusing provision from a lessor proposal:

**Sample Provision: Another Confusing
Commitment Fee Approach**

Commitment Fee:

In the event the Lessee does not utilize this commitment prior to its expiration, Lessee will pay Lessor a fee equal to 1% of the unused portion of the commitment amount* within 30 days after the expiration of the commitment, provided Lessor has received all necessary approvals.

*Commitment amount is the dollar amount of lease
 funding committed by the lessor.

Here, as in the previous example, the lessor does not characterize the fee properly, calling what in effect is a nonutilization fee a "commitment fee." The misleading characterization, coupled with the proviso, once again leaves unnecessary room for misinterpretation. Under this provision, if the equipment costs a penny less than the funding commitment, the full fee is owed.

Here's a more acceptable way for the provision to be written:

Sample Provision: No Fees Permitted

Commitment and Nonutilization Fees:
None.

Now there's no doubt as to what is intended.

If no commitment or nonutilization fee is permitted in a transaction, it's advisable to have the Lessor clearly so indicate in its proposal.

What Tax Benefits Is the Lessor Claiming?

Many lessors take equipment tax benefits into account when determining transaction rents, and some require contractual assurances from lessees that the benefits will be available. If there is a loss for which the lessee is responsible, loss computation formulas measure the amount of money due as compensation for the loss. The "Tax Assumptions" clause in our sample underwritten proposal addresses the tax issue:

Sample Provisions: Underwritten Proposal Tax Assumptions

Tax Assumptions:

A. The rent is calculated based on the assumptions that:

1. The organization created by the Trust will be treated as a partnership for Federal income tax purposes
2. The Lessor will be entitled to 7-year MACRS deprecation on 100% of the Equipment Cost, 200% declining balance switching to straight-line
3. The Lessor will be entitled to deduct interest in the Indebtedness under Section 163 of the Internal Revenue Code
4. The Lessor will be entitled to amortize the transaction expenses over the Interim and Primary Lease Terms using a straight-line method
5. The effective federal income tax rate of the Owner Participant is 34%
6. The Lessor will not recognize any income from the transaction other than from Lessee rental, termination value, stipulation value, and indemnity payments to the Lessor

Tax Ruling:

The Lessor plans to obtain an Internal Revenue Tax Service ruling with respect to the tax assumptions stated above. The Lessee shall agree to indemnify for the tax assumptions above. Such indemnity shall remain in effect until a favorable ruling has been obtained.

In this case, the lessor wants to be indemnified against tax losses until it has received a favorable tax ruling from the IRS confirming the availability of the benefits. If the ruling is not forthcoming, the indemnification stays in effect for the term of the lease. The problem with the tax-ruling approach is that, if the IRS fails to issue a favorable tax letter, attention has been brought to a transaction that might otherwise have escaped without IRS review. And if the IRS does at some point successfully challenge the lessor's tax benefits, the lessee will have to pay under the indemnity. If an aggressive tax position has been taken, the lessee may be better off letting the indemnity run the entire lease term and suggesting that an IRS ruling not be requested. Tax indemnification is discussed further in the next chapter.

If you don't want to indemnify the lessor for any tax losses, have that stated in the proposal. Some lessors simply ignore the issue in the proposal but insert a tax indemnification provision in the lease. The sample nonunderwritten proposal letter provision leaves the indemnification door open as follows:

> **Sample Provision: Nonunderwritten**
> **Proposal Tax Indemnification Issue**
>
> Tax Benefits:
>
> The rent is calculated based on the assumption that NLC will be entitled to:
>
>   a. Three-year MACRS depreciation on the full Equipment Cost, 200% declining balance switching to straight-line
>
>   b. A corporate income tax of 34%

To be on the safe side, if you have no intention of agreeing to a tax indemnification, it's best to require the following addition to such a provision:

> **Sample Provision: Requiring No Tax Indemnity**
>
> Lessee shall not provide Lessor with any indemnification for loss of, or inability to claim, any of the Tax Benefits stated in Section 7.

Have You Considered the Risks of Highly Conditioned Offers?

In reviewing your lease offer, you must pay particular attention to any offer conditions that must be satisfied as a prerequisite to a firm deal. The greater the number of conditions, the greater the risk that your financing won't come together. Common lessor offer conditions, for example, are:

- Necessary governmental or regulatory approvals, licenses, or authorizations
- Favorable opinions of counsel
- The effective placement of the debt, in the case of a leveraged lease
- Acceptable financial covenants, such as a minimum debt-to-equity ratio
- Satisfactory audited financial statements

- Mutually satisfactory documentation
- Formal transaction approvals by the prospective equity participants and lenders
- A minimum dollar participation of equity and debt participants
- A detailed equipment list
- Favorable equipment appraisals justifying the equipment's residual value

The "satisfactory documentation" condition gives all parties the most latitude to back out of the deal if they so desire. The reason is simple: Unless you and the lessor can reach agreement on each term and condition contained in the lease documents, either party can elect not to go through with the transaction. This condition leaves room for some wide-open discussions on issues not even anticipated in the proposal stage, such as whether the lessee should pay for the equipment's return to any location by the lessor. But be careful. If you decide to back out, make sure you've got a solid reason; otherwise, a good lawyer may successfully argue that you should hold to the deal as substantively reflected by the negotiations prior to the time you walked away.

Although an accepted proposal letter is usually not legally enforceable because of these conditions, it's important to the leasing transaction that it be comprehensive, detailed, and in writing because:

- The parties will almost always make significant efforts to complete the deal once the proposal letter has been accepted.
- It serves as the guideline and reminder for the parties and their lawyers when they draft and negotiate the financing documents.
- It is possible that, if a party unreasonably backs out of the deal after the proposal letter has been accepted, it could be used as the basis of a successful legal action—particularly if financial obligations have been incurred on the other side.

Let's examine the offer conditions in our two sample proposal letters.

Sample Provision: Nonunderwritten Proposal Conditions

This offer is subject to the execution of mutually satisfactory lease documentation and expires as of the close of business on March 15, 19XX.

The execution of mutually satisfactory lease documentation is a standard proposal qualification. It gives each party room to change its mind and walk away if agreement can't be reached on the terms and conditions of the lease documents. Theoretically, a standard of reasonableness is applied by the courts in reviewing this type of proposal "out," so each party must act in good faith when using this as a basis to back out.

Now, let's take a look at the offer qualification in our sample underwritten proposal:

Sample Provision: Underwritten Proposal Conditions

This offer expires at the close of business on March 20, 19XX, and is subject to the approval of the Owner Participant's Board of Directors and mutually satisfactory lease documentation.

In addition to the satisfactory documentation qualification, the lease underwriter also provides that, after acceptance by the proposed lessee, the proposal must be approved by the lessor-investor's (owner participant's) board of directors. The board approval condition is typically not governed by any standard of reasonableness, so a prospective lease investor could back out for any reason. It's always a good idea in this situation to follow up actively to see whether the board has acted in a timely manner. If there are board problems, some lease brokers say nothing while trying to locate a new lease investor—exposing the prospective lessee to detrimental delays. It's also not unheard of in these situations for a lease broker to say that the deal has been approved when it's been turned down, simply to gain additional time to locate a replacement investor.

One way to handle any risk is to request that the lease investor write a letter stating its board approval schedule and, when the proposal is approved, to send written verification of the approval, along with any new approval conditions. And it is further advisable for a prospective lessee to call the lease investor directly from time to time to check on progress.

Here are some other examples of actual qualifications found in lessor proposals:

Sample Provision: Adverse Law Change Condition

Proposal Condition:

From the date of this letter to the date of each equipment lease delivery and acceptance, there shall not have occurred any change in federal income tax law, regulations, or administrative interpretations thereof that would have an adverse impact on Lessor.

This qualification allows a lessor to walk away, or have a good reason to raise the lease rate, if there is a tax change that the lessor determines in its sole judgment would affect its economic return. Chances are good that, if a change occurs and the other lease bidders are no longer in the picture, any rate increase will be higher than necessary to maintain the lessor's profit if the lessee has no way to verify the adjustment.

**Sample Provision: Adverse Financial
Change Condition**

Proposal Condition:

From the date of this letter to the date of drawdown, there shall not, in Lessor's opinion, have occurred any adverse change in Lessee's financial condition.

This qualification allows a lessor to walk away, or raise lease rates, if any change takes place in a lease's financial condition that would not be to its liking. And in any company, changes are always possible.

The key to reducing proposal condition risks is to read each condition carefully and keep the conditions uppermost in your mind as the deal progresses. If there is any possibility that you will not meet one of the conditions, immediately formulate a backup plan.

The Lease Award

Following any negotiations concerning the proposal letter, the lessee accepts the offer by acknowledging its willingness to proceed on the basis of the terms as presented. If the proposal is written, it can be accepted by an appropriate officer signing his or her acceptance directly on the letter or in a separate writing referencing the proposal letter. Any acceptance condition should be clearly a part of the acceptance and identified as such. For example, if the acceptance is made by signing in a designated space, the condition should precede the signature. It's always best to "accept" directly on the proposal letter, rather than in a separate writing, particularly if the acceptance is conditioned. Separate papers can be readily lost or misplaced. Our sample nonunderwritten and underwritten proposals have an appropriate lessee acceptance provision at the end of each letter.

A Few Final Comments

This chapter devoted considerable discussion to the lessor's proposal. The proposal outlines your business deal, the terms of which are then incorporated in detail into a lease agreement drafted and negotiated after you've made the lease-financing award by accepting the proposal.

As mentioned earlier, your greatest negotiating leverage as a prospective lessee is during the proposal discussion stage. A prospective lessor knows that unless its offer is what you want, it will not get the lease award. So it will stretch to meet your requests. Therefore, the time spent in carefully analyzing the lessor's offer to ensure that it addresses every business issue and all key legal aspects of your deal will not only save considerable lease document negotiating time and expense but also reduce any possibility of the lessor's changing the deal you thought you had, by claiming, for example, that it misunderstood what you asked for.

As you can see from this chapter's discussion, there is only one way to evaluate a lessor's proposal: very carefully. There are no standards in proposal writing. The lessor's proposal objective is to provide an offer that beats any competition and gives it some room for negotiation in the event you want a better deal.

The best advice I can give you in evaluating a lessor's proposal is to read it thoughtfully. If you don't understand something, ask for a written clarification. And if the proposal overlooks a deal aspect that is important to you or your company, don't let the lessor talk you into having it handled as part of the lease document negotiation. Have the proposal revised to incorporate what you need.

Chapter 7

Negotiating Your Lease Agreement

Your Ongoing Lease Negotiation Job

Once you've decided which leasing company you're going to do business with, it's time to turn your negotiation attention to the lease documents. If you've handled your proposal negotiation properly, all major business and important legal issues will have been agreed on in principle; incorporating them into your lease agreement would seem to be a mere formality. Unfortunately, that is often not the case. Although a comprehensively negotiated lease proposal will reduce potential documentation problems, typically a number of important legal, and possibly some business, issues will arise that must be agreed on.

As suggested in Chapter 4, documenting your lease financing will be less problematic if you've developed (and the lessor has agreed to use) your own form lease. If that isn't possible, you will still be ahead if you've at least reviewed the lessor's form lease and, as a condition to the lease award, obtained the lessor's consent to necessary changes. Keep in mind that, at this stage, the lessor's negotiating leverage has increased simply because the other bidders are no longer around.

One of the biggest mistakes businesspeople make at this stage is thinking that putting together the lease agreement is a mere formality, relying solely on the lawyers to draft the business provisions properly and put the deal to bed. Some lessee business managers are so lulled into a sense of completion once the lease award has been made that they do nothing more than show up for the closing and sign the financing documents without review. A lessee that relies solely on its lawyers to translate the business deal properly into a legal format is making a significant mistake. If a lessor senses that may happen, you can bet there is a good chance it will go out of its way to include tricky or misleading provisions in an effort to gain solid business advantages. So if you're the businessperson on a lease deal, carefully review the documents well in advance of the anticipated closing date to ensure that your lawyers have adequately incorporated all business points and that nothing has been inserted by the lessor's lawyers that could reduce your rights or increase your obligations.

The Lease Agreement's Simple Objective

Although a lease agreement typically involves many complex, highly technical, and sometimes overwhelming concepts, its objective is very simple: It's a contract whereby a property owner, the lessor, transfers the right to use specified equipment to another, the lessee, for an agreed-upon period of time. The lessor retains title to the property.

A lease is different than a conditional sale, an outright sale, or a mortgage type of transaction. In a conditional sale transaction, the property owner sells the property, not merely its use, to the purchaser for a price to be paid in installments over time. When the agreement is signed, the seller only physically transfers the property to the purchaser, retaining title until certain conditions are met—typically, the payment of all installments—at which time, title is transferred to the purchaser.

In an outright sale, the property owner unconditionally transfers the property, including title, to the purchaser in return for the purchaser's simultaneous, or near-term, payment of the full purchase price. In a mortgage situation, a property purchaser borrows some or all of the necessary purchase funds from a third-party lender. The lender, or mortgagee, as security for the loan repayment, requires the borrower, or mortgagor, to provide a security interest in the property. In this case, the borrower has possession of, and title to, the property subject to the lender's right to foreclose on the property in the event of a loan default.

Advantages and Disadvantages of Common Lease Formats

Leases fall into one of two basic formats: the single-transaction lease format and the master lease format. Although both follow the same fundamental structure, the lessor's format choice is dictated by the type of financing transaction, the relationship the lessor anticipates, and its document negotiation strategy. If the lessee has its own lease forms, the format choice is typically dictated by which is more cost-effective for a given relationship or transaction.

The Single-Transaction Lease

Lessors, particularly in small transactions and "vendor" programs, frequently use a "standard" preprinted single-transaction lease. The standard lease form has fill-in blanks for those aspects, such as rent, that typically vary with each transaction. Although this type of lease format can be tailored to meet certain required variations, too many changes squeezed into the document margins, or attached as riders, can result in an unreadable document. Traditionally, preprinted single-transaction leases are used in small-ticket lease financings.

The preprinted lease format, whether it's the lessor's or the lessee's, is particularly attractive in small-dollar lease transactions because it cuts down on drafting and negotiation and thus helps keep documentation costs, such as legal fees, to a minimum. That can help both parties because the greater the expenses, the less the profit to a lessor and the greater the overall cost to the lessee. However, using a lessor's preprinted form lease can be risky for a lessee. Such form leases are often one-sided, giving few benefits to the lessee and containing many traps hidden in the fine print. Lessors use preprinted leases to create the impression that their document is standard in the industry and one that all lessees sign. Unfortunately, that is not true. Preprinted lease terms and conditions vary widely among lessors.

A few sophisticated lessees have recently begun to use lessor document strategies, developing and requiring the use of their preprinted standard form lease as a condition of a lease award. This approach not only saves documentation costs but also eliminates the potential for falling into lessor document traps. And it's always worth keeping the documentation cost issue in mind in approaching a lease financing because these costs can be the same regardless of the dollar amount financed. A $10,000 legal fee may be reasonable for a $500,000 transaction, but it will not be for a $20,000 transaction.

The Master Lease

A lease format set up to make it easy to add equipment that will be delivered in the future is commonly referred to as a master lease. It may be in a preprinted form or specifically prepared—typed—for a particular transaction (a custom lease approach). Traditionally, master lease formats are used in middle-market and large-ticket lease transactions.

A master lease has two parts. The main, or "boilerplate," portion contains the provisions that will remain the same from transaction to transaction (such as basic representations, warranties, tax obligations, and maintenance responsibilities); and the second part, sometimes called the "schedule," contains the items that will vary among transactions (such as equipment type, rent, and options). Typically, the schedule will be short—often only one or 2 pages—while the main portion may be 40 to 50 pages. The advantage of using a master lease format is that the parties can document future transactions with a minimum amount of time and expense by merely adding a schedule containing the information pertaining to the specific transaction.

Strategically, a lessor with a master lease in place with a particular lessee has a competitive advantage over other prospective lessors in any new bidding situation. Because documenting new equipment additions on an existing master lease is simpler than negotiating an entirely new lease, companies having master leases frequently go out of their way to let an existing lessor win by, for example, giving the lessor the last opportunity to match a lower offer.

Companies that frequently lease large-ticket items of equipment have increasingly developed their own master lease format and require its use as a condition of a lease award. Where multimillion-dollar financings are concerned, this can substantially reduce legal fees and other documentation and negotiation costs.

Subjects to Address in Negotiating the Lease

Before starting the lease negotiations, a lessee negotiator must have a thorough understanding of all legal, financial, and practical aspects of a lease and also know on which issues he or she must seek expert advice to avoid the ever-present lessor pitfalls. Without that, it's easy to give up inadvertently on what in fact is an important issue, be too adamant about a point of little consequence, or miss an issue altogether. The lease document discussion in this section identifies and describes issues that should be addressed in reviewing and negotiating a lease—and offers suggestions for resolving requirements that a lessor may initially insist on incorporating.

Always keep in mind in a lease negotiation that compromise will invariably be necessary on both sides to reach an effective and favorable conclusion. If the lessor with which you're dealing becomes inflexible, seriously consider bringing in another as soon as possible. And never forget, the more time you invest in negotiating a lease, and the closer the equipment delivery date, the greater the lessor's negotiating leverage.

The document discussion in this section centers around a typical form of lease, a net finance lease, because it's generally the most comprehensive and complex form. Being able to understand and handle net finance lease issues will enable you to deal with virtually any other type of equipment lease. A word of advice: In approaching the negotiation of a lengthy lease, always insist that an index be compiled containing all the topic headings and page numbers so you can quickly locate relevant provisions. It will save time and money.

One final point before we get started: Some of the issues addressed in this section are the same as those addressed in Chapter 5 on negotiating the lease proposal and are repeated to the extent necessary to give you a solid lease agreement negotiation overview.

Identifying the Parties to the Lease

As mentioned in Chapter 6, not only should the proper lessee entity be accurately specified in the proposal, but it must also be so identified in the lease. The lease, however, must go a step further: It must clearly state both the lessee's and the lessor's full legal name, the jurisdiction in which each is organized, and the mailing address of their principal places of business. This will prevent disputes as to who is intended to be bound by the contract.

Sample Provision: Lessee and Lessor Identification

This lease is made as of the 20th day of January, 19XX, by and between GASU Leasing Corporation, a Delaware corporation, having its principal place of business at 200 Peabody Street, New York, New York 10022 (hereinafter called "Lessor") and the Peterson Corporation, a California corporation, having its principal place of business at 100 Seminole Street, Los Angeles, California 11589 (hereinafter called "Lessee").

At times, problems occur when a company leases equipment to be used exclusively by one of its divisions. When such a division has been organized as a "profit center," the company may want it to be the named "Lessee." However, if the division is not a separate legal entity, it cannot be bound by a contract. But if the "division" is a corporate subsidiary, there are no problems because it has a separate legal existence, and the lessor, assuming the financial strength of the subsidiary is sufficient, will have no objection to having the division named as lessee.

Summarizing the Financing Facts

When the lease document is typed specifically for the transaction, and is not a preprinted form, it's always a good idea for it, at the outset, to summarize the basic facts surrounding the transaction. Writing the summary helps each party focus on the overall transaction. And the summary provides a valuable future reference for individuals not involved at the time the lease was negotiated. For example, the summary might describe the equipment purchase contract into which the lessee entered prior to the lease transaction and state that it has been assigned to the lessor as part of the transaction. Typically, the factual summary is incorporated into what are referred to as "whereas" clauses. The factual summary is often followed by a statement of the consideration for the lease, generally stated as the mutual obligations of the lessor and the lessee under the agreement. This is usually done in a "Now, therefore" clause following the "Whereas" section. Stating the consideration for the transaction in this manner is not legally necessary, but many lawyers consider it good form to do so.

Sample Provisions: A Factual Summary

Whereas, pursuant to a purchase agreement (the "Purchase Agreement") dated November 12, 19XX, between Noret Manufacturing Corporation (the "Manufacturer"), a California corporation, having its principal place of business at 715 Signal Road, Los Angeles, California, and the Lessee identified above, the Manufacturer has agreed to manufacture and sell to the Lessee, and the Lessee has agreed to purchase from the Manufacturer, four (4) Model 77-3 product conveyor systems, which are to be financed pursuant to this Lease; and

Whereas the Lessee and the Lessor will enter into an assignment of the Purchase Agreement simultaneously with the execution of this Lease whereby the Lessee assigns to the Lessor all the Lessee's rights and interests under the Purchase Agreement, except to the extent reserved therein. Now, therefore, in consideration of the mutual agreements contained in this Lease, the parties hereto agree as follows:

Making Sure All Key Terms Are Defined

It's always advisable for the lease to contain a definitions section, preferably at the beginning of the document, where the fundamental terms used repeatedly in the lease agreement are defined. For example, terms such as *fair market purchase value, fair market rental value, manufacturer, purchase contract, stipulated loss value,* and *termination value* must be defined in the context of the particular transaction to prevent future ambiguities.

Using a definitions section makes the text simpler to read, permits the parties to locate definitions quickly, and reduces the risk that an important term will accidentally be left undefined. If a preprinted lease does not have such a section incorporated and the definitions are scattered throughout the text, I often suggest including a rider that lists all key terms and the page number and lease section where they are first defined.

Dealing Now With Equipment to Be Delivered in the Future

Often, the parties want to sign a lease well before the equipment is delivered. This, of course, is advisable for a lessee because it can then be sure that no insurmountable problems will arise before it is too late to find another lessor. Doing so is also a benefit to a lessor: It knows that it has a firm deal. There are, however, some points to consider.

Putting the Equipment Under the Lease

When a lease financing is documented before equipment is delivered, there must be a method for putting the equipment under lease when it arrives. Typically, doing so involves nothing more than a formal notification from the lessee stating that the equipment has been delivered and accepted for lease. The notification, often called an "acceptance supplement" or "certificate of acceptance," is a written statement detailing the equipment delivered and stating the date or dates it has been accepted under the lease. If the equipment conforms to the agreement, the lessor automatically puts it on lease and returns a countersigned copy of the acceptance supplement to the lessee.

If the lease is signed prior to the equipment's delivery, the lessor often spells out the lessee's obligation to lease it. This can present problems for a lessee. For example, you, as lessee, may want the option to accept or reject the equipment when delivered. Ambiguous stipulations like, "The lessee must accept the equipment when delivered by executing an appropriate acceptance supplement, attached as Exhibit A to this Lease," may impose an absolute obligation to accept the equipment. If you want flexibility—such as having the financing available but not being obligated to use it if circumstances change—you must make that clear in your lease.

Even a seemingly less ambiguous stipulation, such as, "The lessee may accept the equipment when delivered by executing the appropriate acceptance supplement," can also cause problems. The lessor may have anticipated that the lessee is bound to accept the equipment, while the lessee may not believe it is bound. The key in any lease negotiation is to remove all ambiguities. Here's an improved way to incorporate the acceptance concept and include lease flexibility:

Nonutilization and Commitment Fees

In the event a lessee wants to sign a lease in advance of equipment delivery but still retain the right to reject the equipment for lease when it is delivered, a lessor—to ensure against a complete profit opportunity loss—often imposes a nonutilization fee and/or a commitment fee.

As you now know, a nonutilization fee compensates a lessor for funds committed to equipment scheduled for future delivery that remain unused at the end of the commitment period. Usually, the fee is expressed as a percentage of originally estimated equipment cost and is payable in a lump sum at the end of the commitment period. If all, or an agreed-upon portion of, the funds are used, the lessee owes nothing.

Example: How a Nonutilization Fee Operates

GASU Leasing Company has agreed to give Sable Company a lease line of credit for ten truck trailers. The trailers' total cost will be $1 million, and they will be delivered over a 12-month period. GASU, however, has limited investment funds available and wants to ensure against an opportunity loss if the trailers aren't delivered or Sable Company decides not to lease them. It therefore imposes a 1% nonutilization fee. If only $400,000 worth of trailers are delivered during the commitment period, how much of a fee is due?

Sable Company would owe GASU $6,000: 1% of the funds remaining unused, $600,000. If none of the equipment was put on lease, Sable Company would owe $10,000 (1% X $1 million). If $1 million worth of equipment was leased, Sable Company would not owe anything.

A nonutilization fee arrangement has risks for a lessee. An unexpectedly high equipment purchase cost (whether from a mistaken estimate, a price escalation, or a delivery delay) may permit the lessor to exclude equipment from the lease. If so, a lessee can end up paying a nonutilization fee based on the unused funds remaining at the end of the commitment period. It is not, however, generally considered unreasonable, in cases other than those in which a lessor could arbitrarily choose not to lease certain agreed-upon equipment when it arrives, for the lessee to bear this type of risk. However, as with commitment fees, this is an area of negotiation.

If you're confronted with a nonutilization fee arrangement, remember that you can lessen the payment impact resulting from equipment exclusions by negotiating a fee percentage leeway. For example, the lease can provide for the fee to be payable only to the extent that more than 10% of the committed funds are not used.

The imposition of a commitment fee is another common approach. Under this arrangement, a lessee must pay a flat fee at the time the lease is entered into based on the total funds the lessor has committed to the financing. Generally, the fee is expressed as a percentage of total cost and commonly ranges from 0.375% to 1%. Because the commitment fee pays a lessor for holding funds available, the lessee can freely elect not to put equipment on lease.

Minimum Grouping Requirements

When a lease involves many less expensive items of equipment scheduled for delivery over a long period of time, a lessor can require a minimum equipment acceptance grouping to reduce its administrative handling expenses. For example, in a multimillion-dollar financing, a lessee may be required to accept equipment for lease in aggregate cost groups of not less than $200,000. Typically, minimum acceptance grouping is not required in small-ticket or middle-market lease financings. As with commitment and nonutilization fees, minimum acceptance grouping requirements are negotiable.

A word of caution: If a lessor provides for a minimum acceptance dollar grouping, be careful. If the dollar minimum is set high, you may have to manipulate deliveries to avoid having to pay for equipment that cannot yet be put on lease simply because you haven't reached your acceptance minimum. A solution is to ask for a "best-efforts" qualification. Under this, if, after using your best efforts to assemble the required minimum, it becomes impractical to do so, you may accept a smaller amount.

Specifying the Period of Equipment Use

The lease must clearly define the period of permitted use—the term of lease. Typically, there are two basic periods: (1) a main lease term, referred to as the "base lease term," the "primary lease term," or the "initial lease term"; and (2) a renewal term. Some transactions also call for an "interim lease term," beginning when the equipment becomes subject to lease until the start of a predetermined primary lease term. As mentioned previously, the interim term concept is often used when many equipment items will go on lease at various times. For example, the primary lease term may be designated to start on February 1, 19XX, for all equipment delivered during the prior three-month period. By consolidating the start of the primary lease term to one date after which all equipment will be delivered, administrative work and rent payment mechanics are simplified.

As to the lease renewal issue, the more alternatives the better for a lessee. For example, one five-year renewal term is less preferable than five one-year terms because the shorter periods provide a lessee with the option of periodically reviewing the market rental rate. And the shorter periods give greater flexibility in the event business needs change. For the lessor, a longer renewal period is generally preferable: Long-term rent income is locked in, reducing its residual profit risk. The more renewal rent a lessor receives, the less dependent it becomes on resale profits to reach its anticipated transaction economic return.

Defining the Rent Payment Obligation

When the rent payments are due and how much the lessee must pay are key elements of every lease financing, and the lease must specify these terms in detail. For example, a five-year lease may call for rent to be payable in ten consecutive, level, semiannual, in arrears, payments, each payment to be equal to 4.5% of the total cost of the equipment.

Payment Dates, Amounts, and Form Are Critical

To avoid problems, your lease must specify: (1) where the rent is payable, such as at the lessor's place of business; (2) the form of payment, such as by regular check; and (3) when it is to be deemed received by the lessor, such as when deposited in a U.S. Postal Service mailbox. If these points aren't clearly indicated, you run the risk of the lessor's claiming a technical default based on what the lessor deems to be an incorrect or late payment. A lessor, on the other hand, runs the risk of losing interest it could have earned had the rent been paid in a manner that would have permitted earlier use of the money. For example, if payment is made by regular check on the rent due date, a lessor would lose the interest it could have earned during the time it takes for the check to clear, as opposed to payment by wire transfer, or early payment, so funds are available on the due date.

If your lease requires rent to be payable on the first of the month in immediately available funds, a regular check arriving on that date is a technical lease violation. If you want to pay by regular check, you must either revise the lease to permit it or send the check far enough in advance of the rent due date so that funds are cleared and available to the lessor on the due date. In this regard, it's always advisable to establish appropriate internal rent payment procedures to avoid technical defaults through, for example, accidental late payments. If the rent must be sent to a special post office box number, all individuals responsible for handling the payments should be separately advised so that the rent does not instead get sent to the lessor's regular business address.

The Rental Amount Must Be Fixed

Small-ticket leases often set rent as a fixed dollar amount, such as $345 per month. As discussed earlier, however, it's preferable to have the rent expressed as a percentage of equipment cost, particularly if the equipment will be delivered after the lease is signed, to avoid having to recalculate the rent and amend the lease if there is a purchase price change. For example, if the monthly rent is expressed as 2% of equipment cost, changes in cost will not require a lease adjustment. If, on the other hand, the lease sets rent at $2,000 a month based on a $100,000 item of equipment and the price later turns out to be $95,000, a lease amendment is needed to incorporate the proper rent.

As mentioned in Chapter 4, the equipment-related cost items that a prospective lessor is willing to finance can vary with each transaction, and the ground rules should therefore be defined in the proposal letter to eliminate possible misunderstandings and incorporated into the lease. For example, if rent is expressed as a percentage of equipment cost, the lease should define what expenses may be included, or "capitalized," in the "cost" term. If a prospective lessor has ample funds available, it may be eager to include more expenses, such as sales taxes and freight charges, in the rent computation cost base because it will increase its profit. If, however, its investment funds are limited, it may prefer to exclude the extras. In addition, when "soft" costs, such as installation charges, are substantial in relation to the raw equipment purchase price, the lessor may be unwilling to exceed a certain cost dollar amount because doing so would lessen its collateral value protection. For example, if a leasing company financed installation costs, and they ran 25% of the raw equipment cost, the lessor's collateral position would be diluted to the extent of the soft cost. Installation charges have no remarketing value.

A Tax Law Rental Adjustment May Be Required

If the leasing company's economic return depends in part on anticipated equipment ownership tax benefits, it may require the right to make rent adjustments if unexpected tax law changes occur that adversely affect its return before the equipment is delivered. The lease may, for example, incorporate a provision allowing the lessor to adjust the rent to maintain the transaction's "yield and after-tax cash flow" or, alternatively, "earnings" or "net return."

Some Document Tips: Rent Adjustments

- You should always make sure the lease clearly defines any lessor rent adjustment criterion. Terms such as *yield* or *earnings*, for example, do not have standard meanings and can be subject to many interpretations. The lease, therefore, must set out the exact formula to be used in making any adjustment to enable an independent verification of any of the lessor's computations.
- A lessor having the right to adjust rents in the event of adverse tax law changes will typically have the ability to make adjustments to values based on the rent, such as termination or stipulated loss values. If so, the adjustment criterion

should be disclosed to permit an independent adjustment verification so financial fairness can be maintained in the event, for example, of an early termination or a casualty loss.

- If a lessor can elect to adjust the rent upward in the event of an adverse tax law change to compensate for any loss, you should request the right to a downward adjustment if a tax law change occurs that is economically favorable to the lessor.
- If a specific tax law change looks likely during lease negotiations, it may be advisable to determine in advance what the rents and rent-related values will be should the change occur and incorporate them into the lease agreement. This way everyone knows exactly what to expect before a final commitment is made.

Payment May Be Unconditional

In many equipment leases, particularly finance leases, the lessee's rent obligation is absolute and unconditional, requiring payment of rent in full and on time regardless of any claim the lessee may have against the lessor. Commonly referred to as a "hell-or-high-water" obligation, this condition often shocks first-time lessees. However, it's not negotiable in the case of most lessors, particularly if the lessor intends to leverage its investment through the use of a nonrecourse equipment loan. Without this provision, a lender will not make such a loan to the lessor because, in the event of a lessee/lessor dispute, the lessee could withhold the rent relied on for the loan repayment.

The hell-or-high-water condition makes some lessees so uneasy that they insist on adding a statement, technically unnecessary, in a hell-or-high-water provision that states that any rights of action it may have for damages caused by the lessor will exist regardless of the hell-or-high-water rent commitment. An independent right of legal action always exists.

Some Document Tips: Hell-or-High-Water Obligation

- For a lessor, using nonrecourse debt as opposed to recourse debt is the most desirable way to leverage a lease transaction. For financial reporting purposes, the nonrecourse nature allows the lessor to disregard the loan obligation on its financial books because the lender looks only to the lessee and the lease collateral for loan repayment, not to the lessor's general

> funds. If you want the benefit of such a leveraged lease structure, you'll probably have to accept the hell-or-high-water obligation.
>
> • At times, a lessor's general lending bank requires the inclusion of a hell-or-high-water lease provision in all leases as security for its general loans to the lessor. The requirement is typically included in the lending agreement and is coupled with a right to require an assignment of all the lessor's rights under each lease, including the right to the rent payments, as additional security for its loans. Failure to incorporate a hell-or-high-water provision in any lease will generally trigger a loan default, something a lessor wants to avoid. If this is the case, you'll have to agree to the hell-or-high-water obligation.

Lease Reports

To enable it to monitor a lease transaction, a lessor often requires the lessee to provide pertinent reports. For example, a lessor may require the lessee to send financial reports, accident reports, lease conformity reports, equipment location reports, and third-party claim reports periodically. In some transactions, the reporting requirement may be burdensome and, if so, should be reduced or eliminated.

Financial Reports

Lessors sometimes monitor a lessee's financial condition during the lease term by requiring that the lessee periodically submit financial reports, such as current balance sheets and profit-and-loss statements. With these, lessors can often spot potential financial problems and take whatever early action may be necessary to protect their investment. Most lessees prepare these in the normal course of business, and providing them is not a problem. However, to avoid additional expense, a lessee must ensure that the reports required are ones that are normally prepared and, to avoid a potential lease default, that the time between that period when the information is gathered and when a financial report is due is adequate for its preparation and submission. For example, if a lessee does not prepare audited financial statements, a requirement to do so for a lessor in connection with, say, a $50,000 lease financing may not be cost-effective.

Accident Reports

A lessor will often ask for immediate notification of every significant or potentially significant accident involving the leased equipment, whether the damage is to the equipment or to persons or other property. Since it's not unusual for a lessor to be sued solely based on its ownership interest, these reports enable a leasing company to take action quickly that may reduce or eliminate any liability.

Typically, these reports must include a reasonable summary of the incident, including the time, place, and nature of the accident and the persons and property involved. As with any other lessee lease obligation, failure to submit reports can result in a lease default, so someone charged with the insurance responsibility should be responsible for fulfilling any such obligation.

Some Document Tips: Accident Reports

- Even if the lease only requires you to notify the lessor in writing, it's always advisable to notify it by telephone as well. A lessor's early arrival on the scene can produce facts important to it that might otherwise be lost and assist in the quick resolution of any potential liability.

- Lessees should insist on limiting accident notification responsibility to serious incidents. Minor accidents are easily overlooked, giving rise to a potential lease default, or can create burdensome and unnecessary paperwork. One suggestion is to set an estimated damage dollar amount below which notification is not required. Care must be taken in making an estimate, however, because if you're wrong, you may be held responsible for failure to conform with the reporting requirement. If in doubt, submit a report.

Lease Conformity Reports

Lessors sometimes require the annual submission of an officer's certificate indicating whether any events of default under the lease have occurred during the reporting year and whether there are any existing conditions that could eventually result in an event of default. If there are any, an appropriate factual summary must accompany the certificate. These reports can be a good early-warning technique for a lessor, and in compiling the report, a lessee may uncover something missed that is, or could cause, a lease default and that can be corrected before it becomes a problem. For example, it's not unusual, particularly in larger companies, to discover at the end of a lease that the equipment has been lost, thrown away, or accidentally sold—often too late to do anything about it.

Equipment Location Reports

Equipment location reports may be required. And the lessor may require notification, and possibly prior written consent, before equipment is moved. Knowing the equipment location is important for two reasons: First, the leasing company may want to inspect the leased equipment periodically, particularly if the lessee has an obligation to maintain it. Second, being apprised of the location at all times is essential if a lessor intends to keep security interest or other collateral protection filings up to date, as a location change sometimes necessitates a new filing. An obligation to notify the lessor of the equipment's location, particularly if it's about to be moved, is fair. However, you, as lessee, should avoid having to obtain the lessor's prior written consent if the equipment is to be moved to a location in the United States where security interest filings can be made simply.

A word of caution: If the lease permits the lessor access to your premises for physical inspection, it should be limited to only during normal business hours.

Third-Party Claim Reports

Tax liens or other third-party claims imposed on the equipment, viable or not, can seriously jeopardize the lessor's equipment rights. Accordingly, leases typically require that the lessee notify the lessor of any events that result, or could result, in such an imposition so that it can act to protect its interest in the equipment. From a lessee's point of view, reports of this nature should not be of concern.

Other Reports

More sophisticated leases will contain a right to request yet-to-be-determined reports deemed necessary in the future. For example, the lessor may want to know the circumstances surrounding unforeseeable events in the future that could affect the equipment. In agreeing to a general reporting obligation, it's advisable for lessees to limit it to providing only reasonable information relevant to the equipment or lease transaction.

Equipment Maintenance and Alterations

A lessor relies, at least in part, on the value of the equipment under lease to ensure its investment return. Therefore, a lease will commonly impose strict and explicit obligations and prohibitions as to the equipment's condition.

Equipment Maintenance

Who's responsible for maintaining the leased equipment, and to what standard, is a key issue, particularly if a large dollar amount is financed. The typical long-term lease puts the normal maintenance responsibilities on the lessee. If high-wear, or technically complex, equipment is involved, the maintenance responsibility can be an expensive obligation.

The cost of maintenance can increase dramatically if the lessor imposes a high, or ambiguous, maintenance standard. For example, some lessors sneak in a requirement that the equipment be maintained in like-new condition. Under a long-term lease, that can be an unrealistic burden for a lessee to assume. Less aggressive maintenance provisions often require the lessee to keep the equipment in "good working order, ordinary wear and tear excepted." At first glance, this maintenance standard approach seems acceptable to most lessees. However, to the sophisticated lessee, it is too general and is subject to individual interpretation.

Some Document Tips: Equipment Condition

- Qualify "good working order, ordinary wear and tear excepted" by adding the phrase "for the use intended." For example, the phrase could be rewritten as follows: "good working order, ordinary wear and tear for the use intended by the lessee excepted."
- If the equipment's manufacturer provides maintenance instructions, follow them exactly and keep a detailed record of what is done.

In certain situations, the equipment must be specially maintained. A leased aircraft, for example, must be kept to standards issued by the Federal Aviation Administration. Failing to meet those standards may mean that the aircraft cannot be flown or, even worse, could easily impose liability on the operator, and possibly the lessor, if an accident occurs.

Some Document Tips: Specialized Maintenance

- When specialized maintenance standards are imposed, consider seeking expert advice before committing to meet the suggested standards.
- Keep detailed and accurate maintenance records. In this way, the lessor can check whether the equipment is being properly serviced, and you, as lessee, have greater protection against a lessor's claim of inadequate maintenance.

Equipment Alterations

It's not unusual for a lessor to have the right to prohibit the lessee from making equipment alterations not related to normal maintenance. An alteration, for example, could affect the equipment's market value and thus impair its value to the lessor following the lease end. If you think out-of-the-ordinary alterations may be needed, get consent in advance and incorporate this permission into the lease agreement.

Protection of the Lessor's Ownership

In general, there are certain basic possession, use, and operational conditions that may be imposed so that the lessor's ownership interest in the leased equipment is protected. The essential issues are outlined in this subsection.

Filings Must Be Made

As suggested earlier, in many cases filings will be necessary to protect the lessor's ownership status. The lessor may want to file security interests under a state's Uniform Commercial Code laws to ensure priority over other creditors—typically referred to as "UCC filings." Certain types of equipment require special filings. An aircraft lessor, for example, must make certain filings with the Federal Aviation Administration to protect its interest.

Some lessors require the lessee to make these filings and to then confirm that they have been made. And the lease may then obligate the lessee to pay for any out-of-pocket losses incurred as a result of an improper filing. It's advisable for lessees to avoid these types of filing obligations. It's too easy to make a mistake and end up in a lawsuit or be in default under the lease.

Equipment May Have to Be Marked

A lease may require that the lessee mark the leased equipment with the lessor's name and its principal place of business. Marking the equipment helps fend off any lessee creditor trying to claim the equipment for unpaid lessee debts, and it enables the lessor to identify its equipment more readily during an inspection trip or a reclaiming action. If you, as lessee, have the marking obligation, make sure someone does what's necessary.

Sample Provision: Ownership Marking

GASU Leasing Corporation, Owner-Lessor, New York, New York.

Certain Use Prohibitions May Exist

A lease will usually prohibit the lessee from "using, operating, maintaining, or storing the leased equipment carelessly, improperly, in violation of law, or in a manner other than contemplated by the manufacturer." If, for example, improper handling or storing damages the leased equipment, and the lessor becomes responsible to a third party for damages caused through any of these actions, the lessor may have a basis for making a claim against the lessee.

Some Document Tips: Broad Use Prohibitions

- Because of the scope of some general usage prohibitions, a lessee can easily find itself in technical default for relatively minor violations. The answer is to define the prohibition parameters more specifically, such as pinpointing the exact laws with which the lessee must comply.

- A provision requiring the equipment to be used in conformity with the manner contemplated by the manufacturer can unknowingly get you into trouble. It's not unusual, for example, for equipment to be acquired for a use different from that for which it was originally built because, say, nothing else was available. If so, you must get a use exception—a specific authorization to use the equipment as necessary.

Key Assurances That Will Be Requested by the Lessor

A typical lease will require the lessee to make certain key representations on matters related to a lease transaction. The representations must be true on the date the lease is signed and, possibly, may be ongoing during the lease period. If they're breached, the lessor may declare a lease default. The most common representations are discussed in this subsection.

The Lessee Is Legally in Existence

A lease will ask for an assurance, through an appropriate lessee representation, that it is a legal entity authorized to do business where the equipment will be used. A corporate lessee will, for example, be required to represent that it is properly organized, validly existing, and in good standing under the laws of its state of incorporation and that it is duly authorized to do business in those states where the equipment will be used.

If the lessee is not, the lessor may have a difficult time suing the lessee should it become necessary to do so. Also, any lack of proper legal standing can result in a seizure of the equipment by state authorities, thus jeopardizing the lessor's secured position.

The Lessee Is Authorized to Enter Into the Lease

A lessee will be asked to represent that it is authorized to enter into the lease transaction and that the persons executing the lease, by name and official title, are fully authorized to sign on the lessee's behalf. For example, if the lessee is a corporation and it had not been properly empowered by its board of directors to make the lease commitment, a lessor may be unable to enforce the agreement against the corporation. In that case, the lessor's only recourse may be against the individual executing the lease "on behalf of the corporation," putting the lessor in a precarious position if the individual isn't wealthy enough to satisfy any substantive claim.

No Conflicting Agreements Exist

A lease will invariably include a provision that, by entering into it, the lessee is not violating any existing credit or other agreements restricting a lessee's ability to enter into a lease agreement. A bank credit agreement, for example, could prevent the borrower from taking out additional loans without the lender's consent. If "loans" are defined to include lease obligations, the failure to secure the lender's consent would most likely be treated as a loan default. Generally, under a loan default, the lender would have the right to demand an immediate repayment of the outstanding money, which, in turn, could adversely affect a lessee's financial condition. Any lessening of the lessee's financial strength can jeopardize its ability to meet its lease obligations. The answer is for a lessee to carefully review its third-party agreements to ensure that there is no conflict or violation when the lease is signed.

Necessary Regulatory Approvals Have Been Obtained

In certain situations, a prospective lessee may have to secure regulatory approval in connection with entering into a lease transaction. For example, a public utility may be required to clear certain lease commitments with the appropriate utility regulatory authority. If they are not cleared, the lease commitments may be unenforceable. To protect itself, a lessor will require a representation from the lessee that all necessary regulatory approvals have been obtained or, if none is needed, a representation to that effect. Failure to comply can result in a major problem for a lessee: The lessor may reclaim the equipment if a misrepresentation is deemed an event of default.

Some Document Tips: Regulated Lessees

- Because of the regulatory complexities, it's always worth considering getting written verification from the relevant regulatory authority as to each lease regulatory representation you're asked for rather than relying, for example, on your counsel's opinion. The best written verification is a favorable and official written opinion from the appropriate regulatory authority on the relevant issues.

- Always keep in mind that a favorable opinion from independent counsel expert in the regulatory area may be comforting, but it is not an "ironclad" solution. An opinion of counsel is just that, an opinion. It doesn't release you from the responsibility for a lease misrepresentation if it's wrong.

- Regulatory approval processes frequently take time. To avoid major delays, you should start the process as soon as possible so that, if necessary, you'll be able to deliver the required assurances, such as supplying certified copies of any approvals obtained, at the lease closing.

There Are No Adverse Proceedings

A lease often asks that the lessee represent that there are no pending or threatened legal or administrative proceedings that could adversely affect the lessee's operations or financial condition. If there are, the lessee will have to indicate what they are, in detail. For example, it is not inconceivable for an impending lawsuit to be potentially serious enough to bankrupt a company. If it comes to a lessor's attention after the lease is signed, a no-adverse-proceeding representation would allow it to terminate the transaction.

The no-adverse-proceeding representation is often very broad, and it's sometimes impossible to be aware of all threatened lawsuits or similar proceedings, particularly those involving minor incidents. So any no-adverse-proceeding representation should be qualified by stating that there are no proceedings that would have a material adverse impact on the lessee's operations or financial condition of which it is aware.

The Lessee's Financial Statements Are Accurate

A lessee's financial condition is a critical consideration in a lessor's credit analysis, so a lease will generally require the lessee to represent that all financial statements delivered to the lessor, including those prepared by the lessee's outside accountants, accurately represent its financial condition. This is a fair request and is typically a non-negotiable representation.

Key Assurances That a Lessee Should Require

A lessee should consider asking that the lessor make certain lease representations—a point often overlooked by less experienced companies. The following are ones worth incorporating in the lease agreement.

The Lessor Can Lease the Equipment

Even though a lessor presents itself to the public as being in the leasing business, there may be restrictions, such as in a credit agreement, prohibiting it from entering into particular types of transactions. Also, a leasing company may have to go through prescribed internal procedures before a lease is in fact an authorized transaction. Violating any restrictions or procedures could jeopardize the lessee's right to continue using the equipment. Although an appropriate lessor representation won't guarantee against problems, such as a use interference, it will form an additional basis for a claim in the event of difficulty.

In underwritten transactions, the lessor-investors are frequently not in the leasing business per se. Many corporations, for example, invest in leases on an irregular basis, and if internal investment approval has not been obtained, a lessee may not be able to sue to require the lessor-investor to fund the lease if it backs out at the last minute. The only ground for a lawsuit in such a situation may be to sue for what is referred to as specific performance on the basis that the lessor should be contractually held based on its apparent authority to enter into the lease. The problem for the would-be lessee, however, is that, if the lessor-investor is not regularly in the leasing market, it may not prevail on this ground. Thus, in underwritten transactions, it's particularly important for a lessee to have the lessor-investor represent that the transaction has been duly authorized.

The Equipment Will Be Paid For in Full

A lease should include a statement by the lessor, particularly when the lease is executed in advance of equipment deliveries, that it will fully pay for and lease the equipment to the lessee. While a firm commitment won't guarantee that investment funds will be available, it will assist in a legal action for damages in the event that the lessor fails to follow through. A lessor, in turn, will want the commitment to be subject to the lessee's fulfilling certain obligations, such as equipment inspection and acceptance. As long as those conditions are within the lessee's capability, they should not be of concern.

Some Document Tips: Lessor Payment Representation

- A lessor payment commitment representation is particularly important when dealing with smaller, less well financed leasing companies. It should not, however, be relied on exclusively if the equipment dollar amount involved is substantial, particularly if last-minute funding problems could cause a budgeting disruption.

- The reputation and financial background of a prospective lessor should be investigated to ensure that funding risk is at a minimum. A cheaper rental rate from a lesser-known leasing company, or an equity participant in the case of an underwritten transaction, will quickly lose its appeal if the funds aren't available when needed.

- The lessor should be asked to represent that the equipment will be, and will remain, free of all liens and encumbrances, except those of which the lessee is aware, such as the debt in a leveraged lease. This representation helps assure that the lessor's third-party creditors won't interfere with the equipment use.

There Will Be No Interference With Equipment Use

Your right, as lessee, to the quiet enjoyment and peaceful possession of the equipment during the lease period is fundamental, provided, of course, that you're not in default under the lease. A lessee should never sign a lease without such a lessor representation.

A Document Tip: Right to Quiet Enjoyment

- A lessor may ask that its quiet enjoyment representation be limited to its own acts or omission; otherwise, it will, in effect, guarantee to hold the lessee harmless against any third party causing a use interference not claiming directly or indirectly through the lessor—even a creditor of the lessee. This is a perfectly acceptable request.

Disclaimers of Product Responsibility by Lessors

If the lessor is not the equipment vendor, it won't want to be responsible to the lessee for anything that goes wrong with the equipment. Typically, it doesn't have legal responsibility, but to be on the safe side, a lessor will make a product warranty disclaimer against defects in the equipment's design, suitability, operation, fitness for use, or merchantability. This disclaimer should generally be acceptable to a lessee, unless the lessor is also the product vendor, because it can rely on the usual manufacturer's, subcontractor's, or supplier's product warranties.

Why It's Advisable for Lessees to Get a Product Warranty Assignment

Where equipment is supplied by a manufacturer, subcontractor, or supplier, the lessee has no recourse against the lessor under a typical finance lease—and must continue paying rent even though the equipment is defective and cannot be properly used during the lease term. And in many cases, the lessor, as equipment owner, is the only one entitled to sue an uncooperative equipment vendor for damages or to correct the defect. To avoid a serious problem, therefore, a lessee should obtain an assignment of any rights that the lessor would have as equipment owner against any manufacturer, subcontractor, or supplier during the lease term. If these rights are not assignable because, for example, of a warranty restriction, a lessee should have the power to obligate the lessor to sue on its behalf if the lessee deems it necessary.

Some Document Tips: Product Warranties

- If you, as lessee, find it necessary to have the right to require the lessor to sue in its name because, for example, the product warranty rights cannot be assigned, that right should be coupled with a right to control the legal action, including the selection of counsel and the grounds of the lawsuit.
- A lessor willing to let you sue in its name may also ask that all expenses be for your account. That is generally a fair request.

Specifying the Party Having the Risk of Loss

Generally, a lessee must bear the risk of equipment loss—whether due to damage, theft, requisition, or confiscation—because it has physical possession of the equipment. Net finance leases, for example, frequently require that the lessee guarantee that the lessor will receive a minimum amount of money, commonly referred to as the "stipulated loss value" or "casualty value," if there's an equipment loss. The stipulated loss value, which decreases as the lease term runs, is computed so that the lessor won't have to report a loss in its financial statements. Such a lessee obligation basically puts the lessee in the position of being the equipment's ultimate insurer.

Some Document Tips: Stipulated Loss Obligations

• Request an offset for any insurance proceeds or other awards resulting from a loss.

• Make sure the lessor's obligations, including rent, under the lease as to the affected equipment terminate as of the *loss* date.

• Insist on a clear definition of the term *loss,* because it's susceptible to various interpretations. Generally, unless a defined *loss* has occurred, the rent must continue, with the possible result that the lessee would be paying on unusable equipment. Typically, *loss* means destruction to the extent that the equipment is no longer usable to the lessee. Keep in mind that loss for the use intended may be somewhat less than actual total destruction, so be careful when agreeing to the loss ground rules.

One last lessee point about equipment damage: If you're required to repair equipment damaged by a third party at your own expense, insist on incorporating the right to claim any money received, at least up to the cost incurred, from the damaging party.

Evaluating General Tax Responsibility

In a typical net finance lease, the lessee assumes full responsibility for paying taxes imposed by any local, state, or federal taxing authority. These payment obligations should be taken into account in assessing your effective leasing cost. Some taxes can be substantial.

**Some Document Tips: General Tax
Payment Obligations**

• Leases frequently require the lessee to pay equipment-related taxes that, by law, the lessor is obligated to pay. If a lessor is improperly assessed by a taxing authority and refuses to institute a proceeding to correct the problem, you may have to pay the incorrect assessment. So insist on a right to have any tax assessment contested or reviewed.

- A lessor, in granting a tax imposition contest right, may fairly require you to deliver an opinion from your counsel setting out a legitimate basis for the action and to put up a reasonable amount of money in advance to cover the expenses.

- The lease should require that you, as lessee, be timely notified of every potential or actual imposition of any taxes or similar assessments on the equipment, so you can participate at the earliest possible time.

Ways in Which a Lessor May Aggressively Protect Its Tax Benefits

Generally, parties to a lease will want the transaction to be classified as a "true" lease for federal income tax purposes. It is absolutely essential, therefore, that it be drafted to ensure that the desired tax treatment will not be endangered.

If a "lease" doesn't qualify as a true tax lease, the lessor would lose its ownership tax benefits, such as depreciation. Since such a loss can turn a favorable transaction into a highly unfavorable one, sophisticated tax lessors build protections into a lease in two basic ways: by prohibiting inconsistent actions and filings and by requiring tax indemnification.

Inconsistent Actions and Filings

There is nothing wrong with a lessor's prohibiting you, as lessee, from taking any action or filing any documents, including income tax returns, that would be inconsistent with the true lease intent, because by so doing, you could lose your right to deduct the rent charges as an expense, creating a substantial tax issue.

Tax Indemnifications That Protect Lease Economics

The second way that lessors seek to protect against tax benefit losses is through tax indemnification provisions. Typically, these provisions require the lessee to pay the lessor an amount of money that, after taxes, will put it in the same economic position as before the loss.

Tax indemnification provisions can be extremely complex, and to properly assess their effect and workability, you have to know how the ownership tax benefits can be lost. Basically, there are three ways:

through acts or omissions of the lessor; through acts or omissions of the lessee; and through a change in law. If a lessor can get away with it, and for obvious reasons, its preference is to put the economic burden of a loss or an inability to claim expected tax benefits on its lessees, regardless of the cause. Sophisticated lessees, however, refuse to assume the entire burden, instead agreeing to something much less.

Acts or Omissions. It's not unusual to find in true leases a tax indemnity for losses or inability to claim expected tax benefits resulting from a lessee's acts or omissions. It's generally considered a nominal lessee risk. In today's competitive climate, however, it is unusual to find a lessee tax indemnity based on the lessor's acts or omissions. It's a significant lessee risk. As lessee, therefore, you should never agree to such an indemnity unless the transaction provides significant other benefits that no other lessor is willing to provide.

Tax Law Changes. The third situation giving rise to potential tax problems, a change in law, can go either way, usually depending on the overall bargaining position of the parties. To understand this issue, you must be aware that the risk of tax benefit losses resulting from changes in tax law breaks down into a *retroactive* risk and a *prospective* risk—that is, changes that affect equipment already delivered and those that affect equipment to be delivered in the future.

In the past, sophisticated lessees have, at times, successfully shifted the burden of a retroactive change in tax laws to the lessor, arguing that it is a "normal" leasing business risk that a lessor should assume. There is some logic to this position.

What about prospective tax law changes, those affecting equipment that a lessor has made a commitment to lease but that has not yet been delivered? In this case, the risk doesn't have to be assumed by either party. For example, the lessor could be given the right to adjust the rent upward by an appropriate amount if there is an adverse change in the tax benefits before the equipment arrives or have the right to exclude affected equipment. The lessee, in turn, could exclude the equipment if the adjusted rent is too high. Alert lessees make sure, if a rent adjustment right is given, that the lessor must make a downward adjustment if there is an increase in available tax benefits.

Some Document Tips: Tax Benefit Changes

- At times, lessors are unable to use additional tax benefits and will refuse to agree to adjust the rents downward if there is an increase in tax benefits affecting equipment to be delivered in the future. For such lessors, a downward rent adjustment will erode their economic return.

- If the parties agree to provide for a rent adjustment and couple it with a mutual exclusionary right if the adjustment is unfavorable, certain disadvantages must be considered. A lessor can lose alternate investment opportunities if a lessee excludes equipment at the last minute, and a lessee may not have enough time to find substitute lease financing if the lessor exercises its rights.

- If the leasing company has the right to exclude equipment based on a tax law change and the lease incorporates a nonutilization fee, a lessee must ensure that the nonutilization fee trigger amount will be automatically and appropriately adjusted downward by the dollar amount of the excluded equipment. For example, if the lessor provided a $1 million lease commitment and excluded $100,000 of equipment, the fee should be based on a $900,000 commitment. If this is not provided for, a lessee will have to pay a fee on funds that remain unused as a result of the lessor's exclusion election.

Tax Indemnity Payment Formulas. A lease containing a tax indemnification provision will—or should—incorporate a precise formula for determining the amount the lessee must pay. Because the indemnity formula's purpose is to make the indemnified party "whole," the formulas are typically broad in scope and provide for a payment that— after deduction of all fees, taxes, and other charges payable as a result of the indemnification payment—will put the indemnified party in the same economic position as before the loss.

Typically, the standard for making a lessor economically whole is expressed as paying the lessor enough money so that its "net return" is maintained. This has risk for a lessee because the term *net return* is subject to many interpretations, such as total earnings, discounted rate of return, or after-tax cash flow. If confronted with a vague adjustment standard, a lessee must insist on making it more precise as well as having an exact formula for determining the amount of the loss.

Tax loss formulas, as you might already suspect, can become very complicated, particularly if the lessor is a large multinational corporation. A loss payment may affect many aspects of the corporation's tax picture. Therefore, where significant sums are involved, it's usually advisable to retain experienced tax lawyers to work out the formulas.

The Tax Loss Date. In any tax loss payment formula, a key aspect is when a tax loss is deemed to have occurred, thereby triggering an indemnity payment. A lease tax indemnity provision, therefore, will identify the date when the lessee becomes obligated to pay the indemnity. For example, the lessee may become responsible to pay for a tax benefit loss when the lessor discovers the problem or when a court rules on it. In many situations, the "loss date" is defined as the time when the tax benefit loss has been established by the final judgment of a court or an administrative agency having jurisdiction over the matter.

Some Document Tips:
Tax Losses

• As lessee, you should never agree to any provision that obligates you to make any tax indemnification payment until the lessor has actually incurred, or is about to incur, an out-of-pocket expense.

• A lessor may want the right under a tax indemnification clause to make justifiable tax adjustments without prompting from the IRS and call on the lessee to pay if it realizes that it may not properly claim a tax benefit. However, it may not always be clear what is a justifiable adjustment, and without some means of making that interpretation, you should not agree to a provision that, in effect, gives the lessor a right to receive payment solely at its discretion. A solution is to insist that the provision allow the lessor to claim indemnity payment only after receiving the opinion of a jointly chosen lawyer or under some other similar arrangement whereby you are reasonably assured of a fair outcome.

• You should always have the right to require the lessor to contest any tax claim that will trigger an indemnification payment; otherwise, a lessor could decide not to contest it, and you will have to pay.

Reimbursement for Erroneous Tax Loss Payments. A lessee should have the right to be reimbursed for any money incorrectly paid under a tax indemnification provision. For example, if, after payment, it's determined that the tax loss did not exist, the lessor should be obligated to promptly return any money paid.

A Document Tip: Tax Loss Reimbursement

- If you, as lessee, ask for the right to force a lessor to contest a tax claim, you should also have a right to the return of any amount that you had to pay before a final resolution if the lessor later, without justification or consent, settles or discontinues the action. If you don't, there is no way to be sure the claim will be fully contested.

The Equipment Return Obligation

The condition in which, and the place where, leased equipment must be returned to the lessor are important considerations. Overlooking either can be costly.

As lessee, when you return the equipment at lease end, you want to avoid any possibly of a lessor claim that the equipment's condition does not meet the lease return standards. If it doesn't, the lessor may insist that you pay for repairs necessary to restore the equipment. Thus, the lease should provide a means to determine whether you have met the standard-of-care criteria defined in the lease.

The best approach is to set an objective, easy-to-measure "outside" standard—for example, agreeing that an aircraft under lease will be returned with no less than 40% of remaining engine operation time before the next major overhaul. Where an easily measurable objective criterion is not available, the parties might agree to use an independent equipment appraiser to assess the equipment's condition. The lease can either identify the equipment appraiser or set out a method to select appraisers if their services become necessary. A selection method, for example, can call for each party to pick an appraiser at the appropriate time, and if the two selected appraisers cannot reach an agreement, the appraisers will then jointly select a third, independent appraiser whose opinion will be final and binding.

The lease should specify where the equipment is to be returned and who will bear the delivery expense. If, at the lease's end, you, for example, unexpectedly had to pay for the transportation of 20 trucks to ten different lessor delivery points scattered up and down the East Coast, your cost of leasing those trucks would increase. Although who pays for shipping expenses varies with each transaction, it is not unusual for a lessee to pay only for shipping charges to a general transportation shipping point near where the equipment is used.

Some Document Tips:
Equipment Return

- Be careful about giving a lessor the right to store equipment on your company premises at the end of a lease until a buyer or new lessee can be found, unless you can do so without cost or with minimal cost. If you do agree, put a time limit on how long the equipment may be so stored and make sure you have no responsibility for insurance or loss while it is in storage. And you may want to consider charging the lessor a storage rent.

- Carefully consider the potential expense in agreeing to return equipment to a particular return point, especially when many items are involved. For example, a trucking pickup location may be much closer, and therefore less expensive, than the nearest railhead. Having the right to choose between alternative return locations may also be advisable. Circumstances can change, and it may turn out to be more practical to transport the equipment to, for example, the nearest railhead instead of the nearest truck pickup point.

Events of Default

If a problem arises that would jeopardize a lessor's rights or interest in the lease or the equipment, the lessor will want to be able to end the lease and take other appropriate action, such as repossessing the equipment. The various "problem" situations, commonly referred to as "events of default," that could give rise to such a lessor right will invariably be detailed in your lease agreement.

Nonpayment of Rent

Your failure, as lessee, to pay the lease rent, when and in the amount due, will always be a specified event of default. Rent payment is a fundamental obligation, and a lessor should expect the fullest attention to it, perhaps allowing for a reasonable overdue payment grace period for unavoidable delays.

A Document Tip: Rent

- Always ask for both a reasonable overdue rent payment grace period and a lessor notice requirement. For example, the lease could provide that the failure to pay rent will not result in an event of default until a period of time—say, ten days—after the lessee has received written notice of such failure from the lessor.

An Unauthorized Transfer

A lease will typically provide that, if the lessee assigns or transfers the lease agreement or the equipment without the lessor's consent, there will be an event of default. From the lessor's standpoint, it enters into a lease transaction generally on the basis of the financial strength and reputation of the lessee, so if assignments or transfers were freely permitted, the equipment could end up in the hands of an unacceptable third party. A sublease, for example, to someone who intended to use the equipment in a high-wear operation could seriously jeopardize the equipment's antici- pated residual value. By controlling transfers and assignments, a lessor can protect its investment position.

Failure to Perform an Obligation

A leasing company will attempt to have the broadest possible definition of events of default. Accordingly, it will endeavor to be able to declare a lease default if the lessee fails to observe or perform any condition or agreement in the lease. Whether or not a court would allow a lessor to actually terminate a lease agreement, no matter how minor the failure, may be open to discussion; however, the potential threat may keep a lessee in full compliance. Lawsuits are expensive, even for the winner.

Some Document Tips: Events of Default

- Many conditions and obligations in a lease may not be fun- damental to the essence of the lease financing, such as the correct marking of the equipment. So it's always advisable for a prospective lessee to minimize the default risk by re- quiring that the breach be "material" before it gives rise to a default event.
- Consider, to avoid inadvertent lease defaults, requiring the lessor to provide at least 30 days' prior written notice before a default can be declared. Lengthy notice requirements, how- ever, may hinder a lessor's ability to move quickly to protect its equipment and are usually resisted.

A Material Lessee Misrepresentation

As suggested earlier in this chapter, the lessor will generally ask the lessee to represent certain facts that a lessor deems critical to its deci- sion to enter into the lease. Any misrepresentation material in nature could subject a lessor to a risk that it would not otherwise have assumed had it known the actual facts. For example, in most cases, lessors rely on a lessee's representation that no adverse changes in the lessee's financial condition have occurred between the date of the latest financial statements and the transaction's closing date. If the lessor discovers after the lease is signed that the representation was not true, it should be entitled to terminate the lease even if the misrepresentation was inadvertent.

A Lessee Bankruptcy

To cover any type of lessee financial problem that could seriously jeopardize the lessor's lease rights, a lease usually provides, as events of default, a court order or decree declaring the lessee bankrupt or insolvent; the appointment of a receiver, liquidator, or trustee in bankruptcy for a lessee under any state or federal law; any similar action that would expose the leased equipment to a third-party claim or otherwise endanger the lessor's position; or any voluntary act by the lessee that would lead to any of these events. Once again, the lessor is entitled to tight control on the critical issue of a lessee's financial strength.

Lessor Remedies Following an Event of Default

A lease typically sets out a broad array of remedies that a lessor can pursue if a lessee defaults on any of its obligations. Although, by so doing, a lessor has no guarantee that a court will permit it to pursue any particular remedy if the parties end up in court, it will put a lessee on notice and thus may weigh heavily against any lessee objection.

As you'll see in this subsection, the lease default remedies are usually nothing more than a commonsense approach to dealing with the default issue. In addition, you'll also note that various remedies sometimes overlap, but from a lessor's viewpoint, it is better to be somewhat redundant than to risk a claim that a certain course of action was waived by implication because it was omitted.

Court Action

The most obvious lease default remedy is a right to bring a court action to require the lessee to perform any breached obligation or to get money damages for the failure to do so. This is a standard remedy available in any basic contract action.

Termination of the Lease

A lessor's right to terminate a lessee's rights under the lease, including its right to use the equipment, is a basic default remedy. Usually included within this right is the lessor's ability to enter the lessee's premises immediately and take possession of the equipment. The reclaiming right is particularly critical if lessee creditors are trying to attach assets as security for their claims.

Redelivery of the Equipment

Lessors generally have the right to require a lessee to redeliver the equipment in an event of default. The default redelivery obligation usually imposes a greater burden than if the lease ran its course normally. For example, a lessee may have to redeliver the equipment at its own expense and risk to any location that the lessor designates rather than to the nearest general transportation pickup point. In an adversary proceeding, however, this expanded right may mean little more than helping to measure damages because it's unlikely a lessee will cooperate at that point.

Equipment Storage

If an unexpected event of default occurs, the lessor may not readily have a place to store the equipment. As a result, lessors often require that the lessee store the equipment on its premises, free of charge, until the lessor can dispose of it. Whether or not it is actually advisable to let a lessee retain control over the equipment is a separate issue that a lessor should seriously consider when a default occurs. For example, a lessor may run the risk that other creditors would seize the equipment. Even though the creditors did not have a valid claim, the inability to get the equipment to ship it to a buyer or new lessee and possible equipment deterioration could endanger the lessor's investment.

Some Document Tips: Equipment Storage

- As in the normal end-of-lease return situation mentioned earlier in this chapter, to avoid a prolonged storage obligation, a lessee should put a time limit on any lessor default storage right. If a time limit cannot be negotiated, the lessee should insist that the lessor be obligated to proceed diligently to sell, lease, or otherwise dispose of the property.
- Any lessor right to have a lessee store the equipment might be accompanied by a right to enter the storage area for any reasonable purpose, including inspection by a prospective buyer or new lessee. This entrance right should be limited to normal business hours and only after reasonable written notice.

- If you, as lessee, are obligated to store the equipment, make sure your responsibility for equipment damage is detailed and limited.

Equipment Sale

A lease will permit the lessor, after a lessee defaults, to sell or otherwise dispose of the leased equipment, free and clear of any of the lessee's rights. A lessee, however, should seek the right to have an offset for any proceeds received against any damages it otherwise owes.

The more a lessor receives from an equipment disposition, the less default damages a lessee owes if it has a right to an offset. Therefore, a lessee should insist on an accounting of the disposition proceeds to help ensure that the lessor undertakes the maximum disposal effort.

Right to Hold or Re-Lease the Equipment

In addition to being able to dispose of the equipment, the lessor often requires the right to "hold, use, operate, lease to others, or keep idle" any repossessed equipment. Ideally, then, a lessor could take what action it deems to be in its best interest. Of course, if a court finds that the lessor did not act in a manner to minimize the damages suffered, the court may limit the lessor's recovery against the lessee.

Liquidated Damages

A "liquidated damage" provision is typically included as an alternate default remedy. Under this provision, the parties agree in advance on the method for determining what damages the lessor is entitled to if a default occurs. Generally, courts uphold a liquidated damage arrangement if it fairly anticipates the losses that may result from the lessee's nonperformance and is not a penalty.

Although there is no industry-standard formula used to measure a lessor's damages resulting from a lessee's default, there are two generally accepted approaches. One calls for the lessee to pay an amount equal to the present worth of the aggregate remaining rentals that the lessor would have received, but for the default, reduced by the equipment's fair market sales value or the present worth of the equipment's fair market rental value over the original remaining lease term. The other provides for the payment of an amount equal to the equipment's stipulated loss value as of the date of default, reduced by the equipment's fair market sales value or the present worth of the equipment's fair market rental value over the original remaining lease term. A prescribed per annum discount rate, such as the prime commercial lending rate in effect at the time of termination, is incorporated into the liquidated damage "formula" for present-worth computation purposes.

A word of caution about discount rates: The discount rate agreed on to compute the present worth of the remaining rental stream can significantly affect what will be owed. Too often, lessees agree to arbitrary rates without considering the consequences. The higher the rate, the less the offsetting credit and the greater the damage amount payable.

Example: Liquidated Damage Formula Computation

GASU Leasing Company leased a $1 million vessel to River Delta Company for a ten-year term. As part of the agreement, the parties incorporated a liquidated damage formula that they considered to be a fair measure of the damages GASU would suffer if River Delta defaulted. The formula provided that GASU would be entitled to an amount equal to the present worth of any remaining rents that would otherwise have been due but for the default, offset by the present worth of the vessel's fair market rental value over the original remaining lease term. The per annum discount rate to be used to compute the present worth was specified as 10%, the current prime lending rate at River Delta's bank. At the end of the fifth year, River Delta defaulted. For simplicity, we will assume that the rents are payable annually, in advance. The facts are:

Unexpired lease term:	5 years
Annual rent:	$120,000
Annual fair market rental value:	$100,000

The present worth of the remaining rents under the lease, calculated using a 10% discount rate, is $500,384. The present worth of the aggregate fair market rental value over a five-year period is $416,986. The amount that River Delta owes is $83,398, the difference between the present worth of the unpaid rents and the fair market value rents.

If the parties had agreed on a discount rate of 8% instead of 10%, River Delta would owe $86,242 instead of $83,392. On the other hand, if the discount rate were 12% instead of 10%, River Delta would owe $80,747. As you can see, the discount rate should not be treated lightly.

Lessor Requirements Regarding Certain Assignment Rights

Leasing companies frequently ask for a general right to assign their interest in a lease and the equipment at any time during the term. This right sometimes makes prospective lessees uneasy but, if properly negotiated, should not cause any concern. To begin with, it's usually advisable for a lessee to have a general statement inserted to the effect that the lessor will be prohibited from making any assignment that will adversely affect the lessee's lease rights. Now, let's examine the specifics.

Assignment to a Lender

A key purpose of a lessor lease assignment provision is to enable a lender to take over the lessor's leases as security if there is a loan default. For example, in many cases, a lessor's lender will require as part of its credit arrangement that the lessor incorporate in all leases a provision giving the lender a right to an assignment of the lessor's lease rights, including title to the equipment, if certain loan restrictions are violated. If an assignment requirement exists in a lessor's loan agreement, it must be in each lease agreement, and it is not a negotiable point between the lessor and the lessee.

In certain situations, a lessor may want the ability to borrow a portion of the equipment purchase cost from a lender on a nonrecourse basis. To do that, the lessor is typically required to assign the lender all of its lease contract rights, such as the right to receive uninterrupted rentals. And this requires each lease to have an appropriate lender assignment clause.

A Document Tip: Lease Assignment

- Anytime you must agree to allow a lessor to assign any or all of its interest in a lease to its lenders, you should also require that any such transfer be subject and subordinate to the terms of the lease. So if there is an assignment, your rights as lessee, including the right to continued use of the equipment, will not in any way be jeopardized by the lessor's assignment of its rights to its lender. It's also a good idea to provide in the lease that any transfer will not relieve the lessor from any of its obligations under the lease to ensure that you'll always have what you originally bargained for.

Assignment to an Investor

Lessors, at times, want the ability to "sell" the lease, including the equipment, to a third party. Under such an arrangement, the third-party buyer would become the equipment owner, would become subject to the terms and conditions of the lease agreement, and would therefore become the "lessor." Typically, the original lessor would then no longer have any lease rights or duties.

A broad assignment right can be risky for a lessee. For example, if the lease was sold to a financially unstable lessor, it could endanger the lessee's right to the continued use of the equipment because of, say, creditor actions against the new lessor. Also, an assignment to a lessor historically difficult to deal with can create problems, for example, if a lease modification becomes desirable.

A Document Tip: Investor Assignment

- You should negotiate into your lease a reasonable amount of control over a lessor lease assignment. For example, if the lessor assigned the lease to any of your banks or lending institutions, that assignment could restrict your future borrowing capability. The answer is to insist on the right to veto any potential transferees or, if that's not acceptable to a lessor, to incorporate in the lease prohibited lender assignees.

The Importance of Lessees' Requiring Equipment Sublease Rights

As lessee, you should always incorporate the right to sublease the equipment to lessen or eliminate the impact of having to pay rent on assets that become unproductive because of changes in use needs during the lease term. The best sublease rights contain no restrictions. Ones that limit transfers to, say, affiliated lessee companies don't ensure much flexibility.

Some Document Tips: Sublease Assignment

- Lessors consenting to a subleasing right often insist that the lessee remain primarily liable under the lease agreement during the sublet period, and some want the right to pass judgment on any proposed sublessee. This is generally a fair request. A transfer, for example, to a financially unstable sublease sublessee that misuses the equipment can jeopardize a lessor's security, and a sublessee's bankruptcy could interfere with the lessor's ability to repossess the equipment.
- Lessees negotiating subleasing rights should avoid agreeing to any exercise conditions, such as having to obtain the lessor's prior written consent. Time wasted waiting for a consent could result in lost revenue.

Lessor Options to Renew, Sell, or Terminate

There are a few situations when a lessor will attempt to get, or want, certain nontypical rights, such as a right to terminate the lease in a nondefault situation, a right to force a sale of the equipment to the lessee, a right to force the lessee to renew a lease, or a right to abandon the equipment. These rights can create substantial tax problems or be otherwise undesirable from a lessee's viewpoint. If your lease contains any of these lessor rights, carefully consider their impact before signing. Let's look at some specifics.

The Right to Terminate the Lease

It's conceivable, although extremely unlikely, that a leasing company would want to be able to terminate a lease for any reason it chooses during its term without the lessee's consent. For example, it may want to have the ability to go after a better rate if it believes the rental market will rise before the end of the negotiated lease term. For obvious reasons, a lessee should not put itself in a position in which a lessor could prematurely terminate the lease without its prior consent and without reason.

The Right to Force a Sale of the Equipment

In certain situations, a lessor will insist on having the right (commonly referred to as a "put") to force a lessee to purchase equipment under lease at the end of the term. Generally, the put is expressed as a fixed percentage of the original equipment's cost rather than a defined dollar amount. For example, a lessor may have the right to sell the equipment to the lessee for an amount equal to 10% of original cost. In effect, a put eliminates any risk that a lessor will not realize its assumed residual value, and that, in turn, protects its anticipated profit. Transactions involving certain types of store fixtures or equipment that will be difficult or uneconomical to move, such as certain heavy storage tanks, sometimes incorporate a forced sale right.

Some Document Tips: Puts

- The use of a put may impair the tax status of a lease transaction and should be agreed to only with the advice of tax counsel.
- If a lessor insists on having a put, a lessee should consider requiring that the lessor indemnify it for any loss of tax benefits it suffers if the put causes the lease to fail to qualify as a true tax lease.

The Right to Abandon the Equipment

In the past, equipment abandonment rights were readily used in leases of equipment that would be difficult and costly, if not totally impractical, to reclaim if the lessee decided not to buy it at the end of the term. A good example was leases relating to certain kinds of commercial storage tanks that were so large that the only way to move them was to cut them into pieces and then reweld them at the new site. Abandonment was preferred because the lessor's removal expenses were often greater than what it could reasonably recoup in a re-lease or a sale.

A few lessors tried to solve the equipment removal expense problem by requiring the equipment to be delivered to them at the end of the term at the lessee's expense. If the lessee refused to agree, however, the lessor's only recourse, without a right of abandonment, was to sue the lessee to force it to live up to its agreement or possibly pay for any resulting damages. If the lessee was in financial trouble, a lawsuit was of little use. Having an abandonment right allows the lessor to drop the property in the lessee's lap and rid itself of any lingering responsibility or expense exposure.

Now, for a variety of reasons, including tax considerations, abandonment rights are rarely requested.

The Right to Force a Lease Renewal

In situations in which an abandonment right or a put might be considered, a lessor may instead use a forced lease renewal right. Under this right, a lessor could make the lessee re-lease the equipment at a predetermined rental. Once again, as with a forced sale right, a lessor's ability to force a lessee to renew can create serious tax lease treatment problems and is rarely requested. If you find such a provision in your lease, seek the advice of tax counsel before agreeing to it.

Lessee Options to Buy, Renew, or Terminate

As discussed in the chapter on proposal negotiation, a lessee should insist on having certain equipment rights, referred to as "options," that enable it to maintain flexibility and some form of control over the equipment's use, such as an equipment purchase right, a lease renewal right, a lease upgrade financing right, or a lease termination right. Generally, options of this nature, although at times not offered by leasing companies, are willingly granted if requested.

A Right to Buy Equipment at Fair Market Value

As lessee, you should always have the ability to buy the leased equipment at the lease's end. Typically, this is done through a fair market value purchase option. Basically, the option gives the lessee the right to buy the equipment for whatever its fair market value is at the time the option is exercised.

Although the term *fair market value* appears self-explanatory, as discussed in Chapter 6, in fact it is not, and you should incorporate a method in the lease for its determination. Generally, the "fair market value" of an item of equipment is the amount that a willing buyer under no compulsion to purchase would pay a willing seller under no compulsion to sell in the open market. As a practical matter, the value is often determined between a lessor and a lessee through an equipment appraisal. At times the lease designates a specific independent appraiser who will evaluate the equipment at the appropriate time or a mechanism for selecting one or more appraisers in the future to provide the necessary evaluation. A typical approach is to select one appraiser to evaluate the equipment, and if both the lessor and the lessee are not happy with the result, each can select an independent appraiser to come in and make an assessment. If the two appraisers cannot agree on a satisfactory value, then they must jointly select a third appraiser, whose opinion will be binding.

A Document Tip: Fair Market Purchase Options

• A fair market value purchase option can be an expensive way for a lessee to acquire equipment with a typically strong resale value. So if your equipment could maintain a high resale value, consider negotiating a purchase price "cap" to limit how much you would have to pay. For example, you might negotiate the right to buy the equipment at fair market value or 30% of the equipment's original cost, whichever is less. A cap, however, can present tax problems, and tax counsel should be consulted before fixing the amount.

A Right to Buy Equipment at a Fixed Price

When equipment has traditionally maintained a favorable resale value, many companies refuse to lease because, if they want to acquire the equipment at lease end, paying fair market value on top of the lease rents is not economically attractive. As a result, some lessors offer fixed-price purchase options to induce them to lease. Under a fixed-price purchase option, commonly referred to as a "call," the lessee can buy the equipment at the end of the lease for a predetermined price, usually expressed as a percentage of the equipment's original cost. For example, a lessee may have the right to buy designated equipment for 35% of cost. A fixed-price option limits how much a lessee has to spend if it wants to buy when the lease is over.

A Document Tip: Fixed-Price Purchase Option

- A lessee fixed-price purchase option may cause a lease to fail to be characterized as a lease for federal income tax purposes. If the exercise price is so low that the lessee has, in effect, a bargain purchase right, the IRS may be able to challenge successfully its status as a true tax lease. Fixed-price purchase options, therefore, should be incorporated with care, and only with the advice of tax counsel, if it is important that a lease qualify as a true tax lease.

A Right to Renew at Fair Rental Value

Incorporating a lessee right to renew a lease at the equipment's fair market rental value at the end of a lease term is acceptable, both from the standpoint of the IRS and, generally, from the standpoint of a lessor. It is advisable, however, for a lessee to insist that an approach be agreed on in the lease to determine the fair rental value. Using an approach similar to that of the determination of the fair market purchase value, through independent appraisal at the time of the intended renewal, is commonly acceptable.

A Document Tip: Fair Market Lease Renewal

- If equipment is vital to your operations, make sure the lease renewal terms are adequate to cover any anticipated needs. For example, if a four-year renewal is desirable, an option that would allow a selection of two two-year periods, four one-year periods, one one-year period followed by a three-year period, or a four-year period would provide a great deal of flexibility as to term and rental rate. A structure such as this provides you with the ability to limit your renewal costs in a high rental market or to "lock in" for a longer period of time in a low rental market. From a lessor's viewpoint, of course, too much latitude on the lessee's side can lessen its chances of maximizing its renewal profit, and therefore, too flexible an arrangement may be resisted.

A Right to Renew the Lease at a Fixed Price

It's sometimes advisable for a lessee to request a fixed-price renewal option. By knowing in advance the exact dollar amount of the renewal rents, a lessee can be assured of its renewal cost if continued use of the equipment becomes necessary after the lease term ends. This would, of course, not be possible with a fair market renewal option.

A Document Tip: Fixed-Price Renewal Option

• A fixed-price renewal right may result in adverse tax consequences and should be incorporated only with the advice of tax counsel.

A Right to Terminate the Lease

Business needs change, and therefore, it's always preferable for a lessee to have the right to terminate a lease early, particularly when it believes the equipment could become technically obsolete or surplus to its needs before the lease would normally end. Under an early termination right, a lessee is required to pay the lessor a predetermined amount of money, commonly referred to as the "termination value," on exercise. Although the termination payment is generally high, it's usually less costly than continuing to pay rent for the remaining term.

A Right of First Refusal

A purchase "right of first refusal" is sometimes used as an alternative to a fair market value purchase option. Under this option, the lessee has the right to buy the leased equipment at the end of the lease term under the same terms and conditions as offered by an unaffiliated third party. The disadvantage of a first-refusal right to a lessee is that a competitor may bid for the equipment simply to push the price up.

**Sample Provision: Right of
First Refusal**

Unless an Event of Default shall have occurred and be continuing at the end of the term of this lease, or any event or condition that, upon lapse of time or giving of notice, or both, would constitute such an Event of Default shall have occurred and be continuing at such time, the Lessor shall not, at or following the end of the term of this lease, sell any item of equipment (including any sale prior to the end of such term for delivery of such equipment at or following the end of such term) unless:

1. The Lessor shall have received from a responsible purchaser a bona fide offer in writing to purchase such equipment;
2. The Lessor shall have given the Lessee notice (a) setting forth in detail the identity of such purchaser, the proposed purchase price, the proposed date of purchase, and all other material terms and conditions of such purchase, and (b) offering to sell such equipment to the Lessee upon the same terms and conditions as those set forth in such notice; and
3. The Lessee shall not have notified the Lessor, within 20 days following receipt of such notice, of its election to purchase such equipment upon such terms and conditions.

If the Lessee shall not have so elected to purchase such equipment, the Lessor may at any time sell such equipment to any party at a price and upon other terms and conditions no less favorable to the Lessor than those specified in such notice.

A Right to Upgrade Financing

At times, companies lease equipment, such as computer systems, that require upgrading to ensure maximum performance, by adding additional equipment or modifying the original equipment. Typically, such an upgrade may not be done without the lessor's prior written consent, and in some situations, it may be of such a nature—for example, internal equipment modifications that have no stand-alone value—that no one other than the original lessor would consider financing it. In these situations, the incumbent lessor has absolute negotiating control over the financing and can charge the lessee more than the going market rate.

To avoid having to accept whatever rate a lessor offers for upgrade financing, companies leasing equipment that may need to be upgraded before the end of the lease term often insist on an upgrade financing option, a right that allows them to require the lessor to finance equipment upgrades during the lease term at a predetermined fixed lease rate or at a rate to be adjusted at the time of financing if there is a change in, say, the lessor's debt borrowing rate. Once again, the adjustment verification approach suggested earlier in connection with general rent adjustments should be considered by a lessee.

Loss of Options by a Defaulting Party

Typically, a lease will provide that the party holding an option forfeits its exercise right if it is in default under the lease. For example, a lessee in default under the terms of a lease will lose its right to buy the equipment under a purchase option.

Designating the Law Governing the Lease

The jurisdiction's law that will be applied in determining the parties' lease rights and obligations in the event of a dispute should be designated in the lease agreement to avoid being subject to, for example, the law of a state that may not facilitate a good commercial decision. The parties could, for example, agree that all actions on lease issues will be decided under the laws of New York State, regardless of whether the proceedings are instituted in a New York court.

Severability Clause

Leases should contain what is referred to as a "severability clause," a clause that provides that any lease provision determined to be legally unenforceable will be severed. Under this clause, the severed provision is treated as though it had never existed. This may prevent the entire lease agreement from being held invalid if only certain provisions are unenforceable.

Interest Penalty for Late Payments

The parties to a lease agreement should agree on the interest rate that will be charged on any overdue payments, such as delinquent rent payments. This will eliminate disputes over late charges and will assist in assessing damages if a lawsuit arises.

Some Document Tips:
Interest Penalties

• If the lease specifies an overdue payment interest penalty but does not also incorporate a qualification that the rate will in no event be higher than the maximum enforceable legal rate, a lessee should first check, if an interest penalty payment is demanded, whether the legal limit has been inadvertently exceeded. If so, the lessor may not be able to enforce its payment.

- A lessee should attempt to get interest on overdue obligations to run from the date the lessee receives written notice of the overdue obligation from the lessor. Traditionally, the lessor asks that it run from the date the money is due until the payment date.

Identification of Notification and Payment Specifics in the Lease

Although leases usually provide that all required notifications and payments, such as loss notifications and rent payments, must be promptly made, they sometimes fail to identify exactly where they should be sent. As a result, payments or notifications could be misdirected and money or valuable time lost. For a lessee, it's best to have the appropriate mailing addresses clearly stated, so the lessor cannot claim a default if any payments or notifications are sent to someplace other than that expected by the lessor.

One more point: The lease should also specify the manner in which notification and payment should be sent. For example, it may be agreed that a notice will be deemed given when it is deposited in a U.S. Postal Service mailbox or sent by certified mail.

Correctly Signing the Lease

All parties to a lease should make sure it is signed in the proper capacities. Leases to be signed by an individual representing himself or herself generally do not present any problems. Leases to be signed by an individual representing an organization—such as a partnership, corporation, or trust—sometimes do. If, in the latter case, the signature is not made in the correct representative capacity, the represented firm may not be bound. For example, if a vice president intends to sign on behalf of his or her corporation, the signature block should be set up as follows:

Sample Provision: Signature Clause

River Delta Corporation

By _____

    D. Ducksworth, Vice President

If the signature form is not correct, the signing individual runs the risk that he or she is personally liable on the contract—certainly, a less-than-desirable outcome for all parties concerned.

Checklist for Drafting and Negotiating a Lease Agreement

In preparing a well-drafted lease agreement, the parties should cover all the important issues involved in a transaction. This checklist pinpoints the issues frequently encountered.

What form of lease is appropriate?

• A single-transaction lease
• A master lease

Does the lease agreement cover the following issues?

• Has a page index of all topic headings been included?
• Have the parties been properly identified?
  - Lessor
  - Lessee
  - Is the lessee a valid legal entity?
• Has a factual summary of the circumstances giving rise to the transaction been included?
• Has the consideration for the transaction been stated?
• Have the key terms been defined in a definitions section? For example:
  - Affiliate
  - Business day
  - Buyer-furnished equipment
  - Casualty loss value
  - Equipment delivery date
  - Equipment manufacturer
  - Event of default
  - Event of loss
  - Fair market value
  - Indenture
  - Interim rent
  - Lease
  - Lease period
  - Lease supplement
  - Lessor's cost
  - Lien

- Loan certificates
- Loan participant
- Overdue interest rate
- Primary rent

• If equipment will be delivered after the lease is signed, has a procedure been established for adding the equipment to the lease?
  - If equipment is to be delivered in the future, can the lessee decide not to lease that equipment when it arrives? If so, will the lessee be obligated to pay either of the following?
    • A nonutilization fee
    • A commitment fee
  - Can equipment to be delivered in the future be accepted for lease as it arrives, or must the lessee aggregate a minimum dollar amount?

• How has the lease period been defined?
  - Will there be an interim lease term? If so, when will it begin and end?
  - When will the primary term begin?
  - How long will the primary term run?
  - Will the lessee be permitted to renew the lease? If so, what is the renewal period arrangement?

• How has the rent structure been defined?
  - Will a percentage rent factor be used? If so, what may be included in the equipment cost base?
    • Sales tax
    • Transportation charges
    • Installation charges
    • Other
  - How much rent must be paid?
  - When will the rent be due?
  - How must the rent be paid?
    • Check
    • Wire transfer
    • Other
  - Where must the rent be paid?
    • Has a post office box or other address been specified?
  - Can or must the lessor adjust the rent charge if there is a tax law change affecting, favorably or unfavorably, the lessor's economic return?
    • If a rent adjustment is provided for, has the exact criterion for making it been clearly specified?
    • If the tax law change applies to equipment to be delivered in

the future and a rent adjustment is not acceptable, can the
party adversely affected elect to exclude the equipment?
  - Will the rent obligation be a hell-or-high-water obligation?

• What is the lessor's total dollar equipment cost commitment?
  - Will a percentage variance be permitted?

• Will the lessee be required to submit reports? For example:
  - Financial reports
    • Profit-and-loss statements
    • Balance sheets
    • Other
  - Accident reports
    • Has a minimum estimated accident dollar amount been
      agreed upon below which a report is not required?
    • Will the lessee be obligated to telephone immediately if an
      accident occurs?
  - Lease conformity reports
  - Equipment location reports
  - Third-party claim reports

• Has a time been established for when lessee reports are due?

• Has a general lessee reporting requirement been imposed as to
  reports that may be deemed necessary by the lessor in the future?

• What equipment maintenance requirements are involved?
  - Who has the responsibility for ensuring proper maintenance?
    • Lessor
    • Lessee
    • A third party
  - Who must bear the cost of the maintenance?
    • Lessor
    • Lessee
  - Will maintenance records be required?
    • Will the lessor be permitted access to the maintenance
      records? If so, at what times?
    • During normal business hours
    • Anytime access is requested

• Will equipment alterations be permitted? If so:
  - Will the lessor's consent be required before the following types
    of changes are made?
    • An addition that may impair the equipment's originally in-

tended function or that cannot be removed without so impairing such function
  - Any change
- Who will have title to any addition or other alteration in the following cases?
    - If the addition or other alteration can be easily removed without equipment damage
    - If it cannot be removed without function impairment
- What rights will the lessor have to buy the alteration?

- Will certain lessor ownership protection filings be necessary?
  - Federal regulatory agencies, such as the Federal Aviation Administration
  - Uniform Commercial Code
  - Other

- If lessor ownership protection filings will be made, who has the responsibility for making them, and who must bear the expense?
  - Lessor
  - Lessee

- If the lessee must make required filings for the lessor, will the lessee have to confirm that they have been made?

- Will the equipment be marked with the lessor's name and address? If so, who will have the marking responsibility and expense?
  - Lessor
  - Lessee

- Has the lessee been specifically prohibited from using, operating, storing, or maintaining the equipment carelessly, improperly, in violation of the law, or in a manner not contemplated by the manufacturer?
  - If the lessee must use the equipment for a purpose other than intended, an exception should be negotiated.

- If certain key lessee representations are required, can they be validly made? Such representations can include the following:
  - That the lessee is properly organized, validly existing, and in good standing
  - That it has proper authorization to do business in the state where the equipment will be located
  - That the lessee has the transactional authority to enter into the lease
    - That necessary board of director approvals have been ob-

tained covering the transaction and the person signing the lease on behalf of the lessee
- • That any other required approvals have been obtained
- - That there are no conflicting agreements
  - • Bank credit agreements
  - • Other loan agreements
  - • Mortgages
  - • Other leases
- - That all necessary regulatory approvals have been obtained
- - That there are no pending or threatened adverse legal or administrative proceedings that would affect the lessee's operations or financial condition
- - That there have been no adverse changes as of the lease closing in the lessee's financial condition since the latest available financial statements

• What key representations is the lessor required to provide? Such representations can include the following:
  - - That the lessor has the transactional authority to lease the equipment
    - • That any necessary board of director approval has been obtained
    - • That any other approvals have been obtained or, if none is required, a statement that none is required
  - - That the lessor will pay for the equipment in full
  - - That the lessor will not interfere with the lessee's use of the equipment
    - • Has an exception when the lessee is in default been negotiated by the lessor?

• If the lessor has no equipment defect responsibility, has the lessee required product warranties to be assigned?
  - - If the warranties are not assignable, the lessor should be required to act on the lessee's behalf.

• Who has the responsibility for equipment casualty losses?
  - - Lessor
  - - Lessee

• Are the casualty loss values competitive from the lessee's viewpoint?

• As of what time will a casualty loss be deemed to have occurred?

Has a "loss date" been defined?
  - What obligations change or come into effect on the loss date?

• When is the casualty loss value payable, and when does interest on the amount payable begin to run?

• What taxes must be paid?
  - Sales tax
  - Property taxes
  - Rental taxes
  - Withholding taxes
  - Income taxes
  - Other

• Who must pay the taxes?
  - Lessor
  - Lessee

• In the case of any taxes for which a lessee must reimburse a lessor for payment, does the lessee have the right to have the taxes contested?
  - What happens if the lessor does not fully pursue its contest remedies?

• Is each party required to notify the other immediately of any tax imposition for which it will be responsible?

• Do the parties intend a true tax lease? If so:
  - Have inconsistent actions and filings been prohibited?
  - Will tax loss indemnifications be required?
  - Will any tax indemnity cover all lessor tax losses or only those resulting from the lessee's acts or omissions?

• Who has the economic risk of a change in tax law?
  - For equipment delivered in the past
  - For equipment to be delivered in the future
    • Can either party elect not to lease if the economics are no longer favorable?

• Has a formula been agreed upon for measuring the amount of any tax benefit loss and the amount of any required reimbursement?
  - Does the formula make the indemnified party whole?
  - Is the formula absolutely clear?

• Has the tax loss date been determined?

- Who has the expense responsibility for the equipment return, and to where must it be returned in the following cases?
  - If the lease ends normally
  - If the lease ends prematurely

- May either party designate an alternate return location? If so, what is the expense responsibility?

- Under what situations may the lessor be able to terminate the lease early or take other protective action?
  - When the rent is not paid
  - When the lessee makes an unauthorized transfer of the equipment or any of its rights under the lease
  - When there is a general failure to perform the obligations under the lease
  - When the lessor discovers that the lessee has made a material misrepresentation
  - When there is a bankruptcy or similar event that would jeopardize the lessor's position

- What actions may the lessor take in the event of default?
  - Court action
  - Termination of the lease
  - Requiring the lessee to redeliver the equipment
  - Requiring the lessee to store the equipment
  - Selling the equipment under its own terms
  - Being able to hold or re-lease the equipment
  - Being entitled to a predetermined amount of money as damages for a lease default

- What lessor assignment rights are required?
  For example:
  - To a lender as security
  - To an investor

- Will the lessee be able to sublease the equipment? If so:
  - Will the lessee remain primarily liable under the lease during the sublease period?
  - Will the lessor have any control over who the sublessee will be?

- Have any lessor options been included? For example:
  - Right to terminate the lease
  - Right to force a sale of the equipment
  - Right to abandon the equipment
  - Right to force a lease renewal

- Have all the lessee's options been included? For example:
  - A purchase right
    - Fair market purchase value
    - Fixed purchase price
  - A renewal right
    - Fair market rental value
    - Fixed-price rental
  - A termination right
  - A right of first refusal
  - An upgrade financing right

- Will a defaulting party retain any of its option rights under the lease?

- Has the law of a jurisdiction been specified to control any issues that may arise under the lease?

- Is there a severability clause?

- Is there any interest penalty for overdue payments?

- Has each side specified how and where any required notifications and payments will be made? Points to be specified include:
  - The address where notifications and payments must be sent
  - The manner in which notifications and payments must be made
    - By U.S. Mail
    - By other means

- Has the signature section been set up properly for:
  - An individual
  - A corporation
  - A partnership
  - A trust
  - Other

- Has the signature been made in the proper capacity?

Chapter 8

Closing Your Lease Financing

Closing a Lease Financing

Once you've negotiated the terms and conditions of your lease agreement, it's time to have it put in final form and prepare for what's referred to as the lease "closing." At the closing, all parties will sign the lease agreement and, in addition, fulfill any closing conditions identified or requested in accordance with the lease or other governing papers, such as the lessee's delivering to the lessor any specified "collateral," or supplemental, documents requested. These collateral documents range from those that essentially provide comfort on specified issues, such as opinions of counsel, to those that define critical supportive arrangements, such as guarantee agreements. And if the equipment has not yet arrived for lease, you, as lessee, will be requested to deliver certain additional documents when it does. All the collateral documents are an integral part of the finance closing. If you are unable to provide one, the lessor is no longer obligated to finance your equipment.

As you'll see, the leveraged lease closing is the most complex because, as explained in Chapter 1, of the added participant—the third-party equipment lender. Although the actual leveraged lease agreement does not differ radically from that of a nonleveraged lease, additional supplemental closing documents are usually involved, such as a security and loan agreement, to accommodate the loan arrangement requirements.

Although drafting the supplemental papers will be the responsibility of the transaction's lawyers, the businesspeople should understand the fundamental concepts involved so the papers can be meaningfully reviewed to ensure that they accurately reflect the agreements reached. That is the purpose of this chapter: to provide you with a closing document overview so you know in advance what to expect and can facilitate a smooth closing.

One final point before we begin: Although this chapter provides a general working knowledge of the typical collateral lease documents, keep in mind that most transactions have their own unique aspects that must also be taken into account.

Legal Opinions

In large-ticket, and at times middle-market, lease transactions, legal opinions are typically required by lessors and, in some cases, by sophisticated lessees. Before going into the various opinions possible and what they might address, let's take a moment to discuss what the practical value of such an opinion may be from a business point of view. To begin with, it's important to understand what a legal opinion does not do. It does not guarantee that the conclusions expressed in the opinion are correct. Regardless of the quality of the lawyer's work in preparing the opinion, a court or an administrative agency may interpret the law or facts differently—and its decision, not the legal opinion, will be controlling. A legal opinion, however, does provide the recipients with value in the following respects:

- It provides the participants with a significant degree of comfort, because the lawyer's opinion usually will be correct.
- In drafting the opinion, the lawyer will need access to relevant information, and therefore, writing the opinion may bring to light transaction trouble spots that can be corrected.
- If a court or an agency disagrees with the opinion, having it may help show that the parties exercised due care in entering the transaction and may prevent the imposition of any penalties.

The problem with legal opinions is that they are invariably qualified by, for example, stating a very specific set of facts on which they are based. To the extent that the relevant facts aren't properly conveyed to the lawyer providing the opinion, therefore, the opinion may be of little value.

Some Closing Tips: Legal Opinions

- Although legal opinions often make the recipient feel secure on the issues covered, there are times when more certainty is required. For example, a lessor or lessee concerned about whether a certain lease structure qualifies as a lease for federal income tax purposes is often well-advised to consider getting an Internal Revenue Service ruling on the issue.

• The "expertness" of the lawyer providing an opinion is a critical consideration, particularly when complex legal issues are involved. Therefore, if you need a legal opinion in a lease transaction, choose a lawyer with solid leasing experience.

The Lessor May Require a Transaction Opinion

In many situations, a lessor will ask that the lessee's attorney deliver an opinion that, in effect, provides the lessor with assurances that no legal issues exist that will undermine the lease transaction. For example, the lessee's lawyer might be asked to opine on whether:

• The lessee has been properly organized, is validly in existence, and is in good standing under the laws of its state of incorporation
• The lessee has the authority to enter into the lease
• The lessee has the ability to perform all of its lease obligations
• All the lessee's lease commitments are legally binding
• Any consents, such as those of the shareholders or lenders, are necessary and, if so, whether they have been obtained
• Any regulatory approvals, such as by a state public utility commission, are necessary and, if so, whether all the proper action has been taken
• There are any adverse pending or threatened court or administrative proceedings against the lessee and, if so, their probable outcome
• By entering into the lease arrangement or complying with any of its terms, the lessee would violate any law, rule, or provision of any of its existing agreements

An Opinion From the Lessor's Lawyer Might Be Advisable

In certain situations, the lessor's attorney will, or should, be asked to deliver a legal opinion.

Why the Lessee May Want an Opinion

A lessee should consider, particularly in large-ticket underwritten leveraged lease transactions, getting an opinion from the lessor's lawyer concerning the legal consequences of the lessor's ability to enter into and perform its obligations. The opinion should minimally confirm that the lessor is properly:

- Incorporated or organized, as the case may be, at the time the lease is signed
- Qualified to do business in the state where the equipment will be used, to avoid, for example, any risk that the equipment could be attached by the state authorities for the nonpayment of any taxes that the lessor may owe

Why the Lender May Want an Opinion

An equipment lender should always request a written opinion from the lessor's lawyer on key issues relating to its loan arrangement with the lessor. This type of opinion generally covers the same issues as those covered in the opinion given to the lessee—for example, whether:

- The lessor is duly organized, validly existing, and in good standing in its state of incorporation
- All the necessary transaction authorizations have been secured
- The lessor's obligations under the loan documents are fully enforceable

If the equipment loan is to be nonrecourse to the lessor, permitting the lender to look only to the lease payments and equipment for repayment, the lender will want an opinion stating that:

- The lessor has good and marketable title to the equipment covered by the lease
- The equipment is free and clear of any liens or encumbrances other than those of which the lender is aware
- The lessor has not made any other lease assignments
- The lender has a free and unencumbered right to receive all payments, such as rent, under the lease agreement

Although unlikely, the lessor may ask that the lender's counsel provide an opinion confirming that all the necessary action in connection with the loan's authorization has been taken. A loan without proper authorization may be withdrawn.

An Opinion From the Guarantor's Lawyer May Also Be Required

It's not unusual for the lessor to ask a third party to guarantee the lessee's lease obligations. For example, the parent company of a financially weak corporate lessee may be asked to guarantee the lease obligations as a condition to the lessor's lease commitment. In that case, the strength and viability of the guarantor's commitment are critical to the lessor and any nonrecourse equipment lender. To help confirm the guarantee's worth, a lessor will typically request a favorable opinion from the guarantor's lawyer on the applicable aspects.

The guarantor's legal opinion will address legal issues that relate to the guarantor's ability to fulfill the guarantee. For example, the opinion may be required to state whether:

- The guarantor is duly organized, validly existing, and in good standing
- Anything exists that could adversely affect the guarantee's quality, such as material litigation
- The guarantee has been fully and properly authorized
- The guarantee is a legally enforceable obligation

The Vendor's Lawyer May Be Asked for an Opinion

Although this is unusual, sometimes the lessor asks that the equipment vendor provide a legal opinion confirming that the vendor has, upon equipment payment, delivered clear title to the equipment, particularly if the equipment cost is substantial. In most situations, however, the lessor will rely solely on the vendor's bill of sale, provided it gives the typical seller representations and warranties as to good title.

The Need for Current Financial Information

The financial strength of the lessor, the lessee, and any third-party guarantor is a key factor in a lease financing, and therefore, it's important that reliable and up-to-date financial information be obtained. The amount of detail necessary depends on the transaction's size: A lease of a $900 office copier will not warrant the same degree of investigation as the lease of a multimillion-dollar printing press.

Although financial information is requested and reviewed when the lessor makes its lease commitment decision, well before the lease closing, certain financial updates are often required at the lease closing, ranging from lease representations as to no adverse changes in the financial information reviewed to supplying of updated financial statements.

Should the Lessor Provide Financial Information?

The financial condition of a lessor is an important lessee consideration: A solid lessor contractual commitment to lease is worthless if the lessor doesn't have funds available when the equipment arrives for lease. All too often, a prospective lessee fails to check the lessor's financial condition, apparently assuming that a lessor always has adequate funds and that, once the deal has been signed, there is nothing to be concerned about. This may not be true. A financially weak lessor may not have purchase money available when the equipment is ready for lease. And even if the equipment has been paid for and put on lease there's a risk—albeit a small one—that the lessor's creditors may seize the leased equipment as security for an unpaid obligation.

The availability of adequate funds for equipment purchase is of particular concern if a lease line of credit is involved—that is, when the lessor has committed to buy and lease many items of equipment to be delivered over a long period. Any lack of available lessor financing could be a serious problem for a would-be lessee.

The Lessee's Financial Information Is Critical

As mentioned several times earlier, the lessee's financial condition is a critical element in the lessor's decision as to whether to enter into a particular lease financing, particularly if a multimillion-dollar, long-term lease is involved. So at all times, the lessor, particularly at the lease closing and when it must advance funds, will want to be assured that the lessee has the financial capability to meet all of its contractual obligations, including payment of rent, for the full lease term.

The Financial Condition of a Controlling Corporation May Be Important

If the lessee is owned by another company, very often a lessor will want to review the parent company's financial statements—even if the parent does not guarantee the lease obligations and regardless of the financial strength of the lessee. The weaker the financial condition of an owning company, the greater the possibility that it will drain the lessee's cash to deal with any of its financial problems.

In addition to reviewing the parent company's financial condition, when there may be a risk that the owning corporation could drain a lessee's funds, the lessor might go a step further. For example, it could impose a restriction on the amount of dividends that the lessee can declare and distribute to the controlling corporation.

Any Guarantor Will Need to Supply Financial Information

If the lessee's financial condition is inadequate, the lessor may, as a condition of going forward with the financing, ask for a transaction guarantee from a financially solid entity, such as a parent company or an equipment vendor. In this event, the guarantor's financial strength is of primary importance, and relevant financial information will be included in the closing.

The Type of Financial Information That May Be Required

Typically, the financial condition of a company can be adequately assessed in a review of its past and present financial statements, including profit-and-loss statements and balance sheets. A lessor may also require bank and trade references to further verify the financial integrity of the company being reviewed. And it may check, particularly in the case of smaller companies, with credit-reporting services, such as Dun & Bradstreet and TRW, to see whether there is any adverse information on file.

Often, the lessor's financial review is done prior to its issuing a lease proposal offer, but sometimes, it is not done until shortly after the lease award. In any event, it's always done well in advance of starting the documentation negotiation. In those cases, the lessor will ask that the financially reviewed entity, particularly if there's a long time between the review and the lease signing, bring its financial information up to the closing date as well as provide the financial statements as a closing document.

One of the most common ways a participant's financial picture is brought up to the transaction's closing date is to require the reviewed entity's financial officer to deliver a certificate at the closing presenting relevant financial information since the last published statements. For example, if the most current financial statements reflect a company's condition as of June 15, 19XX, and the transaction does not close until September 25, 19XX, the certificate must essentially provide that, as of the closing date, September 25, 19XX, there have been no materially adverse financial changes since the date of the latest financial statements, June 15, 19XX. Of course, it would be more comforting to get the company's independent accountants to issue the certificate, but this is generally not practical.

It's always wise for any other party concerned to request updates as of the lease signing from any party whose financial condition may affect the transaction's viability. So, for example, you, as lessee, should require a financial update from a lessor whose financial condition you thought it necessary to review before making an award. This may also be done through a financial certificate from the lessor's financial officer.

Transaction Authorization Documents That Are Part of a Lease Closing

When a corporation participates in a lease transaction, the other parties should require a copy of the corporation's board of directors' resolutions authorizing the transaction. The resolutions will have to be certified by the corporate secretary or assistant secretary and delivered at the closing. The typical lessee resolution, for example, will state that the lessee has been duly authorized to enter into the transaction for the specified dollar amount and that a certain person has been authorized to execute the documents on behalf of the corporation.

Although lessors and lenders usually require lessees to deliver appropriate board of directors' resolutions at a lease closing, lessees rarely ask for authorizing resolutions from the other parties. They should seriously consider doing so, however, particularly from corporate lessors and lenders not regularly engaged in leasing or lending.

Some Closing Tips: Transaction Authorizations

- If the participant is not a corporation, but is, for example, a limited partnership, your attorney should be consulted about what authorization assurances might be advisable.

- If, after the lease has been signed, you discover that a key party failed to get the necessary, say, board of directors' transaction approval, you should immediately request that it deliver, in the case of a corporation, appropriate resolutions approving, ratifying, and confirming all actions that have been taken.

- While board of directors' resolutions should be reasonably broad in scope, corporate directors must be careful not to grant more than is necessary. For example, if a lease transaction is to involve a large conveyor system, its cost should be specified with leeway for reasonable changes. Unless the cost is designated, an individual representing the corporation may be able to bind it to a lease even if there were unexpected and significant cost increases.

Guarantees

A lessee wanting to lease more equipment than its credit capability justifies will be asked for additional credit support. Very often, the lessor will suggest that a financially strong third party be brought in to guarantee the lessee's obligations. The guarantee request may vary anywhere from a full guarantee of all the lease obligations to something significantly less.

The most favorable guarantee for a lessor would be a full lessee guarantee, where the guarantor unconditionally obligates itself to ensure the lessee's full and prompt performance of all the lease obligations, covenants, and conditions. For example, if the lessee fails to pay the rent, the lessor could go directly to the guarantor for payment.

Under a partial guarantee, the guarantor may, for example, only be responsible for the repayment of 15% of the total lease payments. Partial guarantees are usually acceptable to a lessor if the proposed transaction is very attractive, and it is willing to compromise.

Proof of Insurance Documents

Lease agreements generally ask that the lessee have personal injury and property damage insurance covering the leased equipment. In these cases, the lessor will want the lessee to confirm that the insurance will be in effect when the equipment is accepted for lease. That confirmation is required to be delivered at the lease closing and takes the form of a certificate of insurance from the lessee's insurance company stating that the necessary coverage will be in effect.

Some Closing Tips: Insurance

- Obtain and carefully review the proposed certificate of insurance well in advance of the lease closing to verify that the coverage outlined is proper and that it will be in effect when necessary. Be particularly careful about any coverage limitations, such as restricted equipment usage, because the lessor may find those limitations unacceptable. Finding out at the closing that the insurance certificate is inadequate will not only be embarrassing but also delay closing. The best approach is to send a draft certificate to the lessor weeks ahead of the closing for its review and acceptance.

- A lessor will often insist that the required insurance coverage cannot be canceled without prior written notice to it and only after an adequate grace period, to give it an opportunity to take out insurance if the lessee fails to keep it in force. Insurance companies are willing to make such a commitment when asked.

Equipment Purchase Agreements

Unless the equipment has been built, or is already owned, by the lessee, the lessor has to purchase it from a third-party supplier. If the equipment is available at the time the lease is signed, and it's ready for lease acceptance, the lessor simply buys it at that time.

What if the parties enter into the lease agreement before the equipment is ready to be delivered and accepted? When equipment is to be delivered in the future, particularly if it's a major dollar item, it's not unusual for a lessee to enter into an equipment purchase agreement. At times, vendors, knowing that the equipment will be put on lease, ask the lessor to enter directly into the purchase agreement.

For a variety of reasons, that is rarely a good idea, for either the lessor or the lessee. If the lessee, with or without justification, refuses to accept the equipment for lease, the lessor may still be legally obligated to buy the equipment. So sophisticated lessors, if a purchase agreement must be executed early, insist that the lessee be the signing party.

From a lessee's viewpoint, it's always advisable for it to enter into the purchase agreement directly with the equipment vendor and then assign only its right to purchase the equipment to the lessor, subject, of course, to the lessor's fulfilling its lease commitment. In this way, the lessee has direct contract rights with the supplier on warranty or other equipment-related claims, and the lessor has what it needs: the right to purchase the equipment directly from the supplier.

Here's how a purchase agreement and assignment might work: The lessee and the equipment supplier enter into the necessary purchase agreement, and then the lessor and the lessee enter into an assignment of this agreement. Under the assignment, the lessor generally acquires the lessee's contract purchase right but not its obligations. The assignment may also provide that the lessor will acquire additional rights, such as service or training, as well as all buyer warranties or indemnities, as of the time the lease ends and the equipment is returned to the lessor. Further, the assignment often states that the lessee shall remain liable on the purchase contract as if the assignment had not been made and requires the supplier's written consent to the assignment. The supplier is also often asked to specifically acknowledge that the lessor will not be liable for any of the purchase contract duties or obligations.

The Fundamental Importance of an Equipment Bill of Sale

A lessor often requires that the equipment seller deliver a bill of sale when it pays for the equipment. Typically, the bill of sale is a warranty bill of sale in which the seller not only transfers equipment title but also warrants that it has delivered to the purchaser full legal and beneficial ownership of the equipment, free and clear of any encumbrances, mortgages, or security interests. Such a bill of sale commonly has a seller representation that it has the lawful right and the appropriate authority to sell the equipment. Some lessors insist that the bill of sale also contain a seller representation that it will defend the lessor's title to the equipment against any person or entity claiming an interest in the equipment. It is often an important closing document.

Landowner or Mortgagee Waivers

Very often, leased equipment will be located on real property that is leased from a third party or that is subject to a mortgage. In this case, statutory lien rights may exist that, for example, permit a landlord to attach any equipment on its land, including leased equipment, if its rent is not paid. Similarly, the holder of a mortgage on a lessee's building may, under a general mortgage claim right, be able to go after leased equipment located in the building. In these situations, the lessor will require, as a closing document, a waiver from the landlord or mortgagee of any claim to the leased equipment.

Security Interest Filings

Although not technically necessary in most lease situations, a lessor will generally want to file appropriate Uniform Commercial Code (UCC) financing statements to ensure priority over other parties that may claim an interest in the equipment, particularly the lessee's creditors. If the UCC statement is not correctly filed, the lessor's claim to the equipment will not be perfected as to third parties, such as the lessee's general creditors, and won't give the desired protection. Simple in form, the statement basically requires nothing more than a description of the parties and the equipment. The UCC filing will be a condition of the lease closing. The filing procedures are routine and the expenses are nominal.

Participation Agreement Found in Underwritten Leases

A participation agreement, a closing document setting out the lease financing's structural terms and conditions, is frequently used in underwritten lease transactions, particularly leveraged transactions. The parties to such an agreement may include the lessee, the equity participants, the debt participants, and any trust established for the debt or equity participants. The participation agreement states the terms under which the debt participants must make their loans and the equity participants must make their equity investments. It also generally incorporates a method for substituting any defaulting participants and may include any prescribed tax indemnification provisions.

Owner's Trust Agreement

It's not unusual for a trust to be established for equity participants in a leveraged lease transaction, particularly if more than one equity participant is involved. The trust arrangement, referred to as an owner's trust, provides the equity participants with corporatelike liability protection and partnershiplike income tax treatment and thus can be a desirable ownership vehicle. It will be a closing document.

To set up a trust, the equity participants enter into a trust agreement with an entity, such as a bank, that will act as the trustee, referred to as the "owner trustee." The agreement sets out in detail how, and to what extent, the trustee will act on behalf of the equity participants.

As a part of its trust obligations, the trustee will execute all relevant documents—including the lease, any participation agreement, the indenture, and any purchase agreement assignment—on behalf of each equity participant. The right, title, and interest in the equipment, the lease, any purchase agreement, and any purchase agreement assignment are collectively referred to as the trust estate, and legal title to it is held in the owner trustee's name. The owner trustee is, however, only a figurehead owner, the beneficial interest in the trust estate residing with the equity participants. The equity participants' interests are represented by certificates, referred to as owner certificates, issued by the owner trustee.

Lender's Trust Agreement

If the financing is structured as a leveraged lease, the debt participants will typically act through a trust arrangement that enables them to receive favorable tax treatment and liability protection. The arrangement is typically set up through a trust indenture and mortgage agreement entered into between the equity participants and debt participants. A trust indenture and mortgage agreement defines the basic debt-financing parameters and provides for issuing loan certificates that set out the debt repayment obligations. The agreement also grants a security interest in the equipment and the lease to the lenders while the loan is outstanding. As with a participation agreement, it will be one of the lease-closing documents.

The debt trust structure is similar to the equity trust structure. The debt participants are represented by a trustee, referred to as the "loan trustee," and it stands in the same position to the debt participants as does the owner trustee to the equity participants. As the lender's "watchdog," the trustee can take any prescribed action that may be necessary to protect the debt participants' interests, such as foreclosing on the lease in case of default.

Using a Partnership Instead of a Trust Arrangement

At times, multiple equity or debt participants find it undesirable or impractical to act through a trust arrangement. In that case, they frequently use a partnership structure instead. Here, the "lessor" or "lender," as the case may be, is the partnership, with the equity or debt participants as partners in the partnership. It's usually advisable for a formal partnership agreement to be entered into that defines each partner's rights and obligations. The agreement will be a part of the lease closing.

Underwriter's Fee Agreement

In underwritten transactions, the lease underwriter will be responsible for bringing together the equity participants, the lessee, and if the transaction is leveraged, the debt participants. For its services, the underwriter will be entitled to a fee, typically varying with each transaction and each broker, and typically payable by the equity participants. To protect itself and prevent later misunderstandings as to the payment terms, the underwriter may ask that the equity participants enter into a formal fee agreement clearly defining the fee arrangement, which will also be included as a closing document.

A Supplemental Document Closing Checklist

Although the type of additional closing documents required in a lease transaction will vary with each situation, this checklist can provide general guidelines.

- What should you look for in reviewing legal opinions?
  - Is the lawyer rendering the legal opinion thoroughly experienced in the area to be covered by the opinion? Fox example, if an opinion is required on complex tax issues, is he or she fully knowledgeable on all the relevant aspects?
  - How much has the legal opinion been conditioned? In other words, has the lawyer left so many outs as to his or her position that the legal opinion really has provided little comfort?

- To the extent that the legal opinion is based on facts supplied to the lawyer, are the facts accurate and complete?

- Does the opinion of the lessee's lawyer, to be delivered to the lessor, address the following issues?
  - Proper organization, valid existence, and good standing of the lessee
  - The lessee's full authority to enter into the lease
  - The lessee's complete and unrestricted ability to perform all obligations
  - Whether all the lessee's lease commitments are legally binding
  - Whether all necessary consents have been obtained
  - Whether all necessary regulatory approvals have been obtained
  - Whether there are any pending or threatened adverse court or administrative proceedings and, if so, what the potential impact may be
  - Whether any law, rule, or collateral agreement will be violated by the lessee's entering the lease transaction

- Does the opinion of the lessor's lawyer, to be delivered to the lessee, address the following issues?
  - Whether the lessor is properly organized, validly existing, and in good standing
  - Whether the lessor is properly authorized to do business in the jurisdiction where the equipment will be located
  - Whether the transaction has been fully authorized by the lessor. For example, have all necessary committee and board of director approvals been secured?
  - Whether all the lessor's commitments are binding
  - Whether the lessor's ability to perform its obligations is unrestricted
  - Whether any shareholder, lender, or other consents are necessary. If so, have they been obtained?
  - Whether the transaction will violate any law, rule, or collateral agreement as to the lessor

- Does the opinion of the lessor's lawyer, to be delivered to a third-party lender, address the following issues?
  - Whether the lessor is properly organized, validly existing, and in good standing
  - Whether all necessary authorizations, as to both the lease financing and the loan financing, have been obtained
  - Whether the loan obligations are fully enforceable against the lessor

- Whether the lessor has good and marketable title to the leased equipment
- Whether the equipment has any liens or encumbrances on it
- Whether the lessor's rights under the lease are unencumbered, including its right to receive the rent payments

- Does the opinion of the guarantor's lawyer, to be delivered to the lessor, address the following issues?
  - Whether the guarantor is properly organized, validly existing, and in good standing
  - Whether all necessary authorizations as to the lease financing have been obtained
  - Whether the lease obligations are fully enforceable against the guarantor

- Does the opinion of the vendor's lawyer, to be delivered to the lessor, address the following issues?
  - Whether the title to the equipment will be delivered free and clear to the lessor
  - Whether all necessary internal authorizations have been obtained

- Has the lessor been supplied with the required lessee, lessee controlling corporation, and guarantor financial statements?
  - Profit-and-loss statements
  - Balance sheets
  - Officer's certificate updating information to the closing

- Have adequate lessor financial statements or information been obtained?
  - Profit-and-loss statements
  - Balance sheets
  - Officer's certificate updating information to the closing

- Have all the critical financial statements been certified by an independent certified public accounting firm?

- Has a certified copy of any relevant corporate board of director resolutions been delivered?

- If the lease obligations will be guaranteed by a third party, will it be a full and unconditional guarantee? If not, is the limited extent of the guarantee understood?

- If personal injury and property damage insurance is required, does the insurance company's certificate of insurance properly represent the required insurance?

- If the lessor must enter into an equipment purchase agreement directly with the vendor, is it prepared to buy the equipment if the lessee backs away? If not, can a purchase agreement assignment be used?
  - Does any equipment purchase agreement assignment specifically provide that only the rights, not the obligations, will be transferred to the lessor?
  - Under an equipment purchase agreement assignment, will the lessor be entitled to all vendor-supplied services, training, information, warranties, and indemnities?
  - Has the vendor's consent been obtained as to the purchase agreement assignment? If so, does it acknowledge the following?
    - That the assignment has been made
    - That the lessor will not have to buy the equipment if the
    - lessee backs out before the lease is executed

- Has an equipment bill of sale been included? If so:
  - Is it a warranty bill of sale?

- Does it contain a representation that the seller has the lawful right and authority to sell the equipment?

- If the equipment will be located on leased or mortgaged property, has the landowner or mortgagee supplied a written waiver of any present or future claim to the leased equipment?

- Have appropriate UCC financing statements (UCC-1s) been prepared for filing?

- If the transaction is underwritten:
  - Has a participation agreement been prepared?
  - Through what will the lenders and the equity participants each act?
    - A trust arrangement
    - A partnership arrangement
    - Has a fee agreement been prepared to formalize the underwriter's fee arrangement?

Chapter 9

Some Wrap-Up Advice and Thoughts

Putting What You've Learned to Work

To get the best possible lease deal, you must be part technical expert, part salesperson, and part negotiator. After reading this book, you have the necessary business and negotiation background to take on the best lessor negotiators. With a quick turn of the page, you can access the most effective lease negotiation tips, strategies, and insights learned through many years of trial-and-error negotiation—on both the lessor's side and the lessee's side.

Your next two challenges will be to massage into your own style the tips, strategies, and suggestions offered throughout the book and to sell the leasing community on your company's upcoming lease as a solid financing opportunity. The many guidelines you've been given will help you quickly organize an effective and comprehensive negotiation approach. In doing so, keep in mind that negotiation is a give-and-take process, each side having to accept less than it would like in order to reach final agreement. And I can't emphasize enough that your strategy in a given situation must be well-thought-out and simple. It must have the support of every individual in your organization, particularly management. If it doesn't, you may be forced to make changes in midstream. Doing so can signal a weakness in your bargaining approach that a lessor negotiator will use to his or her advantage. This, of course, doesn't mean that you shouldn't be prepared to make approach changes that will clearly better your leverage. One final point: Resist any temptation to make changes or concessions simply because you're tired of negotiating or in a hurry to get the deal done.

In order to get the best possible lease financing for your company, you have to be prepared to set the negotiating stage in your favor. Although it's difficult to provide a set of general rules that will guarantee success in a given situation, there are some basic considerations that will increase your bargaining leverage with a lessor. The following section explores these to ensure that you are properly prepared.

Getting Leverage When You Have None

The first thing you must realize is that you will never encounter a lease—or for that matter, any other negotiation situation—in which your actual negotiating leverage is zero. You may, however, face situations in which your perceived bargaining leverage is less than your opponent's or even zero. Many of you may disagree, saying that there are times when you've had little or no negotiating leverage. However, if you think about those situations, undoubtedly you'll find that they were ones in which either you were unwilling to compromise or you felt so uncomfortable for one reason or another that you simply gave in to your opponent's demands.

If you are willing to make an effort in any lease situation, you can put yourself in a bargaining position that is equal, or superior, to that of a lessor. How? Well, there are three basic ways to do this:

1. Develop alternative strategies in the event you encounter insurmountable problems.
2. Put your financing needs in a lessor-attractive package.
3. Develop a good, organized negotiation style.

Let's first discuss developing options. Having alternatives will allow you to negotiate from strength.

Developing Alternatives

Being able to negotiate effectively means having alternatives in any given situation. Finding alternatives is often simply a matter of detaching yourself from what you think you need or want long enough to explore what else may be available. It may, for example, mean being willing to buy instead of leasing the equipment, or starting negotiations with your backup lessor.

Developing alternatives that shore up your bargaining leverage often takes effort. But if you're able to make the effort, and live with the feeling, possibly for a day or two, that you can't imagine what other alternatives exist, some will invariably pop into your mind. If, however, you're so intent on proceeding a particular way, you will block your ability to come up with other options. If you perceive that your bargaining power is weak, an experienced negotiator will spot that in you—regardless of how well you think you've hidden it. So alternatives are a must.

Here's an example of what I mean: Assume your company wants to lease a $65,000 computer system. It currently is experiencing serious financial problems. If you're like most people looking for lease financing in this situation, you'll feel that you're going to have to take what a lessor offers—having little, if any, room to negotiate more favorable terms. Feeling that way going into a lease negotiation will affect your demeanor in subtle, and often unconscious, ways—something an experienced opponent will quickly identify and use against you.

For example, your speech pattern may vary slightly, pausing for a fraction of a second in response to delicate or probing questions. Your deal requests may belie a lack of confidence or uneasiness: You may, for example, be a little too polite. And your body language may give you away: Your facial muscles may sag ever so slightly, your face may be marginally pale, your eyes may move unnaturally, or your shoulders may slump slightly. Worse yet, even if you've managed to cover up everything, an experienced negotiator can still sense when something is amiss.

So what do you do to avoid handing your opponent an edge? Change your attitude rather than trying to cover it up. Not so easy, you might say. After all, when we're afraid or concerned, most of us know that our anxieties take on a life of their own, dominating our ability to think and feel differently. Have you ever tried to stop worrying when you're afraid? At best, it's difficult, and often, it's impossible.

How do you change your attitude? Learn to accept possible loss. And having alternatives is one way to free yourself to do so. For example, take time before negotiations begin to decide what you would do if the lessor to which you've given an award refuses to go along with an important concession. And be realistic about each negotiation issue, so you don't hold on to any for the wrong reason. For example, assume it was important that your company be able to deduct the lease payments as a rent expense. In order for your company to do so, the lease would have to qualify as a true lease for federal income tax purposes. In your case, the rent offered is extremely low, but the lessor has insisted on having a put option, something that may cause the lease to fail to qualify as a true lease. The choice facing you is whether to risk IRS discovery and lose the rent deduction or walk away from the deal. Although generalizations are not possible, if the lease is for a small dollar amount, it may be worth the risk.

In evaluating risk, it will also help if you can identify the underlying basis of your fears or concerns. Is the risk one you can assess based on your own experience, or must you rely on a third party to evaluate it? And if you must rely on a third party, is he or she generally negative?

Keep in mind that finding alternatives to increase your bargaining power in a lease negotiation is no different than buying a car. If you need a new car and, for example, are dealing with several dealers, it's less likely you'll be backed into a corner. Or if you can make do for, say, another year with your existing car, you'll also negotiate from strength.

To get you started in thinking about alternatives, here are some considerations that will open possibilities in most lease situations:

- Are there funds available to purchase the equipment outright?
- If long-term funds aren't available to purchase the equipment outright, is short-term money available to buy the equipment so a sale/leaseback can be pursued at a leisurely pace?
- Is there a backup lessor ready and willing to finance the equipment, even if the deal is somewhat less favorable?
- Can the equipment supplier finance the equipment on a short-term or long-term basis?
- Is there access to an investor willing to put up equipment equity funds, so a long-term equipment loan is more accessible?
- Will a parent or affiliated company or third party, such as the equipment vendor, provide any lease payment guarantee?
- Is there cheaper, used equipment available that might do the same job?

Packaging Your Financing So a Lessor Wants to Buy

Getting a lessor interested in providing lease financing is no different than coming up with a sales strategy for any product. To sell its product, for example, a manufacturer must determine what its prospective customer wants. It might be the lowest price or the highest quality—or a compromise between the two.

As a prospective lessee, your prospective customers are leasing companies. To get the best possible deal, you have to know how to package your lease opportunity so a lessor wants to invest in it. The lessor must feel that the potential lease offers an attractive balance between profit and investment risk. The less investment risk a lessor perceives it has, the better the deal you'll get. So your job is to create an investment scenario that motivates as many lessors as possible to want your business. The more attractive the investment opportunity, the more lessors will be interested in it and the easier it will be to get a lessor to stretch—or compete—to do business with you.

What does a leasing company want? Well, you now know from Chapter 2 that it wants huge profits at no risk. And you also now know that, in today's market, that's not possible. So to stay in business, a lessor must accept something less. You, as lessee, however, must not forget that you are competing with other prospective lessees for the lessor's dollar, in the same way any product or service seller competes for the consumer's dollar. To get the best available deal, therefore, your package must be perceived as relatively more attractive than the packages offered by other potential lessees in your prospective lessor's market.

If your company has an AAA financial rating, this is easy, and a lessor will cut its profit requirement to the bare minimum to finance your equipment. On the other hand, if your company has severe financial problems, this will be a challenge. In the latter case, you must develop a story that sells the lessor on aspects of your company or market situation that help offset the financial risk. If, for example, your company has maintained a product market niche for years or has an exclusive long-term customer contract or relationship, make that known. If the financial downturn can be explained as a historic anomaly, do so. Your financial officer or adviser will be of help in coming up with aspects that will increase a lessor's comfort. Very simply, use anything that will help convince a lessor that its investment is secure—that funds will be available to pay the rent. The more secure the lessor feels, the better deal you'll get. And remember, security is often a subjective determination.

Developing Your Negotiation Style

Although it's impossible to provide a basic lease negotiation philosophy that will increase your bargaining power in every situation, experience has shown that, by following certain basic rules, even people with little or no lease negotiation background can increase their bargaining leverage.

You've been given a lot of negotiation tips, strategies, and tactics throughout the book. They will all help. The following suggestions are what I consider my top 20 tips, strategies, and tactics. At a minimum, use them as guides in approaching any lease situation. They work. Modify them as necessary to further enhance your bargaining position and personal negotiating style.

1. *Use competitive bidding.* Create an environment in which the lessor must compete for your business, even when the financing transaction is small. As discussed at length earlier, nothing is more powerful than open competitive bidding—asking a number of leasing companies to bid on your financing and letting each know it's a competitive bid situation.

2. *Always have a fallback leasing company.* Nothing creates more negotiating leverage than having another lessor in the background ready to begin negotiations with you in the event existing negotiations break down—provided the lessor with which you're negotiating is aware of your backup lessor. So take the beauty contest approach and have a runner-up.

3. *Fully disclose financial problems.* Never attempt to hide a financial problem. If it's discovered—and you can bet it will be— chances are good that the embarrassment of discovery will seriously damage your ability to negotiate effectively and credibly. It's better to be

open and direct because the person or committee making the lessor's investment decision will feel more comfortable with, and have more confidence in, you and your company.

4. *Never acknowledge the seriousness of a financial problem.* Disclose financial problems when asked, but never confirm their seriousness to the lessor; let the lessor make its own determination. This means, for example, matter-of-factly delivering your financial statements in which the problem is disclosed. And never verify any lessor concern or express your own. Let the hard facts speak for themselves and by themselves.

5. *Create a sense of investment security.* If you're not a *Fortune* 500 company, create an attractive financial and business story about your company. Highlight the positive growth aspects. Make the lessor feel that your lease deal is a solid financing opportunity. That means putting together a comprehensive, but not overwhelming, information package about your products and/or services that portrays an exciting and secure business.

6. *Never state that the final lease decision is yours.* Even if you are the person with full responsibility for making the lease decision, always indicate that some person or group, not a party to your negotiations, must review and approve the results of your final negotiations. For example, make it known that your boss, board of directors, accountant, or lawyer must approve the final deal before you can sign the lease. If need be, make up an imaginary person. And if there is such a third party, make sure your opponent never has access to him or her.

7. *Use a written request for lease quotes.* If you want lease quotes from a lessor, use a written request for quotes. You'll look as if you know what you're doing and will be taken seriously. Experienced lease negotiators always use written RFQs.

8. *Insist on written lease offers.* If a lease offer is not in writing, you can be manipulated. Asking for written offers makes you look as if you know what you're doing and intend to carefully review what's offered.

9. *Develop your own form lease.* Develop and deliver your own form lease with your RFQ.

10. *Put together a deal timetable.* Nothing shows you mean business more than creating a written deal timetable, keeping it updated, delivering it to all parties involved, and complaining when it's not being met.

11. *Always read the proposal and lease carefully and question everything.* When you get a lessor's lease proposal, and if you must use a lessor's

form lease, question everything that is not clear. If you're self-conscious about asking, it will be apparent, and your opponent may use that against you. In my experience, even experienced lawyers don't understand every single lease provision. And rarely is anyone completely secure that what he or she has written is perfectly clear. So question anything you don't understand with confidence. Doing so will increase your leverage.

12. *Always have a third-party expert on call.* It's a good idea to have ready access to a leasing expert in the event difficult issues arise. More important, letting your opponent know that you may be seeking the advice of a leasing expert in the event difficult issues arise will help keep his or her bluffing and tactics to a minimum. Do this even if you are a leasing expert. Having an unknown finance specialist in the background can be intimidating.

13. *Keep requests simple.* Winning often means keeping issues simple—ensuring that your opponent knows what you want.

14. *Always ask for more than you need.* Asking a lessor for more than you need provides you with points that cost little to concede in the bargaining process.

15. *Don't let pride get in the way of closing a deal.* There are times in a negotiation when having to make a concession costs little but hurts a lot if it looks as if you're being run over. Accept when you've been outmaneuvered and don't get emotionally hooked on winning a point for winning's sake. Pride can complicate, and risk, closing what may otherwise be a reasonable lease deal.

16. *Be willing to change lessors.* Always be willing to start over with another lessor if negotiations become unacceptable. Often, stating that the deal is off is enough to bring your opponent to his or her senses. But if you use this negotiation trump card, be prepared to follow though.

17. *Don't focus on crushing your opponent.* People preoccupied with crushing their opponent simply to feel good are rarely effective negotiators and often unnecessarily cause deals to collapse. Your objective must be solely to get the best possible—and most reasonable—business deal.

18. *Never feel that the lessor is doing you a favor.* Lessors need your business to stay in business. Don't forget that.

19. *There is always a deal.* It may take some effort and creativity, but most deals can be done if you're willing to make the compromises necessary. Don't give up until you've explored every possible alternative in a difficult situation.

20. *Don't let your perceptions get in the way.* The negotiation process starts the minute you begin thinking about your lease deal. Don't assume that a lessor won't give you something. Ask and be turned down. If you don't, you'll be helping your opponent.

Some Comments About Issues Often Overlooked

In approaching a lease situation, prospective lessees often fail to consider three important issues: (1) a possible lessor bankruptcy, (2) selecting a lease negotiator or adviser, and (3) the actual lease commitment.

The Risk of a Lessor Bankruptcy

In today's economic climate, bankruptcies are not uncommon. A lessor bankruptcy can create difficulties for a lessee. So before entering into a lease with a particular leasing company, consider the following points: The lessor, not the lessee, actually owns the equipment. Typically, that ownership interest has been put up, commonly referred to as encumbered, in some way as security for loans the lessor took out to finance either your particular deal or its business operations in general. The arrangement with a lessor is a long-term, fixed relationship, so you're locked in for the duration. And if the lessor goes under, generally you'll still have to keep making rent payments to either a trustee in bankruptcy or the lessor's bank. For most lessees, this won't be a problem because, under the typical lease agreement, which the trustee or creditor must abide by, there is a right of quiet enjoyment for as long as the rent is paid. But if a lease modification is needed, you may find that dealing with the trustee or bank is difficult or impossible.

How can a lessor go bankrupt? There are a number of ways. If its major leases are assigned to a lender, along with the rent payments, and the lessees go bankrupt, the resulting failure to pay rent may throw a lessor into involuntary bankruptcy. Or a lessor may simply mismanage its finances and be unable to pay its bills. There is no way to avoid the risk of lessor bankruptcy, but by dealing with financially strong lessors, you can minimize it.

Picking Your Lawyer or Lease Adviser

One of the biggest mistakes lessees make is hiring lawyers or lease consultants who have little or no leasing experience. Now, you might say, everyone has to start somewhere, and that's not a fair position. Unfortunately, leasing is technically complex: There are many legal pitfalls and hidden traps. An experienced counsel or adviser, even if he or she charges a higher hourly rate, can save you money and headaches in the long run. Inexperienced ones are rarely able to assess difficult lease issues properly, unnecessarily running up hourly charges or risking the deal. If you're going to hire a lease lawyer or adviser, check out his or her background thoroughly by, for example, calling former or existing clients.

The Lease Commitment

As discussed in Chapter 1, the typical finance lease contains a "hell-or-high-water" obligation that states that the rent is unconditionally due for the entire lease term, without offset for any reason whatsoever, including the failure of the lessor to live up to any of its lease obligations, such as, for example, the failure to fulfill any upgrade-financing commitment. Unless the lessee was improperly induced into signing the lease, courts generally enforce the payment obligation, allowing a lessee to sue the lessor on separate grounds for any such contract breach, of course.

What if the lease does not contain a hell-or-high-water payment obligation? In that case, a lease is no different than any other contract: If one party fails to fulfill any of its obligations, then the other party has a right, among other remedies, to terminate the contract. Although generalities are not possible when dealing with a particular lease, chances are good that if it does not contain a lessee hell-or-high-water commitment, it's conceivable that a lessee may be able to declare the contract in default and legally stop paying rent. You are referred to my equipment lease forms book, *Complete Book of Equipment Leasing Agreements, Forms, Checklists, & Worksheets* (published by AMACOM), for examples of typical hell-or-high-water rent commitments that a lessor can enforce in a court of law against a nonpaying lessee.

Generally speaking, then, it's unlikely that a lessee can get out of a finance lease unless the agreement contains clear rights to do so, such as termination rights. The best insurance against having to continue to lease equipment that is no longer needed, or for which funds are not available, is to ensure that the lease agreement contains a termination option and/or a sublease right.

Tactically, there is one more possibility that might be considered—only, however, on the advice of competent counsel. As a practical business matter, lawsuits are expensive and time-consuming, and there is always a risk that they could result in an unfavorable decision even against the party that clearly has been damaged. A skilled lawyer can often concoct a credible defense from the situation facts that can tie up the parties for years in court.

Although I'm not suggesting that someone flagrantly violate another party's contract rights without cause, if you, as lessee, have had your rights violated by the lessor, even in a hell-or-high-water finance lease situation, it's often a good business tactic, if you intend to bring a lawsuit against the lessor on a breach, to stop the rent payments. Doing so cuts the lessor's cash flow and can put pressure on it to compromise merely to have some revenues available. One way of putting financial pressure on a lessor if you're unwilling simply to withhold rent is to pay the rent into an escrow fund pending the outcome of litigation. Although the funds will still be available to a defaulting lessor, by so doing you've put financial pressure on it, particularly if not timely receiving the rent proceeds could put the lessor under pressure to come to a reasonable compromise.

The Results Are Now Up to You

Now you have the background to negotiate the best possible lease deal. If you take full advantage of the information and techniques, you will be in the driver's seat. The advantage that lessors have had in the past over prospective lessees is that lessees rarely knew what issues were of real concern to a lessor and where there might be room to compromise. If a lessor bluffed, claiming that it was impossible to provide a certain concession, uninformed lessees often bought the statement hook, line, and sinker.

Good luck on your next equipment lease financing.

Appendix A

Negotiation Objectives Checklist

Rating Points

1–4 = *deal point:* No compromise accepted. This request must be granted or the deal is off.

5–8 = *compromise considered:* Depends on what is given in return.

9–10 = *throwaway issue:* The issue is not worth arguing about but, after appropriate resistance, can be conceded to show good-faith negotiating.

Negotiation Objectives Checklist

Negotiation Objectives	Priority Rating
1. Lessor must not be a broker.	_____
2. Lessor must provide financial statements.	_____
3. Lessor must put up a performance bond.	_____
4. Lessor must submit a written bid.	_____
a) Bid must be firm.	_____
5. Lessor must accept all lessee business requests as an award condition.	_____

6. Lessor must hold the lease rate firm
for three months.   _____

7. Lessor must pay all transaction expenses:
   a) If deal goes through   _____

   b) If deal collapses:
      (1) For any reason   _____

      (2) Due to lessor's failure   _____

8. Lessor must offer ±15% equipment
cost latitude without penalty.   _____

9. There must be no commitment fee.   _____

10. There must be no nonutilization fee.   _____

11. Lessor must accept the lessee's
form of lease.   _____

12. Master lease is required.   _____

13. Lessor must submit its form
lease with its bid.   _____

14. Operating lease characterization
is required (for accounting purposes).   _____

15. Lessor must be a tax lessor.   _____

16. Single-investor lease structure
is required.   _____

17. Leveraged lease structure is required.   _____

18. Lowest rental rate should be obtained.   _____

19. Lease term should be as long as possible.   _____

20. Lease term should be as short as possible.   _____

21. No interim rent should be required.   _____

22. There should be no rent payment
    obligation until the vendor is paid.   _____

23. Rent may be paid by regular check.   _____

24. Rent should be expressed as a percentage of
    equipment cost (automatic adjustment for cost changes). _____

25. Lease term must start on
    a specific monthly date.   _____

26. There should be a fixed-price
    renewal option.   _____

27. There should be a fair market
    renewal option.   _____

28. There should be no automatic
    renewal provision.   _____

29. There should be a fixed-price
    purchase option.   _____

30. There should be a fair market
    purchase option.   _____

31. Lessor should have no right to require
    the lessee to purchase at lease end.   _____

32. There should be an early lease
    termination option:
    a) Beginning at lease term start   _____

    b) Beginning after one year   _____

33. Lessor must supply early termination
    and casualty schedules with its bid.   _____

34. Early lease termination should be
    permitted without penalty.   _____

35. There should be a right to sublease.   _____

36. There should be a right to sublease
    without lessor consent.   _____

37. Lease default should not be permitted
    without prior written notice from the lessor.   _____

38. Lessee should have the right to
    upgrade financing.   _____

39. Lessor should cooperate in
    upgrade financing.   _____

40. Lessee should have the right to
    self-insure equipment.   _____

41. Lessee should have the right to
    self-maintain equipment.   _____

42. Lessor must pass through all
    manufacturer warranties.   _____

43. Lessor can make no lease assignment
    without the lessee's consent.   _____

44. Lessor can assign its lease interest
    for security purposes only.   _____

45. Lease may not be assigned to:
     a) A lessee line bank   _____

     b) A lessee competitor   _____

46. No lessee income tax indemnities
    should be required.   _____

47. Lessor income tax indemnifications should
    be required only for lessee's acts or omissions.   _____

48. Lessor must pay all equipment costs
    (sales taxes, installation, etc.).   _____

49. There should be no lessee end-of-lease
    equipment redelivery cost.   _____

50. End-of-lease equipment return
    should take place at the lessee's site.   _____

Appendix B

Request for Quotations to Lease Equipment

A Formal Request for Quotes Letter

Request for Quotations to Lease Equipment

April 12, 19XX

SunBird Corporation is issuing this Request for Quotations (RFQ) to obtain equipment lease bids from prospective lessors. This RFQ is not an offer to contract. SunBird Corporation will not be obligated to lease the specified equipment until a mutually satisfactory written lease has been executed by all parties.

A. Proposal Request—General

In accordance with the terms and conditions specified below, SunBird Corporation wishes to receive proposals from equipment leasing companies (Lessors) to provide lease financing for certain data-processing equipment.

In the evaluation of each proposal, SunBird Corporation will rely on all written and verbal representations made by each prospective Lessor, and each representation will be incorporated into any and all formal agreements between the parties.

No Lessor receiving this RFQ is authorized to act for, or on behalf of, SunBird Corporation prior to the receipt of written acceptance by SunBird Corporation of a satisfactory lease proposal and then only in accordance with the specific terms, if any, of the acceptance.

B. Proposal Guidelines

1. Your proposal must be submitted in writing and follow the guidelines in this RFQ. If not, it will be rejected.

2. All RFQ requirements must be addressed. Specifically identify any requirements that cannot be satisfied.

3. If you can offer any additional benefits not requested in this RFQ, identify them as "Additional Benefits" and state them in a separate section at the end of your proposal.

4. You must notify SunBird Corporation no later than the Lessor Proposal Intent Notification Due date specified in the Timetable in section D if you intend to submit a proposal in response to this RFQ.

5. SunBird Corporation may, without liability and at its sole discretion, amend or rescind this RFQ prior to the lease award. In such event, each Lessor offering to submit a proposal will be supplied, as the case may be, with an RFQ amendment or a notification of our intent not to proceed.

6. Your proposal will be considered confidential, and none of the contents will be disclosed to a competing Lessor.

7. You shall be responsible for all costs incurred in connection with the preparation of your proposal and any contract(s) in response to this RFQ.

8. Your proposal must be signed by a duly authorized representative of your company.

9. Your proposal must be submitted in triplicate and remain in effect at least until the lessor proposal commitment cutoff date specified in the Timetable in section D.

10. Your proposal should be accompanied by (a) a copy of your most recent annual report or financial statements or appropriate bank references with account officer name and telephone number; (b) a description of any material litigation in which you are currently involved; and (c) a statement of any potential conflict of interest, and plan to avoid it, as a result of an award.

11. SunBird Corporation intends to announce its award decision no later than the Award Announcement date specified in the Timetable in section D.

12. Any questions concerning this RFQ should be sent in writing to:

    SunBird Corporation
    1823 Third Avenue
    New York, New York 11020
    Attn. John Peterson
    Telephone no.: (212) 754-2367

    Any questions and answers that we feel would be of assistance to all Lessors submitting proposals will be promptly distributed to each.

13. SunBird Corporation may enter simultaneously in negotiations with more than one Lessor and make an award to one or more without prior notification to others with which we are negotiating.

14. Any information supplied to you in this RFQ by SunBird Corporation or otherwise by any representative in connection with this RFQ is confidential and may not be disclosed or used except in connection with the preparation of your proposal. If you must release any such information to any person or entity for the purpose of preparing your proposal, you must obtain an agreement prior to releasing the information that it will be treated as confidential by such person or entity and will not be disclosed except in connection with the preparation of your proposal.

15. If you are a selected Lessor, prior to our making the award, you will be supplied with a copy of our form lease document(s) for your review. Your response to the acceptability of the document provisions, with exceptions noted in writing, will be a condition precedent to any award.

C. Equipment Lease Requirements

1. Equipment Description, Cost, and Trade-In

a. The equipment will consist of electronic data-processing equipment (Equipment) acquired from the following designated vendor(s):

Vendor	Equipment Description	Cost
StarByte Computer Corp. StarByte Computer Corp. Buffalo, NY	(1) Model 423 Computer (7) Model 3 Remote Ctrs.	$1,850,000 350,000
Microtech, Inc.	Material Tracking System Installation: Total:	150,000 120,000 $2,470,000

(i) The final cost of the Equipment may vary as much as +(10)% or –(20)%, and your financing offer must permit this leeway without penalty.

b. If you can provide more advantageous financing by supplying equipment you own, have access to, or can acquire through volume discount arrangements with a vendor, please provide the specifics in the "Additional Benefits" section. If you intend to offer to provide any used equipment, the serial number(s), current location(s), and owner(s) must be stated in your proposal.

(i) Any equipment you offer to supply must be delivered to SunBird Corporation at 937 Secour Drive, Buffalo, New York 11342 no later than the Anticipated Equipment Delivery date specified in the Timetable in section D and be ready for acceptance no later than the specified Anticipated Equipment Acceptance date. You must provide a firm delivery date commitment with contractual assurances and remedies for failure to meet such date, which should be stated in your proposal.

c. The Equipment will replace equipment under an existing lease of computer equipment, and SunBird Corporation would like you to propose an additional financing arrangement that would incorporate the buyout of that lease. The specifics of the existing lease are as follows:

Lessor: AmerLease Corp.
Lease term: 7 years
Lease start date: March 1, 19XX
Lease ending date: February 28, 19XX
Monthly rent: $21,324, in advance
Lease termination amount as of August 31, 19XX: $397,000
Equipment: StarByte XTRA Material Tracking Computer System
Original equipment cost: $1,253,000
Right to sublease: yes
Purchase option: fair market
Renewal option: year-to-year, 90 days' prior notice, fair market

(i) If you can provide any other arrangement that would be beneficial, such as subleasing the existing equipment to another lessee, please so indicate.

2. Estimated Delivery and Acceptance Date

It is anticipated that the Equipment will be delivered and accepted for lease no later than the Anticipated Equipment Delivery and Anticipated Equipment Acceptance date(s) specified in the Timetable in section D.

3. Equipment Payment

The Equipment must be paid for by the Lessor no later than thirty (30) days following acceptance for lease.

4. Equipment Location

The Equipment will initially be accepted for lease at our manufacturing plant located at 937 Secour Drive, Buffalo, New York. We must have the right to move the equipment to any location in the United States without the prior consent of the Lessor but upon providing thirty (30) days' prior written notice.

5. Primary Lease Term

Your proposal must provide offers to lease the Equipment for Primary Lease Terms of five (5) and seven (7) years.

The Primary Lease Terms must run from the later of the Equipment acceptance for lease or payment in full by the Lessor for the Equipment.

6. Primary Term Rents

Rent payments must be quoted on a monthly, in advance, and quarterly, in arrears, basis.

The rent payments must be expressed as a percentage of Equipment Cost and be on a consecutive, level basis. The nominal lease interest rate must be provided for each rent quote.

SunBird Corporation shall not be obligated for payment of rent until the Equipment vendor has been paid in full.

7. Interim Lease Term

No Interim Lease Term will be permitted that requires payment of interim rent.

8. Interim Rents

No Interim Lease Term rent payments will be acceptable.

9. Options

a. SunBird Corporation must have the option to renew the term of the lease year-to-year for a total of three (3) years, on a fair market value basis. Offers providing for a fixed-price renewal will also be considered. Any fixed-price offers should be included in an "Additional Benefits" section at the end of the Lessor's proposal.

b. Lessee must have the right to purchase the Equipment at the end of the Primary Lease Term and each Renewal Term for its then fair market value. Offers providing for the right to purchase for a fixed percentage of Equipment Cost will be given favorable consideration and should be included in an "Additional Benefits" section at the end of the Lessor's offer.

c. SunBird Corporation must have the right, beginning as of the end of the first year of the Primary Lease Term, to terminate the lease prior to the end of the Primary Lease Term, or any Renewal Term, in the event the Equipment becomes obsolete or surplus to SunBird Corporation's needs.

(i) In the event of an early termination, SunBird Corporation shall have the right to arrange for the sale or re-lease of the Equipment. Any proceeds from the sale, or anticipated proceeds from the lease, of the Equipment shall reduce any termination penalty payment required.

(ii) A schedule of early termination values must be included with your proposal.

d. SunBird Corporation must have the right to upgrade the Equipment, by adding equipment or replacing components, at any time during the term of the lease, and the Lessor must provide financing for such upgrade for a term coterminous with the term remaining during the upgrade period at a financing rate that will not exceed the Lessor's transaction nominal after-tax yield.

10. Insurance

The Equipment shall be self-insured.

11. Casualty Value Schedule

A schedule of casualty values, expressed as a percentage of Equipment Cost, for both the Primary Lease Term and any Renewal Term(s), must be submitted with your proposal.

12. Transaction Fees

Lessee will not pay financing commitment or nonutilization fees.

13. Accounting Classification

Preference will be given to a lease that qualifies as an operating lease under the applicable accounting guidelines.

14. Single-Source Preference

Preference will be given to Lessors that intend to provide 100% of the funds necessary to purchase the Equipment over those that intend to leverage the purchase with third-party debt. Your proposal must disclose your intent.

(a) In the event you determine it would be advantageous to propose a leveraged lease-financing structure, it should be submitted assuming a long-term debt interest rate of 6.75% per annum. In addition, the following terms will apply:

(i) Our investment banker, Chicago First Corporation, will be responsible for securing the third-party leveraged lease debt at a rate satisfactory to SunBird Corporation, within our sole discretion.

(ii) You must provide assurance that the lease will qualify as a true lease for federal income tax purposes under the current tax rules and guidelines.

(iii) You must state whether your proposal is on a best-effort or firm basis; preference will be given to proposals on a firm basis.

(iv) At the time of submission of your proposal, you must be prepared to identify all lease participants (with contact name and telephone number), including each identified equity and debt participant, so they may be called immediately for verification in the event you are the successful bidder.

15. Broker Disclosure

We will give a preference to lease offers from principal funding sources that do not intend to resell or broker the transaction. In the event that you do not intend to act as a principal and purchase the equipment for your own account, you must disclose that in your proposal.

16. Expenses

Lessor shall be responsible for payment of all fees and expenses of the transaction, other than the Lessee's own direct legal fees in connection with documenting the lease transaction, including fees and expenses incurred in connection with the arranging, or documentation, of the Equipment lease.

D. Timetable

SunBird Corporation will adhere to the following time schedule in connection with evaluating submitted proposals, making the award decision, and negotiating the equipment lease document(s):

Action	Date
Lessor Proposal Intent Notifications Due	_____
Lessor Proposals Due	_____
Lessor Proposal Commitment Cutoff	_____
Lessor Notification of Initial Qualification	_____
Form Lease Document(s) Sent to Qualified Lessor(s)	_____
Lessor Response to Form Lease Document(s)	_____
Lessor(s) Selection	_____
Award Announcement	_____
Lease Negotiations—Start	_____
Lease Signing	_____
Anticipated Equipment Delivery	_____
Anticipated Equipment Acceptance for Lease	_____

Glossary

When entering into a leasing transaction, you may encounter unfamiliar terms that have developed along with the leasing industry. This glossary defines leasing terms according to their industry usage.

accelerated cost recovery system (ACRS)—The method prescribed by the Internal Revenue Code that an equipment owner must use in computing depreciation deductions on most equipment placed in service after 1980 and before 1987. Under ACRS, the owner writes off the equipment's cost over a 3-year, 5-year, 10-year, or 15-year period, depending on the recovery period designated for the equipment type.

acceptance certificate—A document in which a lessee acknowledges that certain specified equipment is acceptable for lease. Generally used in transactions in which the parties enter into the lease document well in advance of the equipment's delivery date, it serves to notify the lessor that the equipment has been delivered, inspected, and accepted for lease as of a specified date. The typical form requires the lessee to list certain pertinent information, including the equipment manufacturer, purchase price, serial number, and location.

acceptance supplement—The same as an acceptance certificate.

advance rental—Any payment in the form of rent made before the start of the lease term. The term is also sometimes used to describe a rental payment arrangement in which the lessee pays all rentals, on a per-period basis, at the start of each rental payment period. For example, a quarterly, in advance, rental program requires the lessee to pay one-fourth of the annual rental at the start of each consecutive three-month period during the lease term.

alternative minimum tax (AMT)—A system for taxing individuals and corporations that, in effect, prevents a taxpayer from otherwise reducing his, her, or its tax below a formulated level. If the tax liability calculated under the AMT rules is greater than the taxpayer's regular tax, the excess amount has to be paid along with the regular tax. The AMT is basically an attempt to dampen taxpayers' typical motivation to reduce their tax liability excessively.

antichurning—A concept under the federal tax laws that prevents a taxpayer from taking advantage of more favorable equipment depreciation tax benefits through equipment transaction manipulations that violate the spirit of the tax laws.

asset depreciation range (ADR) indemnity—A type of tax indemnification given by the lessee to the lessor relating to leased equipment depreciated under the asset depreciation range system method. The lessee, in effect, guarantees the lessor against loss of, or inability to claim, anticipated ADR tax benefits under certain conditions.

asset depreciation range (ADR) system—A method prescribed by the Internal Revenue Code that could be used in computing depreciation deductions for certain assets placed in service after 1970 and before 1981. ADR provides a range of useful lives for specified assets that serve as the period over which the asset is depreciated. The lives listed are generally shorter than the period over which an asset may be depreciated under the "facts and circumstances" method of depreciation.

balloon payment—Commonly found in mortgage financings, a balloon payment is a final payment that is larger than the periodic term payments. Usually, it results because the debt has not been fully amortized during the repayment period. For example, a one-year financing arrangement providing for interest-only monthly payments during the year, with the principal plus the last interest payment due on the final payment date, is said to have a "balloon payment," or simply a "balloon," due at the end of the term.

bareboat charter party—A net finance lease relating to vessels. Also sometimes referred to simply as a "bareboat charter." See **net lease.**

base lease term—The primary period of time that the lessee is entitled to use the leased equipment, without regard to any interim or renewal lease terms. The base lease term of a five-year lease is five years.

base rental—The rental that the lessee must pay during the base, sometimes called primary, lease term.

beneficial interest holder—Refers to a beneficial, as opposed to legal (title), owner. For example, when a trust has been created by the equity participants to act as the lessor, the equity participants are deemed the beneficial interest holders. They hold interests in the trust that has title to the equipment.

bond—An instrument that represents a long-term debt obligation. The debt instruments, sometimes referred to as loan certificates, issued in a leveraged lease transaction are referred to as bonds or notes.

book reporting—The reporting of income or loss for financial, as opposed to tax, purposes on the financial records of a corporation or other reporting entity.

book residual value—An estimate of the equipment's residual value that a lessor uses, or "books," to calculate its economic return on a lease transaction.

broker—A person who, or an entity that, for compensation, arranges lease transactions for another's account. A broker is also referred to as a syndicator or an underwriter.

call—The right a lessee may have to buy specified leased equipment for a predetermined fixed price, usually expressed as a percentage of original cost. If provided, such an option commonly does not become exercisable until the end of the lease term, and it lapses if the lessee fails to give the lessor timely notice of its intention to exercise it. For example, a lessee may have a right to buy equipment at the end of the lease term for 30% of original cost, notice of intention to exercise the option to be given not less than 90 days before the lease term's end.

capital lease—Under the guidelines set out by the Financial Accounting Standards Board in FASB 13, a lessee must classify certain long-term leases as capital leases for accounting and reporting purposes. Capital leases are accounted for in a manner that reflects the long-term repayment obligation of such leases.

cash flow—In a lease transaction, the amount of cash a lease generates for a lessor.

casualty value—A predetermined amount of money that a lessee guarantees the lessor will receive in the event of an equipment casualty loss during the lease term. Generally expressed as a percentage of original cost, the value varies according to the point in time during the lease term when the loss occurs. It is also referred to as a "stipulated loss value."

certificate of delivery and acceptance—The same as an acceptance certificate.

charterer—The lessee of a vessel.

charter party—A document that provides for the lease (charter) of a vessel or vessels. Although the format is basically the same as any other lease, there are certain additions and modifications reflecting the requirements dictated by a vessel transaction.

chattel mortgage—A mortgage relating to personal property. Thus, a mortgage on equipment is a chattel mortgage.

collateral—Assets used as security for the repayment of a debt obligation. In a typical leveraged lease, the collateral is the leased equipment.

commencement date—The date the base, or primary, lease term begins.

commission agreement—An agreement between a lease broker and a prospective equity participant providing for the payment of a fee to the broker for services in arranging a lease transaction.

commitment fee—Compensation paid to a lender in return for an agreement to make a future loan or to a lessor for its commitment to lease equipment to a lessee in the future.

conditional sales agreement—A contract, also referred to as CSA, that provides for the time financing of asset purchases. The seller retains title to the asset until the buyer fulfills all specified conditions, such as installment payments. At that time, title automatically vests in the buyer.

cost of money—Commonly, the cost that a lessor incurs to borrow money. This includes the interest rate and any additional costs related to such borrowing, such as fees or compensating balances. In pricing a lease transaction, a lessor factors this cost into the computation.

cost-to-customer—The simple interest rate on a lease transaction.

DDB/SYD/SLM—A technique of switching methods of depreciation to maximize early depreciation write-offs used on property not covered by ACRS or MACRS. Depreciation deductions are initially computed using the double-declining balance (DDB) method, with an appropriately timed change to the sum-of-the-years'-digits (SYD) method, followed by another appropriately timed change to the straight-line method (SLM).

debt participant—A long-term lender in a leveraged lease transaction. Frequently, those transactions have more than one debt participant.

debt service—The aggregate periodic repayment amount, including principal and interest, due on a loan.

default—In a lease transaction, when a party breaches certain material lease obligations.

deficiency guarantee—A guarantee given to a lessor by a third party, such as an equipment vendor or a manufacturer, to induce a lessor to enter into a lease that it would not otherwise enter into, usually because the prospective lessee may be a poor credit risk or the future value of the equipment may be highly speculative. For example, a deficiency guarantor may agree to pay the lessor for any shortfall below a designated amount—say, 20% of original cost—incurred when the equipment is sold at the end of the lease.

delivery and acceptance certificate—The same as an acceptance certificate.

depreciation indemnity—A tax indemnification given by a lessee against the lessor's loss of anticipated depreciation tax benefits on leased equipment.

direct financing lease—A classification for a particular type of lease prescribed under the lease accounting guidelines set out by the Financial Accounting Standards Board in FAS No. 13, applicable to lessors. Those guidelines tell lessors how to report direct financing leases for accounting purposes.

discounted cash flow analysis—The process of determining the present value of future cash flows.

Economic Recovery Tax Act (ERTA)—A 1981 federal income tax act.

equipment certificate of acceptance—The same as an acceptance certificate.

equity participant—The equity investor in a leveraged lease. Frequently, a leveraged lease transaction has more than one equity participant, who jointly own and lease the equipment. An equity participant is also sometimes referred to as an "owner participant."

event of default—An event that provides the basis for the declaration of a default. For example, the nonpayment of rent under a lease agreement is typically prescribed as an event of default, which gives the lessor the right to declare the lease in default and to pursue permitted remedies, such as terminating the lease and reclaiming the equipment.

facts and circumstances depreciation—A method of determining the depreciable life of an asset generally usable on assets placed in service before 1981. Under the facts and circumstances method, the useful life determination is based on the owner's experience with similar property, giving due consideration to current and anticipated future conditions, such as wear and tear; normal progress of the art; economic changes, inventions, and current developments within the industry and the taxpayer's trade or business; and climatic and other relevant local conditions that can affect the taxpayer's repair, renewal, and replacement program.

fair market purchase value—An asset's value as determined in the open market in an arm's-length transaction (one in which there is a willing buyer and a willing seller, under no compulsion to act) under normal selling conditions. It is also referred to simply as the "fair market value."

fair market rental value—The rental rate that an asset would command in the open market in an arm's-length transaction (one in which there is a willing lessee and a willing lessor, under no compulsion to act) under normal renting conditions. It is also referred to simply as the "fair rental value."

FASB—The Financial Accounting Standards Board, the accounting profession's guideline-setting authority, based in Stamford, Connecticut.

FAS Statement No. 13, Accounting for Leases—FAS No. 13 sets out the standards for financial lease accounting for lessors and lessees. FAS No. 13 was initially issued by the Financial Accounting Standards Board in November 1976.

finance lease—(1) The same as a full-payout lease. (2) A statutory lease category that would have permitted leases that otherwise would not have qualified as true leases for tax purposes to be so treated. Although enacted by the Tax Equity and Fiscal Responsibility Act in 1982, the finance lease's effective date was postponed, and it was repealed by the 1986 Tax Reform Act before ever having gone into effect, with limited exceptions.

financing agreement—An agreement commonly entered into by the principal parties to a leveraged lease before equipment delivery. The agreement identifies each party's obligation to the transaction and any conditions that must be satisfied before the obligations are fixed. Typically, it will involve the debt and equity participants, their representatives, and the lessee. It is also referred to as a "participation agreement."

floating rental rate—A form of periodic rental payments that change or "float" upward and downward over a lease's term with changes in a specified interest rate. Frequently, a designated bank's prime rate is the measuring interest rate.

full-payout lease—A form of lease that will provide the lessor with a cash flow generally sufficient to return its equipment investment; pay the principal, interest, and other financing costs on related debt; cover its related sales and administration expenses; and generate a profit. The cash flow is determined from the rental payments, the ownership tax benefits, and the equipment residual value. The lessee typically has the right to use the leased equipment for most of its actual useful life.

gross income tax—A tax imposed by a state or local taxing authority on gross income generated from sources within its jurisdiction. The tax is deductible by the taxpayer for federal income tax purposes.

grossing up—A concept that reimbursement for a monetary loss will include sufficient additional monies so that the after-tax amount will equal the loss. The recipient is said to be made whole for its loss because the amount paid must take into account any taxes the recipient will have to pay as a result of the receipt of the payments from the payor.

guaranteed residual value—An arrangement in which, for example, a broker or an equipment manufacturer guarantees that a lessor will receive not less than a certain amount for specified equipment when it is disposed of at the end of the lease term. It is also sometimes referred to simply as a "guaranteed residual."

guideline lease—A leveraged lease that meets with the IRS's lease guidelines, such as set out in Revenue Procedures 75-21, 75-28, 76-30, and 79-48. Although the guidelines specifically address only private ruling requests, generally a guideline lease should qualify as a true lease for federal income tax purposes.

half-year convention—A concept under the income tax rules for depreciating equipment under which all equipment placed in service during a tax year is treated as having been placed in service at the midpoint of that year, regardless of when during the year it was in fact placed in service.

hell-or-high-water clause—A lease provision that commits a lessee to pay the rent unconditionally. The lessee waives any right that exists or may arise to withhold any rent from the lessor or any assignee of the lessor for any reason whatsoever, including any setoff, counterclaim, recoupment, or defense.

high-low rental—A rental structure in which the rent payments are reduced from a higher to a lower rate at a prescribed point in the lease term.

implicit lease rate—The annual interest rate that, when applied to the lease rental payments, will discount those payments to an amount equal to the cost of the equipment leased.

indemnity agreement—A contract in which one party commits to insure another party against anticipated and specified losses.

indenture—In a leveraged lease transaction, an agreement entered into by an owner trustee (the lessor's representative) and an indenture trustee (the lender's representative) in which the owner trustee grants a lien on the leased equipment, the lease rents, and other lessor contract rights as security for repayment of the outstanding equipment loan. It is also referred to as an indenture trust.

indenture trustee—The representative of the lenders where, in a leveraged lease transaction, the debt is provided through a trust arrangement. As the lender's representative, the indenture trustee may, for example, have to file and maintain a security interest in the leased equipment, receive rentals from the lessee, pay out the proper amounts to the lenders and the lessor, and take certain action to protect the outstanding loan in the event of a loan default.

installment sale—A sale in which the purchase price is paid in an agreed-upon number of installments over an agreed-upon period of time. Typically, title to what is sold does not transfer to the purchaser until the last installment has been made.

institutional investors—Institutions that invest in lease transactions. They can be, for example, insurance companies, pension funds, banks, and trusts.

insured value—The same as casualty value.

interim lease rental—The equipment rental due for the interim lease term. Typically, for each day during the interim lease term, a lessee must pay as interim lease rent an amount equal to the daily equivalent of the primary lease term rent. In a leveraged lease transaction, the lease sometimes instead permits the lessee to pay an amount equal to the daily equivalent of the long-term debt interest.

interim lease term—The lease term period between the lessee's acceptance of the equipment for lease and the beginning of the primary, or base, lease term.

investment tax credit (ITC)—A credit allowed against federal income tax liability that can be claimed by a taxpayer for certain "Section 38 property" acquired and placed in service by a taxpayer during a tax year. ITC is generally not available for property placed in service after 1985.

ITC indemnity—A type of indemnification in which the lessee commits to reimburse the lessor for any financial loss incurred through the loss of, or inability to claim, any or all of the anticipated ITC. If the lessor has "passed through" the ITC to the lessee, the lessor may have to give the indemnity.

ITC "pass-through"—An election made by the lessor to treat, for ITC purposes, the lessee as the owner of the leased equipment. After the election, a lessee can claim the ITC on the equipment covered by the election.

layoff—The sale by a lessor of its interest in the lease agreement, including the ownership of the leased equipment and the right to receive the rent payments.

lease agreement—A contract in which an equipment owner, the lessor, transfers the equipment's use, subject to the specified terms and conditions, to another, the lessee, for a prescribed period of time and rental rate.

lease line—A present commitment by a lessor to lease specified equipment to be delivered in the future. A lease line can cover a variety of types of equipment, at varying rental rates and lease terms. It is also referred to as a lease line of credit.

lease underwriting—The process in which a lease broker arranges a lease transaction for the account of third parties, a prospective lessor and a prospective lessee. This can be on a best-efforts basis or on a firm-commitment basis. In a best-efforts underwriting, the broker only offers to attempt diligently to arrange the financing on certain proposed terms. In a firm-commitment underwriting, the broker in effect guarantees to arrange the financing as proposed.

lessee—The user of equipment that is the subject of a lease agreement.

lessor—The owner of equipment that is the subject of a lease agreement.

level payments—Payments that are the same for each payment period during the payment term. Frequently, rent and debt service payments are paid in level payments over the payment period.

leveraged lease—A lease in which a portion—generally, 60% to 80% of the equipment acquisition cost—is borrowed from a bank or other lending institution, with the lessor paying the balance. The debt is commonly on a nonrecourse basis, and the rental payments are usually sufficient to cover the loan debt service.

limited use property—Leased property that will be economically usable only by the lessee, or a member of the lessee group, at the lease term's end because, for example, of its immobility or unique aspects. The IRS will not rule that a lease is a true lease where the leased equipment is limited use property.

loan certificate—A certificate that evidences a debt obligation.

loan participant—A debt participant.

low-high rental—A rental structure in which the rent payments are increased from a lower to a higher rate at a prescribed point in the lease term.

management agreement—A contract in which one party agrees to manage a lease transaction during its term, including, for example, rental payment processing and equipment disposal.

management fee—A fee that a lease transaction manager receives for services performed under a management agreement.

master lease agreement—A lease agreement designed to permit future equipment not contemplated when the lease is executed to be added to the lease later. The document is set up in two parts. The main body contains the general, or boilerplate, provisions, such as the maintenance and indemnification provisions. An annex, or schedule, contains the type of items that usually vary with each transaction, such as rental rates and options.

midquarter convention—A concept under the income tax rules for depreciating equipment in which all equipment placed in service during a quarter of a tax year is treated as placed in service at the midpoint of such quarter, regardless of when it was in fact placed in service during the quarter.

modified accelerated cost recovery system (MACRS)—A method prescribed for depreciating assets that was introduced by the 1986 Tax Reform Act. It applies to most equipment placed in service after 1986.

mortgage—An arrangement whereby a lender (mortgagee) acquires a lien on property owned by a taxpayer (mortgagor) as security for the loan repayment. Once the debt obligation has been fully satisfied, the mortgage lien is terminated.

negative spread—The amount by which a value is below a certain prescribed amount. Generally, in a leveraged lease, a negative spread is the amount by which the transaction's simple interest rate is below the leveraged debt interest rate.

net lease—A lease arrangement in which the lessee pays all costs—such as maintenance, certain taxes, and insurance—related to using the leased equipment. Those costs are not included as part of the rental payments. Typically, finance leases are net leases.

nonpayout lease—A lease arrangement that does not, over the primary term of the lease, generate enough cash flow to return substantially all the lessor's investment, debt-financing costs, and sales and administration expenses.

nonrecourse debt financing—A loan as to which the lender agrees to look solely to the lessee, the lease rents, and the leased equipment for the loan's repayment. As security for the loan repayment, the lender receives an assignment of the lessor's rights under the lease agreement and a grant of a first lien on the equipment. Although the lessor has no obligation to repay the debt in the event of a lessee default, its equity investment in the equipment is usually subordinated to the lender's rights.

nonutilization fee—A fee that a lessor may impose in return for its present commitment to buy and lease specified equipment in the future. The fee is generally expressed as a percentage of the aggregate unused portion of the initial dollar commitment—for example, 1% of the unused balance of a $1 million lease line of credit. Thus, if all the committed funds are used, no fee is payable.

operating lease—A form of lease arrangement in which the lessor generally commits to provide certain additional equipment-related services other than the straight financing, such as maintenance, repairs, or technical advice. Generally, operating leases are nonpayout in nature. The term also refers to a lease classification under FAS No. 13.

option—A contractual right that can be exercised under the granting terms. For example, a fair market value purchase option in a lease is the right to buy the equipment covered by it for its fair market value.

packager—A person or an entity that arranges a lease transaction for third parties. Also referred to as an underwriter, a syndicator, or, sometimes, a broker.

participation agreement—The same as a financing agreement.

payout lease—The same as a full-payout lease.

portfolio lease—The term commonly refers to a lease that is entered into by a "professional" lessor for its own account and investment.

present value—The term refers to the present worth of a future stream of payments calculated by discounting the future payments at a desired interest rate.

primary lease term—The same as base lease term.

private letter ruling—A written opinion that the IRS issues in response to a taxpayer's request. The letter sets out the IRS's position on the tax treatment of a proposed transaction. In leveraged lease transactions, for the IRS to issue a favorable private letter ruling, the request must comply with the IRS Guidelines.

progress payments—Payments that may be required by an equipment manufacturer or a builder during the construction period toward the purchase price. Frequently required for costly equipment with a long construction period, the payments are designed to lessen the manufacturer's or builder's need to tie up its own funds during construction.

purchase option—The right to buy agreed-upon equipment at the times and in the amounts specified in the option. Frequently, these options are only exercisable at the end of the primary lease term, although they sometimes can be exercised during the primary lease term or at the end of any renewal term.

put—A right that a lessor may have to sell specified leased equipment to the lessee at a fixed price at the end of the initial lease term. It is usually imposed to protect the lessor's residual value assumption.

recourse debt financing—A loan under which the lender may look to the general credit of the lessor, in addition to the lessee and the equipment, for repayment of any outstanding loan obligation. The lender is said to have a "recourse" against the lessor.

recovery property—Property that can be depreciated under the accelerated cost recovery system (ACRS).

renewal option—An option frequently given to a lessee to renew the lease term for a specified rental and time period.

residual sharing—A compensation technique sometimes used by syndicators for arranging a lease transaction. Under this, the equity participants must pay a predetermined percentage of what the equipment is sold for at the end of the lease. For example, on sale, a syndicator may get 50% of any amount realized exceeding 20% of the equipment's original cost.

residual value—The value of leased equipment at the end of the lease term.

right of first refusal—The right of the lessee to buy the leased equipment, or renew the lease, at the end of the lease term, for any amount equal to that offered by an unaffiliated third party.

safe-harbor lease—A statutory lease category enacted as part of the Economic Recovery Tax Act (ERTA) that permitted a lease to qualify as a true lease for federal income tax purposes although it would not otherwise ordinarily qualify. It was repealed by the 1984 Deficit Reduction Act (DRA), with limited exceptions. Under a safe-harbor lease, an equipment owner could essentially sell the ownership tax benefits without giving up other ownership rights.

sale/leaseback—An arrangement in which an equipment buyer buys equipment for the purpose of leasing it back to the seller.

sales tax—A tax imposed on the sale of equipment, similar to any other sales tax on property sold.

sales-type lease—A classification for a particular type of lease prescribed under the lease-accounting guidelines that the Financial Accounting Standards Board set out in FAS No. 13, applicable to lessors.

salvage value—The amount, estimated for federal income tax purposes, that an asset is expected to be worth at the end of its useful life.

Section 38 property—Tangible personal property and certain other tangible property, as defined by Internal Revenue Code Section 38.

security agreement—An agreement that evidences an assignment by the lessor to the lender, as security for the equipment loan, of the lessor's rights under the lease agreement and a granting of a security interest in the leased equipment.

sinking fund—A fund frequently established in leveraged lease transactions by the lessor to accumulate funds to pay for future taxes.

sinking fund rate—The interest rate that a sinking fund is deemed to earn on accumulated funds.

special-purpose equipment—The same as limited use property.

spread—The difference between two values. In lease transactions, the term is generally used to describe the difference between the lease interest rate and the interest rate on the debt.

stipulated loss value—The same as casualty value.

sublease—The re-lease by a lessee of equipment that is on lease to the lessee.

take-or-pay contract—An agreement in which one party commits to buy an agreed-upon quantity of goods or materials from another at a predetermined price. If the goods or materials are not bought, the party making the purchase commitment must pay the other party an amount of money equal to the cost of the goods or materials it had committed to buy. For example, a public utility can agree to buy 100 tons of coal annually from a mining company, and if it does not buy this amount in any year, it will pay an amount of money equal to the coal's sale price.

tax benefit transfer (TBT) lease—The same as a safe-harbor lease.

Tax Equity and Fiscal Responsibility Act (TEFRA)—A 1982 federal income tax act.

tax lease—The same as a true lease.

Tax Reform Act—A 1986 federal income tax act.

termination option—An option entitling a lessee to terminate a lease during the lease term for a predetermined value, the termination value, if the equipment becomes obsolete or surplus to the lessee's needs. The lessor usually requires the lessee to sell the equipment to an unaffiliated third party, and the lessee must pay the lessor any amount by which the sale proceeds are less than the termination value. Typically, any excess sales proceeds go to the lessor.

termination value—The amount that the lessee must pay the lessor if it exercises a termination option. Typically, the termination value is set as of each rental payment period and is generally expressed as a percentage of equipment cost. For example, the lessee may be permitted to terminate the lease at the end of the third year of a seven-year lease for an amount equal to 60% of cost.

time sale—An installment sale.

total earnings—The amount by which the aggregate rentals due the lessor over the entire lease term exceed the total equipment costs, including equity investment and debt-financing costs. This concept does not consider the time value of money.

TRAC lease—A lease of motor vehicles or trailers that contains what is referred to as a terminal rental adjustment clause (TRAC). The clause permits or requires the rent amount to be adjusted based on the proceeds the lessor receives from the sale of the leased equipment. TRAC leases qualify as true leases.

transition rules—Statutory rules enacted when there is a change in the tax laws. The transition rules allow certain transactions to be exempted from the law change. For example, transition rules permitted investment tax credit (ITC) to be claimed on certain equipment placed in service after 1985.

true lease—An arrangement that qualifies for lease treatment for federal income tax purposes. Under a true lease, the lessee may deduct rental payments, and the lessor may claim the tax benefits accruing to an equipment owner.

trust—An arrangement in which property is held by one party for the benefit of another. It is frequently used in leveraged lease transactions.

trust certificate—A trust document issued on behalf of a trust to evidence the beneficial ownership in the trust estate.

trustee—The person or entity appointed, or designated, to carry out a trust's terms. In leveraged lease transactions, the trustee is generally a bank or trust company.

trustee fees—Fees payable to a trustee as compensation for services performed.

trustor—An individual or entity that causes the creation of a trust and for whose benefit it is established.

unleveraged lease—A lease in which the lessor puts up 100% of the equipment's acquisition cost from its own funds.

useful life—Commonly, the economic usable life of an asset.

use tax—A tax imposed on the use, storage, or consumption of tangible personal property within a taxing jurisdiction. For example, in most states, a lessor purchasing equipment has the option of paying an up-front sales tax equal to a specified percentage of the equipment's purchase price or a use tax equal to a specified percentage of lease rents under the equipment's lease.

vendor—A seller of property. Commonly, the manufacturer or distributor of equipment.

vendor program—A program in which an equipment lessor provides a lease-financing service to customers of an equipment manufacturer.

Index

abandonment, equipment, 249
accelerated cost recovery system (ACRS), 303
acceptance certificate, 303
acceptance of equipment
  date for, 132–133
  provision for, in broker's proposal, 174–178
accident reports, 223–224
accounting guidelines, 137
ACRS (accelerated cost recovery system), 303
ADR, *see under* asset depreciation range
advance rental, 303
agreements, lease, *see* lease(s)
alterations, equipment, 227
alternative minimum tax (AMT), 3, 303
alternatives, developing negotiating, 281–283
AMT, *see* alternative minimum tax
annual reports, 23
antichurning, 304
asset depreciation range (ADR) indemnity, 304
asset depreciation range (ADR) system, 304
assignment, 112–113, 245–247
assistance from lessors, 90–91
attitude, pre-negotiation, 70–72
automatic renewal, 109
award, lease, 209

bait-and-switch tactics, 32–33, 170
balloon payments, 304
bank credit agreements, 229
bank leasing companies, 13–15, 28

bankruptcy
  of lessee, 242
  of lessor, 287
bareboat charter party, 304
bargaining strategy(-ies), 69–97
  avoiding common mistakes in, 86–94
  for bid requests, 78–80
  for companies with financial problems, 87–88
  deal timetable as, 76–78
  and delays by lessor, 74–76
  and equipment sources, 89
  in initial telephone calls, 94–96
  limiting information disclosure as, 69–70, 78–87
  planning for financing as, 74
  and pre-negotiation attitude, 70–72
  refusing last looks as, 78
  relationship with salesperson as, 72–74
  and team preparation, 97
base lease term, 304
base rental, 304
beneficial interest holders, 304
best-efforts offers, 166–167
bid requests, *see* requests for quotations (RFQs)
bill of sale, 273–274
bonds, 103, 304
book reporting, 304
book residual value, 304
brokers, lease, *see* lease brokers
business areas, identifying key, 100–101
business drives, 31–32

call options, 305
capital budget restrictions, 82–83
capital leases, 305
captive leasing companies, 11–13
cash flow, 305

casual questions, 69–70
casualty payment obligations, 52–53
casualty value, 137, 305
certificate of delivery and acceptance, 305
charges, *see* fees/charges
charterer, 305
charter party, 305
chattel mortgage, 305
claim reports, third-party, 225
closing, 264–279
  bill of sale provided at, 273–274
  checklist of documents needed at, 276–279
  guarantees provided at, 271–272
  landowner/mortgagee waivers provided at, 274
  and legal opinions, 265–268
  participation agreement provided at, 274–275
  proof of insurance documents provided at, 272
  and purchase agreements, 273
  security interest filings as condition of, 274
  transaction authorization documents for, 271
  trust agreements provided at, 275–276
  and underwriter's fee agreement, 276
  up-to-date information for, 268–270
collateral, 264, 305
collection telephone charges, 62
commencement date, 305
commission agreement, 305
commitment fees, 60, 61, 105, 202–204, 218, 305
competitive quotes, 83–84
compliments, giving, 92–93

compromise, 70
conditional sales, 212, 305
conditioned offers, highly,
    206–209
cost of money, 305
cost(s)
    equipment, 130–131
    of equipment, 105, 108, 113,
        173–174
    of proposal preparation, 127
    transaction, 199–202
    see also fees/charges
cost-to-customer, 306
credit
    and financial requirements,
        30–31
    and interest charges, 40–41
    money-over lessors and
        weak, 25
    as requirement, in lessor's
        proposal, 183–184
    residual-sensitive lessors and
        weak, 24–25
    tax-oriented lessors and good,
        26

DDB/SYD/SLM, 306
deal rewrites, 62–63
deal sheets, 142–144
deal timetable, 76–78, 139–141
debt participant, 306
debt placement fees, 59–60
debt provision, of lessor's
    proposal, 185–187
debt service, 306
default, 111, 240–245, 254, 306
    for bankruptcy, 242
    events of, 306
    for failure to perform
        obligation, 241
    lessor remedies following
        event of, 242–245
    for material
        misrepresentation,
        241–242
    for nonpayment of rent, 240
    for unauthorized transfers,
        241
deficiency guarantees, 306
definitions section (of lease),
    216–217
delays, by lessor, 74–76
delivery and acceptance
    certificate, 306
delivery date, estimated
    equipment, 132–133
delivery of equipment provision,
    in broker's proposal,
    174–178

depreciation, 307
depreciation indemnity, 306
direct financing lease, 306
discounted cash flow analysis,
    306
documentation fees, 55
documents, collateral, 264
drives, business, 31–32
Dun & Bradstreet financial
    reports, 21, 23

early lease termination, 54,
    110–111
Economic Recovery Tax Act of
    1981 (ERTA), 306
equipment certificate of
    acceptance, 306
equipment costs, 113
equipment lease requirements
    section (of RFQ), 130–139
Equipment Lessors Association,
    22
equipment location reports, 225
equity participant, 306
equity placement fees, 58
ERTA (Economic Recovery Tax
    Act of 1981), 306
excess use charges, 57

facts and circumstances
    depreciation, 307
fair market lease renewal
    options, 251
fair market purchase options, 110
fair market purchase value, 307
fair market renewal option, 109
fair market rental value, 307
fair market value, 190
fair market value purchase
    options, 250
FASB (Financial Accounting
    Standards Board), 307
fees/charges, 139
    broker's, 7
    collection telephone, 62
    commitment, 60, 61, 105,
        202–204, 218, 305
    for deal rewrites, 62–63
    debt placement, 59–60
    documentation/filing, 55
    equity placement, 58
    excess use, 57
    late payment, 61–62
    maintenance/repair, 55–57
    nonutilization, 60–61, 105,
        202–204, 218, 311
    redelivery, 63–64, 114
    remarketing, 61
    transaction, 137

trustee, 314
    underwriter's, 276
filing fees, 55
finance leasing companies, 5, 26
Financial Accounting Standards
    Board (FASB), 307
financial leases, 16–17, 307
financial problems, revealing
    information on severity
    of, 87–88
financial reports, 223
financial requirements, preparing
    for, 30–31
financial statements, 23
    of lease broker, 10
    of lessee, 230–231
    of lessor, 103
financing
    closing of, *see* closing
    planning for, 74
    right to upgrade, 253–254
    upgrade, 54, 111–112
financing agreements, 307
firm offers, 167–168
first refusal, right of, 194, 252–253
fixed-price purchase option,
    109–110, 250–251
fixed-price renewal option,
    108–109, 252
flexible leases, 67
floating rental rate, 307
friendships with lessors,
    avoiding, 72–73
full-payout leases, 307
funds, unavailability of,
    81–82

general financing request section
    (of RFQ), 123–124
governing law, 254
gross income tax, 308
grossing up, 308
grouping requirements,
    minimum, 219
guaranteed residual value, 308
guarantees, 271–272
guideline leases, 308
guidelines, proposal, 125–130

half-year convention, 308
handshake agreements, 89–90
hell-or-high-water clauses, 64,
    222–223, 288, 308
hidden profits, *see* profiting by
    lessors
high-low rentals, 308
highly conditioned offers,
    206–209
honesty, 89–90

identification
  of equipment, in lessor's offer, 170–173
  of lessee, in lessor's offer, 168–170
  of parties, in lease, 215
immediate equipment needs, 85
implicit lease rate, 308
income tax indemnifications, 113
indemnity, ITC, 309
indemnity agreements, 308
indenture, 308
indenture trustee, 308
independent leasing companies, 4–7
individual-type lessors, 2–4
information, disclosure of, 78–88
  about capital budget restrictions, 82–83
  about existing financial problems, 87–88
  about future equipment upgrade needs, 85–86
  about getting competitive quotes, 83–84
  about immediate equipment needs, 85
  about lease rate, 85–86
  about tax benefits, 84–85
  about unavailability of funds, 81–82
  checklist for, 79–80
  reasons for avoiding, 78–79
installment sales, 309
institutional investors, 309
insurance
  and casualty occurrences, 52–53
  cost markups for, 53–54
  lessee provision requiring, 189
  proof of, 272
  RFQ provision requiring, 136–137
  self-, 112
insured value, 309
interest charges/rates, 36–42
  attracting customers with below market, 66
  lack of limits on, 40
  and length of lease, 37
  lowball rates, 41
  and market leverage, 37–38
  negotiating over, 38–39
  and overcharging, 41–42
  paying above market, 85–86
  and risk, 40–41

interest penalties, 254–255
interim lease rentals, 309
interim lease term, 309
interim rent, 49–50, 107, 179, 181
internal support, for negotiation, 99–100
introduction section (of RFQ), 124–125
investment bankers, 186
investment tax credits (ITCs), 2–3, 43, 309
invoicing practices, unfair, 50–51
IRS, 205
ITCs, *see* investment tax credits

lack of interest, showing, 91–92
last-look opportunities, 78
late payment charges, 61–62, 254–255
lawyers, selecting, 287–288
layoff, 309
lead times, lease transaction, 75–76
lease advisers, selecting, 287–288
lease brokers (underwriters), 7–11, 27, 103, 200–202, 276
  advantages of, 11
  definition of, 304
  disadvantages of, 11
  disclosure by, 138–139
  equity placement fees charged by, 58
  "hidden," 9–11, 162–166
  role of, 8–9
lease conformity reports, 224
lease lines, 309
lease(s), 211–263
  assignment of, 112–113, 245–247
  award of, 209
  capital, 305
  checklist for drafting/negotiating, 256–263
  closing of, *see* closing
  commitment to, 288–289
  default of, *see* default
  definition of, 309
  definitions section of, 216–217
  direct financing, 306
  equipment maintenance/ alteration provisions in, 225–227
  equipment return provision in, 239–240
  financial, 16–17, 307
  flexible, 67
  full-payout, 307
  governing law clause in, 254

  guideline, 308
  holding rate of, for three months, 104
  identification of parties in, 215
  late payment clause in, 254–255
  lessor ownership protection provisions in, 227–228
  lessor's tax benefits protected in, 235–239
  leveraged, 18, 107, 310
  master, 106, 213–214, 310
  net, 310–311
  nonleveraged, 19
  nonpayout, 311
  nontypical lessor rights in, 248–249
  notifications clause in, 255
  objective of, 212
  operating, 18, 106, 311
  options in, *see* option(s)
  payments clause in, 255
  period of use provision in, 219
  portfolio, 311
  pre-delivery provisions in, 217–219
  primary term of, 134–135
  product responsibility disclaimers in, 233
  product warranty assignment provision in, 233
  renewal of, *see* renewal
  rent payment obligation specified in, 220–223
  reporting requirements in, 223–225
  representations of lessees in, 228–231
  representations of lessor in, 231–232
  risk of loss provision in, 233–234
  safe-harbor, 312
  sales-type, 312
  service, 19
  severability clause in, 254
  signature clause in, 255–256
  single-transaction, 213
  subleasing provision in, 247
  summary section of, 215–216
  tax responsibility provision in, 234–235
  termination of, *see* termination
  term of, 107, 108, 134–135, 219
  TRAC, 314
  true, 314

lease(s) *(continued)*
    types of, 15–19, 198–199
    unleveraged, 314
lease underwriting, 309
Leasing Sourcebook, 24
legal opinions, 265–268
legal proceedings, 230
length of lease, 37
lessee
    bankruptcy of, 242
    definition of, 309
    financial information of, 269
    identification of, in lease, 215
    and legal opinions, 266–267
    material misrepresentation
        by, 241–242
    representation of, 228–231
lessor(s)
    assistance from, 90–91
    bait-and-switch marketing
        used by, 32–33
    bank leasing companies as,
        13–15, 28
    bankruptcy of, 287
    benefits of leases for, 64–66
    brokers as, *see* lease brokers
    business drives by, 31–32
    capabilities/objectives of, 1–2,
        22–24
    captive leasing companies as,
        11–13
    definition of, 309
    financial information of,
        268–269
    financial requirements of,
        30–31
    identification of, in lease, 215
    independent leasing
        companies as, 4–7
    individual-type, 2–4
    investigating potential, 19–29
    and legal opinions, 267
    market reputation of, 20–22
    money-over, 25–26
    niche, 28–29
    ownership status of, 227
    profiting by, *see* profiting
        by lessors
    proposals by, *see* proposals,
        lessor
    protection of tax benefits by,
        235–239
    rental companies as, 26–27
    representations of, 231–232
    residual-sensitive, 22, 24–25
    single-investor, 107
    small-leasing companies as,
        27–28
    tax, 26, 106–107

tips for selecting, 24–29
types of, 2–15
0%, 29
level payments, 310
leverage, gaining, 37–38, 281–287
    through attractive packaging,
        283–284
    through development of
        alternatives, 281–283
    through development of
        negotiation style, 284–287
leverage, process, 118
leveraged leases, 18, 107, 310
limited use property, 310
liquidated damages, 244–245
loan certificates, 310
loan participants, 310
local leasing companies, 28
location of equipment, 133–134,
    187–189, 225
loopholes, in lessor proposals,
    162
lowball interest rates, 41
low-high rentals, 310

MACRS, *see* modified accelerated
    cost recovery system
maintenance, self-, 112
maintenance charges, 55–57
maintenance condition (lease
    agreement), 225–226
management agreements, 310
management fees, 310
manufacturer warranties, 112
market leverage, 37–38
market reputation, of lessor,
    20–22
marking, of equipment, 227
master leases, 106, 213–214, 310
midquarter convention, 310
Million Dollar Directory, 21
minimum grouping
    requirements, 219
misrepresentation, material,
    241–242
modified accelerated cost
    recovery system
    (MACRS), 43, 310
money-over lessors, 25–26
Monitor, 23
mortgages, 212, 274, 310

naming of lessee, in lessor's offer,
    168–170
negative spreads, 310
negative thinking, 70–72
Negotiation Objectives Checklist,
    102–114
net leases, 17, 310–311

niche leasing companies, 28–29
nonbank leasing companies, *see*
    independent leasing
    companies
nonleveraged leases, 19
nonpayout leases, 311
nonrecourse debt financing, 186,
    311
nonrecourse equipment loans, 64
nonunderwritten lease proposal,
    157–158
nonutilization fees, 60–61, 105,
    202–204, 218, 311
notifications required, 255

objective(s), negotiation, 98–117,
    151–153
    checklist of, 103–114, 291–294
    determination of specific deal
        priorities as, 102
    example of setting, 114–117
    identification of key business
        as, 100–101
    internal support for, 99–100
    plan as basis for achieving,
        98–99
offers by lessor, *see* proposals,
    lessor
operating leases, 18, 106, 311
opinions, legal, 265–268
option(s), 190
    definition of, 311
    of lessee, 249–254
    purchase, 192–193, 312
    put, 196–197
    renewal, 193–194, 312
    in RFQ, 135–136
    sublease, 197–198
    termination, 313
    termination option as,
        194–196
outright sales, 212
overcharging
    with interest charges, 41–42
    by vendor leasing
        subsidiaries, 28
ownership status, of lessor, 227
ownership structure, 184

packagers, 311
participation agreements,
    274–275, 311
partnerships, 276
"pass-through," ITC, 309
payment(s)
    for equipment, 133, 231–232
    interest for late, 254–255
    rent, 134–135
    required, 255

penalties, prepayment, 51–52
performance bonds, 103
period of permitted use, 219
period of use provision, in
        broker's proposal,
        178–179
plan, negotiation, 98–99
planning, for financing, 74
portfolio leases, 311
precommencement rent, 49
pre-delivery provisions, of lease,
        217–219
prepayment penalties, 51–52
present value, 311
primary lease term, 134–135, 311
priorities, determining specific
        deal, 102
private letter rulings, 311
processing fees, 55
process leverage, 118
profiting by lessors, 35–64
    through casualty occurrences,
        52–53
    through collection telephone
        charges, 62
    through commitment/
        nonutilization fees, 60–61
    through deal rewrites, 62–63
    through debt
        costs/placement fees,
        59–60
    through documentation/
        filing fees, 55
    through equity placement
        fees, 58
    through excess use charges, 57
    through false financial
        programs, 66–67
    through insurance cost
        markups, 53–54
    through interest charges,
        36–42
    through interim rent, 49–51
    through late payment
        charges, 61–62
    through maintenance/repair
        charges, 55–57
    through prepayment
        penalties, 51–52
    through redelivery charges,
        63–64
    through remarketing fees, 61
    through residual earnings,
        44–48
    through tax benefits, 42–44
    through upgrade financing,
        54
    and windfall profits, 65
progress payments, 311–312

prohibited uses of equipment,
        228
proposals, lessor, 151–152
    acceptance of, 209
    allocation of transaction
        expenses in, 199–202
    and brokers, 162–166
    commitment/nonutilization
        fees specified in, 202–204
    cost of equipment specified
        in, 173–174
    credit support provisions in,
        183–184
    debt arrangement terms in,
        185–187
    detailed review of, 156–161
    equipment/delivery/
        acceptance terms
        specified, 174–178
    equipment insurance cost
        specified, 189
    firm vs. best-efforts,
        166–168
    highly conditioned, 206–209
    identification of equipment
        in, 170–173
    identifying potential
        loopholes in, 162
    lease options in, 190–198
    and lease type, 198–199
    location of equipment
        specified in, 187–189
    naming of lessee in, 168–170
    negotiation objectives,
        151–153
    overview of, 153–156
    and owner structure, 184
    period of use specified in,
        178–179
    rent payments specified in,
        179–183
    tax benefits claimed by lessor
        in, 204–206
purchase agreements, equipment,
        273
purchase options, 192–193, 312
    fair market, 110
    fixed-price, 109–110
put options, 196–197, 312

qualified offers, 10–11
questions, casual, 69–70
quiet enjoyment, 232
quotes, competitive, 83–84

rate sheets, 28
reasonable, appearing, 93–94
recourse debt financing, 312
recovery property, 312

redelivery
    charges for, 63–64
    in event of default, 243
    provisions for, 114
regulatory approvals, 229–230
remarketing fees, 61
renewal
    automatic, 109
    fair market option of, 251
    fixed-price option of, 252
    forced, 249
    option for, 108–109, 135–136,
        193–194, 312
rent
    amount of, 220–221
    interim, 107, 179, 181
    nonpayment of, 240
    payment of, 108, 134–135,
        179–183, 220–223
    as percentage of equipment
        cost, 108
    and vendor payment, 108
rental, advance, 303
rental adjustment clause, 182–183
rental companies, 26–27
rental rates, 107
repair charges, 55–57
reporting requirements (lease
        agreement), 223–225
representations
    of lessee, 228–231
    of lessor, 231–232
requests for proposals, 103–104
requests for quotations (RFQs),
        118–150
    checklist for, 146–150
    deal timetable in, 139–141
    elements of, 119
    equipment specifics in,
        130–139
    example of, 295–301
    formal, 123–141
    format of, 120–121
    general financing request
        section of, 123–124
    ineffective, 121–123
    informal, 142–144
    and information disclosure,
        78–80
    introduction section of,
        124–125
    objective of, 146
    overlooked points in, 146
    and process leverage, 118
    professional-looking, 119
    proposal guidelines in,
        125–130
    scope of, 119–120
    semiformal, 141–142

requests for quotations (continued)
    Summary Response Sheet
        with, 144–145
residual earnings, by lessor,
        44–48
    examples of, 47–48
    through gain in equipment
        value, 46
    through tax pass-through
        claims, 44–45
residual-sensitive lessors, 22,
        24–25
residual sharing, 312
residual upside, 46
residual value, 312
return of equipment, to lessor,
        239–240
return provisions, 56
review, of lessor's offer, 156–161
review copies, of proposal, 128
rewrites, deal, 62–63
RFQs, see requests for quotations
right of first refusal, 312
risk of loss provision (lease
        agreement), 233–234
rulings, private letter, 311

sale/leaseback, 312
sale of equipment
    in event of default, 244
    upon termination, 248
salespeople, avoiding
        friendships/social
        situations with, 72–74
sales tax, 312
sales-type leases, 312
salvage value, 313
Section 38 property, 313
security agreements, 313
security interest filings, 274
self-insurance, of equipment, 112
self-maintenance, of equipment,
        112
service leases, 19
service leasing companies, 5–6
services, value-added, 67–68
severability clause, 254
signature clause, 255–256
single-investor lessors, 107
single-source, preference for,
        138
single transaction leases, 213
sinking fund, 313
sinking fund rate, 313
small leasing companies, 27
social situations with lessors,
        avoiding, 73–74

solid negotiating image,
        maintaining, 92
sourcing, equipment, 89
specialized leasing companies,
        5–6
special-purpose equipment, 313
spread, 313
statements, damaging, see
        information, disclosure of
stipulated loss value, 313
storage, equipment, 243–244
stub period rent, 49
style, negotiation, 284–287
subleases/subleasing, 111,
        197–198, 247, 313
Summary Response Sheet,
        144–145
summary section (of lease),
        215–216
syndicated leveraged lease
        transactions, 162
syndicators, see lease brokers

take-or-pay contracts, 313
tax benefits
    claimed, in lessor's proposal,
        204–206
    false claims of, 44–45
    and money-over lessors,
        25–26
    nonusable, 84–85
    and profiting by lessors,
        42–44
    protection of, by lessor,
        235–239
Tax Equity and Fiscal
        Responsibility Act
        (TEFRA), 313
tax law, changes in, 236–237
tax law rental adjustments,
        221–222
tax lessors, 106–107
tax obligations, lease clause
        specifying, 234–235
tax-oriented lessors, 26
Tax Reform Act of 1986 (TRA),
        2, 43
team
    preparing, for negotiation,
        97
TEFRA (Tax Equity and Fiscal
        Responsibility Act), 313
telephone calls, initial lessor,
        94–96
telephone charges, collection, 62
term
    base lease, 304

of equipment use, 178–179
of lease, 107, 108, 134–135, 219
termination, 136, 248, 252
    for default, 242–243
    early, 54, 110–111
    options for, 194–196, 313
termination payments, 51–52
termination value, 313
Texas, 41
third-party claim reports, 225
time sale, 314
timetable, deal, 76–78, 139–141
total earnings, 314
TRA, see Tax Reform Act of 1986
TRAC leases, 314
trade associations, 23
trade newsletters/magazines, 23
transaction authorizations, 271
transaction expenses, 199–202
transaction fees, 137
transaction timetables, 76–78
transfers, unauthorized, 241
transition rules, 314
true leases, 314
trust agreements, 275–276
trust certificates, 314
trustee fees, 314
trustees, 314
trustors, 314
trusts, 314

UCC (Uniform Commercial
        Code), 274
underwriters, see lease brokers
underwritten lease proposal,
        158–161
Uniform Commercial Code
        (UCC), 274
unleveraged leases, 314
upgrade financing, 54, 111–112
upgrades, equipment, 86–87
useful life, 314
use tax, 314
usury laws, 41

value-added services, 67–68
vendor, 314
vendor programs, 314
verbal promises, 21

warranties, 112, 233
windfall profits, 65
written bids, 103–104

0% financing offers, 29, 45